❧ THE ❧
MIDDLE SCHOOL
CURRICULUM

allyn and bacon, inc. boston, london, sydney

❧ THE ❧ MIDDLE SCHOOL CURRICULUM

a practitioner's handbook

Leslie W. Kindred, Rita J. Wolotkiewicz, John M. Mickelson, Leonard E. Coplein, Ernest Dyson

LIBRARY OF CONGRESS CATALOGING IN PUBLICATION DATA
Main entry under title:

The middle school curriculum.

   Bibliography: p.
   Includes index.
   1. Middle schools.   I. Kindred, Leslie Withrow,
date
LB1623.M52   373.2'36   75–15068
ISBN 0-205-04847-1

❧ CONTENTS ❧

Evaluative Instruments
Marking Student Performance
Reporting Student Performance
Curriculum Evaluation

❧ PREFACE ❧

A strong movement has been underway since the last decade to replace the junior high school with the middle school. The motivations behind this movement are varied, but the one that seems most universal is the desire to bring a more functional type of education to youngsters between ten and fourteen years of age. This desire is predicated upon recent studies of growth characteristics and needs of young people in their prepubescent and early adolescent stages of development.

Unfortunately, too many middle schools have been organized along precisely the same lines as the junior high schools they replaced. Almost identical programs of study are offered, based upon similar philosophical and psychological approaches to the learning process. Such middle schools have missed the real essence of middle school education.

This situation is due in part to the lack of appropriate reference sources to which middle school people can turn for constructive ideas and suggestions. Most references to the middle school contain some helpful information, but they do not provide a full treatment of a curriculum that is fitted to the middle school population and that takes into account innovations that may facilitate the learning process.

It is for these reasons that *The Middle School Curriculum: A Practitioner's Handbook* has been designed. An overview of the curriculum-building process is presented and new avenues of learning are described. The reader is introduced to ways of organizing and utilizing personnel in order to realize as fully as possible the stated objectives of the school. Attention is given to the place of student activities in the curriculum and to the means available for the evaluation of student performance.

The book should be helpful to students who are taking courses in elementary or secondary school curriculum, curriculum development, the junior high school, or the middle school. It should be most useful in the in-service preparation of teachers for the middle school. It can be an important reference book for conferences, workshops, and study committees concerned with the improvement of middle school education.

The authors appreciate the assistance given by colleagues and friends during the preparation of the manuscript and the permission given by publishers and writers to use copyrighted materials.

L. W. Kindred
R. J. Wolotkiewicz
J. M. Mickelson
L. E. Coplein
E. Dyson

❧ 1 ❧

THE RATIONALE

A major question in education today is how to provide children with an education that will not only meet each one's personal needs, but also incorporate social realities, including the perpetuation and realistic interpretation of democratic values. How can we liberate each individual in order to enable him to function at his highest level as a member of our rapidly changing society?

Some people believe that the middle school is a partial solution to these problems. The authors of this book have tried to provide a usable guide for those who are interested in the middle school concept and those who are actively engaged in the development of a middle school. The first chapter provides the reader with an understanding of the factors leading to the middle school's development, a progress report on that development, and an idea of what should be expected of this relative newcomer to the educational scene. Subsequent chapters develop a base for curriculum development in the middle school and then present a comprehensive description of varied means of individualizing instruction, as well as a summary of the most appropriate technological innovations. Activity programs, staff utilization, and assessment of performance are discussed in the final chapters.

GROWTH OF THE MIDDLE SCHOOL

Strong advocates of the middle school regard this new development in American education more as an educational program resulting from a variety of forces than as a rearrangement of grades. Among these forces are strong feelings of dissatisfaction with the junior high setup, changes in the maturation patterns of teenagers, new concepts in educational ideals and values, developments in learning

1

theory, innovations in educational methods and materials, and changes that have been taking place in society. Middle school education must be built upon a philosophy that takes these forces into account and gives direction to the teaching–learning process, recognizing its role in the development of preadolescent and early adolescent youngsters.

A RECENT PHENOMENON   The current concept of the middle school began developing in the late 1950s. The common organizational patterns we know today had come into evidence by 1963.   A study by Zdanowicz in 1965 showed that, of the intermediate school units in his sample, 3.8 percent were organized to include a unit consisting of grades five through eight or six through eight.[1]   His population consisted of a random sample of 414 middle and junior high schools located in the northeastern United States.

Cuff, for purposes of his survey, defined a middle school as a school that included grades seven and eight in its organization and that did not extend below grade four or above grade eight.   In twenty-nine states, he found 446 school districts operating 499 middle schools fitting this description.[2]   Alexander's survey of the number of such middle schools in 1967–1968 indicated that there were about 1,100.[3]   Gross found 960 middle schools in forty-seven states and the District of Columbia. Nearly two-thirds of them were located in the states of Texas, California, Illinois, Michigan, New Jersey, and Ohio.[4]   His information was obtained during the first quarter of the year 1967.

In a more recent study, Raymer found 1,906 middle schools in the United States during the 1973–1974 school year.[5]   There were 521 middle schools housing grades five through eight; 1,092 schools housed grades six through eight.   The remainder housed various grade combinations from grade four to grade nine.

The results of these studies indicate a movement away from

1.   Paul J. Zdanowicz, "A Study of the Changes That Have Taken Place in the Junior High Schools of Northeastern United States during the Last Decade and the Reasons for Some of These Changes," doctoral dissertation, Temple University, 1965, p. 117.

2.   William A. Cuff, "Middle Schools on the March," *The Bulletin of the National Association of Secondary School Principals,* Vol. 51, February, 1967, p. 83.

3.   William M. Alexander et al., *The Emergent Middle School,* 2nd ed. (New York: Holt, Rinehart and Winston, Inc., 1969), p. 9.

4.   Bernard M. Gross, "An Analysis of the Present and Perceived Purposes, Functions, and Characteristics of the Middle School," doctoral dissertation, Temple University, 1972.

5.   Joe T. Raymer, "A Study to Identify Middle Schools and to Determine the Current Level of Implementation of Eighteen Basic Middle School Characteristics in Selected United States and Michigan Schools, doctoral dissertation, Michigan State University, 1974.

the traditional six-three-three organizational pattern along with a new concern for the child at this "in-between" stage of development. The two most common patterns of grade organization are the three-year unit encompassing grades six through eight and a four-year unit including grades five through eight. Proponents of the six-through-eight organization believe that it not only provides more appropriately for children's growth patterns but that it also keeps the four-year senior high school organization intact. Gross found in his study that the five-through-eight unit is more common in urban areas where, in addition to pursuing its educational objectives, it is being used as a device to foster integration.[6] Gross's conclusion was supported by the Kurtzman plan for desegregating the schools of Philadelphia which incorporated the use of middle schools. The report recommended that the district's twenty-one school planning areas be combined into a smaller number of educational service areas to expedite desegregation of the schools and that the school buildings in each area be organized on a kindergarten-to-fourth, fifth-to-eighth, and ninth-to-twelfth basis. It was also recommended that locations for conversions to each grade span be planned to bring about the maximum racial balance possible.[7]

DISSATISFACTION WITH THE JUNIOR HIGH   There has been an increasing awareness of the problems of adolescence and the need to adjust the school program to the needs and interests of children during this transitional period. In the thinking of many people, the junior high school has failed to accomplish these goals. It has frequently become a miniature senior high school with complex senior high school departmentalization, rigid scheduling, and interscholastic athletics, all of which have caused adjustment difficulties for pupils.

The junior high school was originally perceived as a bridge between the elementary school and the senior high school, but its broad exploratory function has been replaced by a preparatory function. With an emphasis on content, it prepares students for senior high school. The adoption of senior high school departmentalization has obliterated to a great extent the transitional function of the junior high school—to help the youngster move from the security of the self-contained classroom to complete departmentalization.

In summary, concern about the purposes, program, and orga-

---

6. Gross, *op. cit.*

7. David Kurtzman's report recommending a plan for desegregation of the School District of Philadelphia, 1974.

nization of the junior high school has been increasing among educators and community members alike.

CHANGES IN MATURATION PATTERNS   Another important factor in the movement toward the middle school is the changing nature of the development of today's young people.   Boys and girls are maturing physically sooner than their parents because of better nutrition and because of scientific advancements, which provide protection against disease and improved medical care.

Along with accelerated physical maturation we find accelerated social maturation.   Mass communications media and other cultural influences are making their mark.   Youth between the ages of ten and fifteen possess much more knowledge of the world about them than their parents and even their older brothers and sisters had at that age.   It is for these reasons that some educators advocate the inclusion of the sixth and sometimes the fifth grade in the intermediate unit.

NEW EDUCATIONAL IDEALS   Today's students are experiencing extreme and rapid change in the social, political, and economic aspects of their lives.   Schools are institutions that exist for social, political, and economic reasons, and these reasons form a basis for educational theory or a philosophy of education.   It is our educational philosophy that tells us why we should have schools, who should be taught, what they should be taught, and how they should be taught.   Recent developments in the philosophy of education imply a new kind of school.

We find in education today a philosophy that is really a conglomerate of basic philosophies mixed with an emphasis on the development and nurturing of creativity.   Pratte refers to the influence of two schools of progressive education.[8]   The first embraces the theory of natural selection, which stresses survival of the fittest, growth, and the need for adaptation.   There is an early emphasis on individual differences and the learner as an active learner.   Current supporters of this school favor real-life situations in the curriculum, vocational guidance, and a life-adjustment approach to education.

The second group described by Pratte comprises the experimentalists, who see education as a means of building a system of

---

8.   Richard Pratte, *Contemporary Theories of Education* (Scranton, Pa.: Intext Educational Publishers, 1971), p. 28.

values. In their view, school is not a vehicle for promoting adjustment to a real-life situation, but rather for promoting a moral experience which will ultimately enhance the quality of human life.

In addition, there are the philosophies of essentialism, perennialism, reconstructionism, and existentialism. The first of these is a conservative position which emphasizes the fact that the function of education includes the development of values and skills plus acquisition of facts and knowledge. Perennialism is similar to essentialism in that the development of the intellect is stressed; education should be stable. It attacks vocationalism and adaptation to the contemporary world as educational goals. In direct contrast to the above groups, the reconstructionists believe that radical societal change is needed and that schools should play a large part in social reform.

Finally, existentialism emphasizes the idea that each person should create his or her own goals and purposes. Man has discovered that he can become more than he ever dreamed. He is gaining an understanding of the almost infinite potential of human capacity to adjust and the importance of becoming a self-actualizing individual. Self-actualization is the capacity to reach the fullest extent of one's potential. It can be achieved only through individual psychological freedom. True self-actualization can be realized only by the "supremely healthy, fully functioning person."[9] A. H. Maslow states that the need for self-actualization is uppermost in the hierarchy of human needs.[10] He defines self-actualization as the capacity "to become everything that one is capable of becoming." Below self-actualization in the hierarchy are physiological security, safety, love and affection, and belonging.

The influence of several of these philosophies is obvious in the trend toward placing more and more emphasis on providing each individual learner with every possible means of self-development through a student-centered curriculum. A whole new approach to education dealing with self-actualization is coming to the fore. It is recognized that the uniqueness of each individual is of prime importance and must be preserved. The learner is looked upon as a whole person who is in a state of developing or becoming. He or she is a complex person and must be recognized as such by the developers of a curriculum. He must be accepted for what he is and where he is, and an attempt must be made to help him become what he might be, that is, to enable him to develop to his fullest

9. Association for Supervision and Curriculum Development, *Perceiving, Behaving, Becoming,* 1962 Yearbook (Washington, D.C.: National Education Association, 1962), p. 2.

10. A. H. Maslow, ed., *Motivation & Personality,* 2nd ed. (New York: Harper & Row Publishers, Inc., 1970).

potential. The school and its curriculum must not demand of him what he is not or attempt to fashion him according to a preconceived pattern. There must be an atmosphere of freedom within which students can make decisions and within which they can know and find themselves.

The school must provide a student-centered curriculum where the role of the learner is an active one. He must have a place to go and goals to achieve, whether they be within the framework of intramurals and newspaper production or through process learning. The child must discover relationships, seek answers to questions, learn where and how to seek information, and then organize and evaluate it. A sequence of experiences in accord with his maturity, ability, and readiness will facilitate his learning.

DEVELOPMENTS IN LEARNING THEORY   During the twentieth century we have witnessed a complete shift in the theory of learning. No longer is the mind viewed as a place for the storage of an endless array of facts. For example, science and mathematics were once considered important subjects because they disciplined the mind. Today's approach, on the other hand, is a behavioral one; school is looked upon as a place for providing experiences to promote desirable behavioral change and understanding.

The behavioral approach is based on stimulus–response conditioning theories. Contemporary behaviorism does not focus on the minute elements of a specific situation, but deals with what is referred to by Bigge as "stimulus situations" or "molar behavior," which involves the total act of an organism.[11] In other words, learning is viewed as a change in behavior resulting from an experience, which might take any number of forms, such as participation in an activity, observation, or directed skill training. It is essential that the learner play the active role of participant in the process taking place. He must learn to organize, interpret, and code information in many ways, sometimes in many complicated ways. Or, as Bruner views the learner, he is an information processor, a thinker, and a creator.[12]

In order to design a curriculum that will provide an opportunity for meaningful experiences that will result in desirable behavioral change, one must take into account the developmental stage of the learner. That is what the middle school is all about!

11. Morris L. Bigge, *Learning Theories for Teachers,* 2nd ed. (New York: Harper & Row Publishers, Inc., 1964), p. 59.

12. Jerome S. Bruner, *Beyond the Information Given* (New York: W. W. Norton & Co., Inc., 1973), p. xxiii.

Figure 1-1. Readiness and Learning

Little good is accomplished and harm can even result if new learnings are introduced before the appropriate level of maturation has been reached.

Learning is affected by the environmental circumstances surrounding an individual. His home, school, social environment, and geographical location all have an effect upon what he learns and, as Gagné indicates, upon the kind of person he becomes.[13] We still do not know the extent of the effects. However, each human being does develop his own ideas about the world around him and adjusts his behavior accordingly. On the basis of his experiences he moves constantly toward higher levels of maturation.

Related to maturity is the concept of readiness. Mastery of simple skills enables the individual to move on to the development of higher-level skills. Concepts are developed in an hierarchical fashion, particularly during adolescence, as language becomes more and more important as a medium of expression. Readiness also implies that the student actively wants to learn. What he wants to learn, of course, is that which he believes will satisfy his needs. The most effective learning experiences help him to recognize his needs and to find means to fulfill them, thus fostering more rapid learning and greater gains in achievement. This, in turn, will lead to the development of a new set of needs to be met. (See Figure 1-1.)

Another important relationship is that of learning experiences and the ability of the learner. As students advance through the various levels or grades in school, individual differences in ability become more obvious. Each pupil's level of aspiration should be

13. Robert M. Gagné, *Conditions of Learning*, 2nd ed. (New York: Holt, Rinehart and Winston, Inc., 1970), p. 2.

raised, but the extent of his mental and physical abilities must not be ignored. There is a point beyond which further additions to the quantity of his experiences could be detrimental to the quality of his learning and even to his health.

INNOVATIONS IN EDUCATIONAL METHODS AND MATERIALS
The comparatively recent development of the middle school makes it an ideal place for innovation and change, since it has no traditions to uphold or break.

Much has yet to be learned about how to bring about optimum learning, but technology is doing its part to improve the learning process. The use of data processing for administrative purposes such as rostering and issuing grade reports is only the beginning. One hears the terms hardware and software applied to educational materials; the former being the physical equipment itself, and the latter being the programs, the data base, and various materials needed by the educational organization. The application of technology to education need not be accompanied by dehumanization. As Colton emphasized, the "people" element is still the keystone of educational endeavor.[14] It is the interaction between students or between students and teachers that makes for humanization, and an appropriate use of technology can free teachers to be more available to learners who need their special, personalized attention.

Another innovation is the increasing development of open classrooms with their completely student-centered approach. Flexibility in the use of space, furniture, and equipment leads to more informal teaching and learning situations. The importance of the individual becomes more apparent in an open classroom where the personal freedom of the student is combined with the necessity for intelligent student decision making.

Curriculum development is no longer considered to be only a local task. National organizations such as the National Science Foundation and the National Council for the Social Studies are producing curriculum models for national consumption. These groups are devoted to the task of providing up-to-date, relative curricula to be used as is by schools or to be used as models which a particular school district can adapt to its own purposes.

Innovations in methods and materials will be successful only to the extent that they are related to the objectives and needs of the teachers. Adaption of any new approaches must be based on the teacher's decision that such approaches will improve his effective-

---

14. Frank V. Colton, "Preservice Programs: The 'What' and the 'How' Technologically," *Educational Leadership*, Vol. 31, February, 1974, p. 47.

ness in the teaching–learning situation. It is essential that fadism be avoided if the middle school is to become an effective institution.

CHANGES IN SOCIETY   Societal changes are accelerating at such a rapid pace that the rate is a geometric rather than an arithmetic progression. We all recognize that the second half of the twentieth century has so far been vastly different from the first half. Not only factual knowledge, but values and attitudes as well are undergoing rapid change.   John W. Gardner summarizes the situation:

> If we indoctrinate the young person in an elaborate set of fixed beliefs, we are ensuring his early obsolescence. The alternative is to develop skills, attitudes, habits of mind, and the kinds of knowledge and understanding that will be the instruments of continuous change and growth on the part of the young person. Then we shall have fashioned a system that provides for its own continuous renewal.[15]

The Nature of the Changes.   A sharp division of labor exists in the current work world. Highly specialized skills are in increasing demand, partly because of the tremendous increase in the amount of knowledge applicable to the world of work. An individual can no longer be an expert in a number of fields. A student must leave school with attitudes, habits, and general work skills that he can apply to whatever he does and upon which he can build.

Technology and advances in other areas are creating a trend toward a shorter work week. The forty-hour week is becoming thirty-five, and there is an attendant increase in leisure time. Interests and hobbies need to be developed; they will influence the life of the middle schooler when he becomes an adult, and they may possibly even carry him through retirement.

Rapid changes in technology and accelerating scientific accomplishments have created increasingly serious environmental problems. The air, water, and land surrounding us are becoming more and more polluted by obsolete products and by waste products man has created. Noise, smells, soot, dirt, and ugliness are apparent as we go about our everyday lives. Natural resources are becoming depleted; means for conserving and replenishing them must be found and suitable substitutes developed.

Problems of pollution are not local. Although the middle school student is made aware that these problems exist when he views his hazy surroundings and smells polluted waterways, he

---

15.   John W. Gardner, *Self-Renewal: The Individual & the Innovative Society* (New York: Harper & Row Publishers, Inc., 1964), p. 21.

must be prepared to recognize these as not only local, but national problems. Indeed, he must see them as international problems.

The United States is in a period of turmoil—it is in the final stages of the shift from a rural to an urban base. Values and ideas that have been accepted as traditional are being questioned and challenged. Church attendance is decreasing, and the divorce rate is climbing. The ties that bound a family together and influenced its members are no longer as strong as before.

Among the major issues in the United States today is that of civil rights. Although this area once focused upon comparatively simple issues such as the right to vote, it has since become more complex. New definitions and new interpretations are appearing; even more are needed. The authority of law enforcement agencies and their representatives is being challenged through new interpretations of constitutional rights.

Another problem area deals with the disadvantaged. In past years, people from many national backgrounds gradually overcame the handicap of prejudices directed against them because of their foreign origins. Unfortunately, this absorption has not and is not taking place for all. We are faced, more than ever, with problems of black versus white. Puerto Ricans are coming to the eastern states with handicaps that make it almost impossible for them to survive in the urban situation into which they are thrust. The influx of Spanish-speaking people in the southwest makes the need for an ethnic adjustment within our society more apparent than ever. The terms *disadvantaged* and *culturally deprived* are being applied to groups among which lack of education is a serious handicap. Adequate nondiscriminatory employment opportunities coupled with improved educational opportunities will lead to the development of self-respect and a recognition of the worth of each individual human being; these qualities are essential to the well-being of our society.

The following quotation provides a very succinct summary of the scope of the changes affecting American society today:

In the United States, the transition involves the following aspects: continued urbanization, with the growth of mammoth metropolitan agglomerations and changes in the nature of city life; the growth of complex and interlocking organizations in the public and private domains, accompanied by increasingly organized regulation of social life; greater homogeneity of the population through a redistribution of wealth, the relative decline of ethnic stratification, and a decline in the polarization of the social classes; increasing similarity between the great regions of America and an enormous increase in the interdependence of the whole nation in the political, economic, and cultural fields. All of this has resulted in the development of new patterns of social stratification which determine the life chances of individuals and require different kinds of skills for successful participation in the society, thus affecting directly every person.[16]

Implications for the Middle School.   A changing society places new burdens on education. Education must respond by becoming a promoter of change and an agent for synthesizing interacting forces. It must provide a basis for participation in decision making, particularly as it affects public policy. Processes for resolving value conflicts must be developed and taught.

Education was once looked upon as a means for transmitting culture; its function today is much broader and more complex. Emphasis on process is apparent. Processes for selection of goals and activities become important; equally important is the process for selecting, with understanding and appreciation, the appropriate responses to an increasing range of phenomena.

Young people today are challenging traditions. They are not as concerned with financial security as previous generations. The influence of television and other mass media upon the preadolescent and early adolescent makes them aware that change is taking place. The school must help them to understand reasons for and outcomes of change. Many Americans are dissatisfied with what exists today and are clamoring for change, but, unfortunately, they have no notion of what the results of change should be or how to go about accomplishing worthwhile, lasting change. No one can deny that continuous change for the better is a desirable goal. However, it should be steady and gradual; precipitous change produces upheavals. Life must be made more meaningful and more satisfying; change just for the sake of change is not desirable. Many changes result from increases in knowledge. The young must learn to use knowledge as a tool to understand how and why change occurs and then how to bring about desirable change.

By the time the child reaches pubescence, he or she should be ready to discover relationships, seek answers to questions, and determine where and how to find the information he needs to develop his ideas. He is ready to learn how to evaluate information and how to organize it. He is now more qualified to be an active participant in the learning process, to make choices, to seek answers, and to work independently. He should be able to go beyond content to the process by which he can attain new knowledge when the need

16. J. Steele Gow, Jr., Burkart Holzner, and William C. Pendleton, "Economic, Social, and Political Forces," *Changing American School,* Sixty-fifth Yearbook, Pt. 2, National Society for the Study of Education (Chicago: Univ. of Chicago Press, 1966), pp. 168–169.

arises. This is the ideal time to emphasize the inquiry approach to learning, which develops the self-activated individual who is able to think objectively and reasonably and to seek new and better solutions to personal and social problems. The task of the teacher becomes more difficult but also more rewarding as he arranges or constructs situations that are challenging to the learner and that help him to find meaning in his experiences. The reward to the teacher will be in seeing his pupils acquire knowledge and, most importantly, in seeing them develop the skills and independence that will enable them to further their own learning.

The fundamental changes taking place in culture and society must be accompanied by a reexamination and reconstruction of its institutions. In the past, the adaptation of social institutions to new needs has been painfully slow; school organization has been particularly resistant to change. The rapidity of today's societal changes calls for equally rapid changes in the organization and administration of the entire educational structure. Applicable knowledge and new techniques must be applied to curricular content and organization and to the methods and materials of instruction. The middle school, with its unique philosophy, can play a very important role in society, for it can assist the young person in making his way in a rapidly changing world. He must be prepared to deal with changing family and community relationships. The development of rational thinking with its methods for comparing sets of alternatives should be a major goal of the middle school. Middle school should prepare the young for the growing trend toward a systems-analysis approach to decision making. New forms of social organization that are more fulfilling to more people must be developed by man.

The prepubescent child cannot help but be aware of the rapidly changing world. Children today have greater talent for dealing with the problems of accelerating knowledge and a better perspective on the social scene than their counterparts had a generation ago. Every available resource is needed to help develop the ability to cope with change. New concepts and new uses of technology are required. New materials must be developed and old ones adapted. Imaginative applications of a multiplicity of media are essential, as are new methods of instruction. There is a basic interdependence among students, materials, and teachers which cannot be denied. A program for self-actualization is essential if the middle school pupil is to grow to possess the capability to cope with an ever-changing society. Such a program must motivate him to think both critically and creatively about himself, the world, and the universe.

Unfortunately, society in the past demanded compliance of the individual rather than self-fulfillment. People anxiously sought the approval of their peers. They tended to conform instead of seeking warm interpersonal relationships. Everything has been on a large scale; the individual and his influence have been lost. Society has been bureaucratic and depersonalized. The educational system can be instrumental in shifting the emphasis.

CHARACTERISTICS OF A MIDDLE SCHOOL

The middle school must be not only a rearrangement of grades but a definite attempt to provide for that period in a child's life referred to by Eichhorn in his book *The Middle School* as *transescence*.[17] This is a transitional period involving late childhood and early adolescence. To harmonize with this developmental stage, the school should also be transitional. The school must make it possible for students to work on the developmental tasks associated with their particular stage of life at a particular point in time.

THE UNIFIED CURRICULUM   Everything that is known today about human development emphasizes the fact that it is a continuous, unbroken process moving from one stage to the next. A predictable pattern can be found in physical, mental, and social development. Just as human development is a continuous process, the school curriculum should reflect a continuous unity. This is what is meant by *vertical articulation*. The middle school can best reflect this by emphasizing the continuation of basic education in the fundamentals while, at the same time, beginning to pave the way for entrance into the senior high school. Concurrently, it can retard the growing up process by removing its students from the influence of the traditional upper grades of the senior high school.

EMPHASIS ON SELF-ACTUALIZATION   The middle school must provide its pupils with opportunities to explore some of their own interests and ideas, encourage them to work independently, and assist them in discovering that learning within the formalized structure of a school can be exciting.

The following quotation focuses on several directions the mid-

---

17.   Donald H. Eichhorn, *The Middle School* (New York: The Center for Applied Research in Education, 1966).

dle school can take in its efforts to help its students work toward the goal of self-actualization:

> Our society now calls for each person to achieve a kind of maturity and depth of understanding that is not commonly achieved—self-actualization. Facilitating self-actualization in pupils is a task of the schools through curriculum content and teacher–pupil relations. In order to accomplish this, creative planning for educational reconstruction is imperative.
> We can make possible "fulfillment" education for all pupils. While a curriculum revolution may be underway in mathematics and science, one of the most significant human needs has been neglected or overlooked. This need is related to self and the human condition. Only when this need occupies a central position in the curriculum will fulfillment education become a reality. To achieve this kind of education, pupils must come to explore and learn independently. Equally important, they must be introduced to ethics and values.
> Specifically, these new directions in education must occur for pupils to become self-actualizing persons.
>
> 1. Pupils must select areas of learning or problems which are significant to them.
> 2. Pupils must learn how to think creatively and flexibly.
> 3. Pupils must learn to generalize from data and to group ideas in meaningful clusters if they are to solve problems.
> 4. Pupils must be taught to generate models and theories to explain phenomena.
> 5. Pupils must learn ways to test hypotheses and make critical judgments.
> 6. Pupils, at some point, must arrive at a decision and take a stand.[18]

DEVELOPMENT OF SELF-DIRECTION   In order to achieve self-actualization, the individual child must be helped through education to establish his values and to use them in determining how he will spend his energies. To accomplish this, he must have a knowledge of himself and the ability to assess his needs and his powers. This assessment becomes the basis from which he works toward the optimum development of his capacities.

The development of self-direction or self-management in children has been a major goal of American education for a long time.

---

18. Association for Supervision and Curriculum Development, *Learning and Mental Health in the School*, 1966 Yearbook (Washington, D.C.: National Education Association, 1966), pp. 97–98. Copyright by the Association for Supervision and Curriculum Development.

The two major components of this goal have been summarized succinctly by Lois Barclay Murphy as follows:

1. Development of capacity for independence in meeting one's own needs and dealing with the environment.
2. Development of capacity for self-control or management of one's own impulses and drives.[19]

The child of middle school age has reached a stage in his development where it is possible to teach him to recognize and understand his needs, the reasons for his attitudes and behavior, and why one direction in which he might go is preferable to another. He can begin to make intelligent decisions about himself and his future. The middle school must provide him with opportunities to act independently and to do creative work, and, at the same time, ensure that he has the time to read, to discover the world about him, and, finally, to discover himself.

USE OF INNOVATIVE TECHNIQUES   Old approaches to the teaching–learning situation will no longer be tolerated. So many new developments in teaching methods are appearing that one cannot help but become aware that exciting things are happening in education. Professional literature abounds with phrases such as computer-assisted instruction, individually prescribed instruction, large-group and small-group instruction, simulation games, modular scheduling, and instructional media centers, all of which are becoming common, everyday terms in some school districts.

Major goals of the middle school should focus on the personal development of the learner with provision for his transitional nature and should include exploration of a wide variety of educational experiences, including work, leisure, and socializing. The program must focus on increasing the self-identity of each individual and on providing him with the skills needed for continuous learning. Absolutely essential for accomplishing these goals is a flexible time schedule. An individualized instructional program that utilizes commercial and quasi-commercial instructional systems such as the SRA materials, Individually Prescribed Instruction, or LAPs (Learning Activity Packages) can help provide the motivating atmosphere that must be characteristic of the middle school.

Because the middle school is a comparatively new organiza-

---

19. Association for Supervision and Curriculum Development, *New Insights and the Curriculum,* 1963 Yearbook, Association for Supervision and Curriculum Development (Washington, D.C.: National Education Association, 1963), p. 107. Copyright by the Association for Supervision and Curriculum Development.

tional unit, it provides a perfect opportunity for introducing some of these innovations. Its students are entering a new stage in their development and are becoming more receptive not only to more independent work, but also to teaching methods that stimulate their motivation through inquiry and learning by doing. The middle school must provide a long-awaited, fundamentally new and different setting for education. The uniqueness of the revised framework should encourage the development of a variety of unique educational concepts.

CULTIVATION OF INDIVIDUAL AND SOCIAL SKILLS It is obvious that two areas of focus are necessary in the development of skills: the development of individualized skills and the development of social skills. One must not overshadow the other; both are important. It is the burden of education to help children prepare for their roles in the society of tomorrow while developing their own abilities to the fullest extent. The two goals are not opposed to one another; they are actually complementary.

In order for society to continue, it must be in a constant state of change. A static society cannot last. A healthy educational system and its curriculum must be ready to change to help its students prepare to live in a changing society. The society will continue to be pluralistic, impersonal, and affluent with large-scale organizations, business, military, unions, and so on. Action will become increasingly collective and effective group membership will be an absolute requirement. Yet the school must continue to develop each student's attitudes and abilities in a way and to a degree that will preserve his individuality.

Today's students will be living in a world that will provide an unknown wealth of goods and services. They will need education as consumers to choose, buy, and use wisely. They will have a stake in an economy that must function well. Wise social policies will become increasingly important in the distribution of income and provision of social services. They will need to understand science and technology and their place in civilization. Their votes will be important in determining the direction of government; they must be prepared to understand the political process, how to reach decisions regarding their votes, and the ramifications of their votes.

There is increasing need for intercultural and intergroup education concerning the nature of prejudice and how to remove it from our society. The increasing importance of international relations points out the need to study ways of living in other countries, a subject that has never before been included in many school curricula. Above all, the student will need to be educated in how to think through and develop his own values.   The school's function is to help him grow to maturity mentally, socially, and emotionally and to release his potential to the fullest.   The particular characteristics of the early adolescent make the middle school a most appropriate vehicle for concentrating on the accomplishment of these goals.

✎ 2 ✎

THE CHILD
TEN TO FOURTEEN

Middle school pupils usually range in age from ten to fourteen. Their growth stages range from late childhood to early adolescence. It is the diversity among the students in physical maturation and in emotional, social, and intellectual characteristics that makes the middle school exciting.   Each child is a challenge to the teacher.

HIS SELF-CONCEPT

Many factors combine to make the middle school child what he or she is.   His stage of growth is reflected physically and emotionally; he must cope with his rapidly changing body and changing perceptions of himself and others.

The child of ten is entering what can be called a preadolescent stage.   When he approaches the age of thirteen or fourteen, he enters early adolescence.   During this period, he is "in-between" childhood and adulthood; he is looking for an adult personality.   He is beginning to view himself as separate from his family and to look inward in his search for an identity.

Preadolescence has also been termed *pubescence,* the point in a child's life when rapid physical changes begin to take place.   The physical changes are accompanied by changes in intellectual functioning; thus this is a period of psychological and social reorientation.

The child is very conscious of his bodily changes, which are very apparent to him and, he believes, are even more apparent to everyone else.   He must understand that growth patterns are highly individualized and that his own rate of change will differ to some extent from that of his classmates. He must also learn to accept and handle the lack of coordination that accompanies rapid growth.

It is a well-accepted fact that negative perceptions of oneself can have a debilitating effect. To be effective, a person must have an adequate concept of self which will enable him to have a healthy outlook on life and to accept his limitations. He must be satisfied with his view of himself; he must feel capable of accomplishing whatever is at hand. In other words, it is the view from within that counts; it is not what you are, but what you think you are.

When an individual can accept himself, he is better able to accept others as well. Acceptance is not an innate characteristic, but something that must be learned by experiencing acceptance and openness from others. The child builds attitudes, habits, and knowledge from his experiential background. His self is shaped in relationship to others and his behavior changes as a result of others. His individuality is derived from his biological inheritance and the effect of all his past experiences, experiences that come from the stimuli of his environment.

The person who views himself as adequate will behave more effectively or intelligently than others, and will set realistic goals for himself. He will be a more responsible person and will have the capacity to work harmoniously with others in whatever role is required of him. He will not be overly concerned with conformity.

The importance of self-concept and its relationship to self-actualization are discussed in the 1962 Yearbook of the American Association for Supervision and Curriculum Development:

> All definitions accept or imply: (a) acceptance and expression of the inner core or self, i.e., actualization of these latent capacities and potentialities, "full functioning," availability of the human and personal essence; and (b) minimal presence of ill health, neurosis, psychosis, or loss or diminution of the basic human and personal capacities.[1]

FACTORS INFLUENCING HIS GROWTH

Numerous factors influence the growth of an individual. During the period of late childhood, the individual experiences his most rapid growth spurt since infancy. His particular development is strongly affected by his heredity and his environment. It has been

---

1. Carl R. Rogers, "Toward Becoming a Fully Functioning Person," *Perceiving, Behaving, Becoming,* 1962 Yearbook, Association for Supervision and Curriculum Development (Washington, D.C.: National Education Association, 1962), p. 36. Copyright by the Association for Supervision and Curriculum Development.

proven that these heredity and environmental factors have their greatest effect prior to the teenage years.

HEREDITY   Certain aspects of an individual's growth pattern are the result of hereditary factors.   Such characteristics as his body structure and his own unique timetable according to which change takes place are probably determined by genes.   Many of his physiological capacities and the latent skills that he has derived from parents, grandparents, and greatgrandparents will appear during adolescence.

Some traits that can be inherited may not appear in every generation or may be modified by the inheritance of opposite traits from the other parent.   It is sometimes difficult for a child to understand why his physical build and abilities are what they are.   His ability to run, his level of muscular coordination, and his basic physical capacities are all part of his basic inheritance, which he must learn to accept, as difficult as that may sometimes be.

Frequently a child who has inherited a small stature also inherits a physiological system with a metabolic imbalance that turns food into body fat at a particularly fast rate.   This characteristic provides an additional handicap which makes it difficult for him to participate effectively in physical activities.   His problem becomes more severe when he enters into the adolescent period of accelerated growth, which is usually accompanied by an increase in appetite.

In the area of mental development, the nature versus nurture debate has continued for many years.   The IQ test does not measure basic inherited intelligence; it measures one's ability to handle verbal symbols and shows a positive correlation with scholastic success.   IQ is not independent of the environment, although recent studies, which are admittedly limited because of the difficulties involved in conducting them under widely different environmental conditions, indicate that the generic component outweighs the environmental component.   Genetic and physical factors combine with nutritional factors to influence mental development.

ENVIRONMENT   It is expected that the current trend in the United States toward earlier physical and social maturation will continue.   This trend is the result of a number of forces in the environment.

Socioeconomic Conditions.   A relationship is apparent between early growth and socioeconomic conditions.   Since socioeconomic conditions have been favorable in the recent past, physical growth has been accelerating. It is estimated that maturation is occurring nine months to one year earlier than it was thirty years ago. This is a direct result of better prenatal care and the various advances of medical science. Advances in our understanding of nutrition, vitamins, immunization against childhood diseases, and reduction of infection and debilitating effects from disease are all making their influence felt. The child between ten and fourteen is extremely healthy. His greatest problem is the possibility of injuring himself as a result of clumsiness or awkwardness arising from his rapid physical growth.

Cultural Variables. Certain cultural variables may slow down or accelerate the child's developmental rate. In the American culture, a child's experiences are very closely related to his socioeconomic class. The social conditions in the midst of which an individual finds himself provide a framework within which he learns to act and to conceptualize. The learner's self-expectations are also culturally based; the middle school child's adjustment to his environment depends upon his growth patterns and their relationship to what his culture expects of him.

A child's parents have more than hereditary influences over his growth. Children show an accelerated intellectual growth pattern when their parents are warm and accepting. These children also tend to be less excitable, more emotionally secure, and more original. If parents actively reject their children, the children tend to be slightly decelerated in intellectual development, to use their abilities relatively poorly, and to be emotionally unstable, aggressive, and rebellious. Family patterns provide a great deal of important information relative to the growth of an individual child.

Parental attitudes toward a child have a tremendous effect on his ways of thinking and behaving and his mental, emotional, and social development. This is very well expressed by the following:

> *How can a person feel liked unless somebody likes him?*
> *How can a person feel wanted unless somebody wants him?*
> *How can a person feel acceptable unless somebody accepts him?*
> *How can a person feel able unless somewhere he has some success?*
> *How can a person feel important unless he is important to someone?*[2]

---

2. Arthur W. Combs, ed., "The Positive View of Self," *Perceiving, Behaving, Becoming,* 1962 Yearbook, Association for Supervision and Curriculum Development (Washington, D.C.: National Education Association, 1962), p. 101.

Another cultural influence on the growth and development of the prepubescent and pubescent youngster is pressure from his peers. He is at a stage where he is beginning to transfer his base for security from his home and parents to his peers. During the early middle school years boys find relationships with the same sex satisfying, but by the time they complete eighth grade boys are beginning to be attracted to girls. The girls, in many instances, have been attracted to boys for a whole year already.

The ten-year-old learns a great deal from the "gang" or group to which he belongs. He feels the pressures of their demands to conform for social acceptance. It is from this relationship that he develops his social attitudes and the ability to participate in and enjoy social and group activities. At the age of ten, the child tends to belong to a gang whose members are of the same sex as himself. As he matures, heterosexual interests, activities, and relationships increase in importance. By the age of fourteen he is beginning to become more interested in himself as an individual and less interested in conformity. He must develop the skills required to conform to the peer culture, but continue his development as an individual with distinct abilities and characteristics.

Technology. Another important influence on growth is the current rapidity of technological change. As David Sarnoff said, "Science and technology will advance more in the next thirty-six years than in all the millennia since man's creation."[3] Although civilization has always been in a state of change, the pace is accelerating much faster now. The increased emphasis on technology is influencing all aspects of life including personal values and moral and religious beliefs.

A period of rapid change tends to widen the gap between the child and adult. Many adults today are still awed by the developments that have made it possible not only for man to walk on the moon, but for viewers on earth to watch him do it. Each launch into space triggers a feeling of excitement in many adults, because they still remember that it once took two days to fly from New York to California. To children growing up in today's world, taking off into space does not create a great feeling of wonder because they have not observed the slow developmental stages.

Today we can view something on the far side of the earth at the same time it is occurring. New stereophonic sound systems, popular among young people, have produced a new vocabulary including words like "woofers" and "tweeters." The effects of these

---

3. David Sarnoff, "By the End of the Twentieth Century," *Fortune*, Vol. 69, 1964, p. 116.

technological advances on school curricula make it almost impossible for parents to assist with the mathematics and science being studied by their children in school.

The current instability of national and international affairs is exerting its pressure on the developing middle school child. International relations are strained by the possibility of a nuclear war. Today's generation is living during a period in which wars have and are being fought, but the horrors of an "all-out" nuclear war are unimaginable. Under such circumstances, even the survival of civilization would be questionable. Add to this the internal struggles between the various subcultures in the United States and you begin to appreciate the difficulty facing the student who is preparing to make his way in this world. Each individual must have an adequate personality in order to survive in a far-from-perfect social world and a rapidly changing physical environment. The more complex society and its cultural forces become, the more strain and stress are placed upon each individual.

Technology, however, is also foremost among the factors aiding in the growth and development of middle school learners. The varied communications media provide unparalleled opportunities for increased intellectual experiences. Television programs such as the underwater explorations of Jacques Cousteau cannot help but make their impact by presenting in a very palatable form knowledge that hitherto was unavailable to children. The effect of *Sesame Street* on the mental development of preschool children is being publicized. These kinds of experiences will have a long-range effect on the middle school child.

The learner can take advantage of many opportunities by himself. A child between ten and fourteen years of age can manipulate the simple machines that put in front of him filmstrips, slides, and tape recordings. Newspapers are becoming an accepted part of the vast array of available teaching materials; in many homes boys and girls have been making use of them since an early age.

We are much more closely linked with people of other lands than ever before. Advances in transportation, communication, and mass media will continue to foster this link with increasing effectiveness. Transportation is allowing us to become a nation of globe trotters; one finds among children in a middle school many who have lived and traveled in other parts of this nation and in other countries. And for boys and girls of middle school age who had not gone beyond their immediate neighborhoods until they entered the middle school because of the inherited disadvantages of being born and raised in a ghetto area, mass media can provide a vital link.

HIS GROWTH PATTERNS

It is essential that the developing and maturing child understand the changes that are taking place within himself and accept them as part of the process of growing up. The term *adolescence* means a period of transition, a time for "growing up" or growing to maturity. As the middle schooler approaches puberty and the subsequent adolescent period, he becomes aware of himself and the small ways in which he is beginning to change. This awareness causes conflicts in his thinking and in his emotions.

PHYSICAL DEVELOPMENT   American youth today are maturing physically much sooner than children did fifty years ago. Today's sixth graders are developmentally comparable to seventh graders of the early 1900s. Increases in height and weight are related to age and stage of pubescence. The most marked changes in height and weight occur at the onset of puberty, which for many occurs at about the age of twelve.

Most boys reach the stage of puberty, the point at which adolescence begins, at the age of fourteen or fourteen and a half, whereas girls reach that point at about age twelve and a half or thirteen. In the approximately three years during which their bodies change most rapidly, girls gain an average of thirty pounds, while boys gain an average of forty. The physical development of girls is about one and a half to two years ahead of that of boys.

One of the results of this rapid physical growth is poor motor coordination. Although adolescents have relatively few health problems, they tend to have difficulties with injuries resulting from accidents. Not only is growth a problem, but its uneven characteristics produce difficulties. Arms and legs may suddenly increase in length and the awkwardness that results can be embarrassing and disconcerting.

The ten-year-old has the motor skills required of him pretty well in hand, but, as he reaches the age of twelve, he becomes more self-conscious about learning new skills. Because of his growth at this time, it is difficult for him to develop new skills. During later adolescence (when girls are fourteen to eighteen years of age and boys range in age from sixteen to twenty) an increase in muscle growth and a decrease in growth in height and weight make the increase in skills more rapid.

The period of most rapid growth leads not only to poor motor coordination, but also to a low tolerance for fatigue. Both boys and girls begin to develop anxieties about their personal grooming, accompanied by feelings of restlessness and irritability. Physical development is a base for other kinds of development which can be seriously affected if one is dissatisfied with his physical development.

MENTAL DEVELOPMENT   Two of the more important areas in which mental development takes place are problem solving and creativity.   The most rapid mental growth occurs between the ages of nine and twelve.   Rapid physiological development at an early age will be accompanied by a correspondingly rapid rate of mental growth.   If physiological development occurs later, mental development will occur at a slower rate.   Among children between the ages of ten and fourteen, one will find a wide range in mental abilities because of the irregularities of physical, social, and psychological growth.

The noted learning theorist Jean Piaget identified several hierarchical stages in intellectual development.   The final two of these are pertinent to the middle school child: the period of concrete operations, which takes place between the ages of seven and eleven, and the stage of formal operations, which occurs between eleven and fifteen years of age.   In the stage of concrete operations, the learner can manipulate ideas only in the presence of actual things and immediate experiences.   In the stage of formal operations, the individual can develop ideas about ideas and handle relationships in the absence of the concrete.   During transescence, most boys and girls enter the formal operations stage.   How an individual student functions depends upon how he is taught.   Mentally, the child of middle school age is ready to move from an understanding of the real and the concrete to the theoretical and hypothetical.   There will be individual differences as to where the stages begin, just as there will be differences in the accomplishment of the same individual in various fields of subject matter.

Everyone is born with some potential for creativity.   Encouragement and nurture are essential to its development; otherwise it may be lost because of the self-consciousness of the individual child involved.   As youth and adults advance in years, the use of creative power seems to diminish, although it is believed that a positive relationship exists between general intellectual ability and creative abilities.   The child of ten or eleven who enters the middle school should not yet have been stifled in utilizing his creative abilities, and development of these abilities should be encouraged with the appropriate school atmosphere.

After a young child in his first years in school watched a garden worm for a while, he came up with the following:

HOW WORMS WALK

Some worms don't have any feet.
They pull themselves out,
And they pull themselves in,
And they pull themselves out,
And they pull themselves in;
And that's the way they get along—
Because they don't have any feet.[4]

Education should nurture in children continued development of their ability to express themselves. If experiences are capitalized on, we will find poems of the calibre of the one below, which was written by a sixth-grade boy.

THE KING

It grew from a thought
And there it stands,
Tall and graceful,

King of steel and cement
Looking down loftily from the high perch
At its far-flung realm.

There, look above you;
In a heaven of blue mist
Waiting to be praised
Stands the finished skyscraper.

It grew from a thought,
And there it stands![5]

Simple short stories, skits, playlets, and songs provide a myriad of opportunities for self-expression. Many delightful songs have resulted from class efforts where individuals contributed individual lines.

The opportunities presented by the many art media from pencil and charcoal to oil paints are endless. Burlap, noodles, rice, and odd beads can be made available as additional materials for self-expression and creative effort. Creative effort gives a child an opportunity to view what he has wrought with pleasure and satisfaction. He needs constant opportunities to be freely creative; he must not be bound by endless rules of proportion, balance, use of

---

4. Hughes Mearns, *Creative Power: The Education of Youth in the Creative Arts* (New York: Dover Publications, Inc., 1958), p. 108.

5. *Ibid.*, p. 111.

color, and perspective. These rules have their place in instruction, but they must not be emphasized to the point of inhibiting the child in his freedom of expression.

Some teachers prefer quiet, complacent conformists for students. However, the most creative youngsters often do not fit this mold. They are inclined to act quickly without considering all possible outcomes, and they tend to be less concerned about how others regard them. With the rapid increase in knowledge, there is a need for divergence and new ways to cope with new circumstances. The creative individual who possesses abilities such as fluency, originality, and flexibility is just the kind of person needed to meet these new situations. Boys and girls must learn to question tradition without being lawbreakers.

SOCIAL DEVELOPMENT   The development of an individual may be affected positively or negatively by the group to which he belongs. He learns much about himself by interaction with others, including his peers. While the social growth patterns of the early adolescent are characterized by many and varied changes and those of early childhood by stability, the preadolescent period appears to be quite unique. It can be described as the "lull before the storm."

During the preadolescent stage, boys are most likely to relate to closely organized gangs. They are boisterous, noisy, aggressive, and often just plain sloppy. They tend to create problems in school by annoying others, rejecting adult direction, and being hyperactive. Girls present an opposite picture. They are friendly, neat, shy with their peers, and less well organized socially. They gradually become more talkative and develop an aggressiveness toward boys in the form of teasing to gain their attention. Girls are more interested in making good grades than boys.

The early adolescent is on the threshold of maturity, physically and psychologically. As a child, he was protected by adults. Now he is vulnerable. He tries to cover up what he feels to be his inadequacies. His peer group's opinions of him are very important and he tries to meet their expectations in order not to feel inferior and, most important of all, to be accepted by them. He makes every effort to be like other members of his group.

The child between the ages of ten and fourteen cannot meet adult standards, so he leans very heavily on his peers; their standards become extremely important to him. Peer groups can provide opportunities boys and girls need to get along with others of their own age; these are the people they will later work with, play with, and marry. The peer group also provides an opportunity to have fun. The child needs to be part of a group that will exert pressure on him to conform. It is a place to escape from family influences.

As the child approaches the age of twelve, thirteen, or fourteen, he discovers himself and his parents. He develops the ability to view his parents objectively and sometimes sees them as authoritarian and demanding. Early adolescents believe their parents to be totally oblivious of their deep feelings and yearnings; bickering and quarreling are not uncommon. The young boy or girl tries in every way to express his new independence and his desire to be less helpless than he feels. In order to conform to demands from outside the home such as those of his peer group, he may abandon a pattern of complete loyalty to his parents.

The middle school child has a kind of world of his own which is reflected in his interests and values. The characteristics of this world are circumscribed by his relationships with his family, by the influences of his school and the world in general, and, as family influence upon him diminishes, by the values of his peer group.

EMOTIONAL DEVELOPMENT The child of ten or eleven is on the threshold of a number of emotional changes. As his body begins to change and it becomes necessary for him to deal with the change, he becomes extremely sensitive. His own assets are not quite adequate to meet the demands on him. He must learn how to control his emotions and refrain from relieving tension by an outward expression such as boisterousness which, in many instances, is considered inappropriate to the situation. Blount and Klausmeier summarize the particular needs of the child during this stage as follows:

1. Understanding socially approved methods for relieving emotional tensions and substituting these for childish or otherwise disapproved methods.
2. Analyzing emotional situations objectively.
3. Obtaining a broader understanding of situations in which disruptive emotions are produced.
4. Acquiring many social skills to meet new situations.
5. Eliminating fears and emotionalized patterns of response that are already firmly established.[6]

Gertrude Noar sees the following as "needs all children experience as they strive to lead emotionally comfortable lives in which they can make normal progress toward maturity":

6. Nathan S. Blount and H. J. Klausmeier, *Teaching in the Secondary School,* 3rd ed. (New York: Harper & Row Publishers, Inc., 1968), p. 45.

1. The need for affection and security, which create feelings of being wanted and a sense of belongingness.
2. The need for recognition and reward.
3. The need for achievement and success, which help to create feelings of adequacy.
4. The need for fun and adventure: new experience.[7]

As he meets the needs above, the child develops an insight into his own behavior which enables him to deal with problem situations without tremendous stress and strain. Thus he moves toward emotional stability. If he is to develop and mature in the school situation, he must be free from anxiety and preoccupation with personal problems; otherwise his achievement can be seriously affected by his emotional disorganization.

GROWTH AND THE CURRICULUM

Human development is a continuous, predictable process. At every stage, an individual is capable of achieving certain competencies, both mental and physical. In other words, one can expect that certain developmental tasks will be acquired within the framework of specific chronological periods.

HAVIGHURST'S DEVELOPMENTAL TASKS   One of the best-known contributors to the concept of developmental tasks is Robert J. Havighurst. He has specifically defined just what the child needs to accomplish at each stage of his development in order to be ready to move on to the next stage. He has even extended this concept to include the various stages of adulthood. The tasks of later childhood and adolescence might be one base for developing a curriculum appropriate for the middle school. Havighurst defines these tasks as follows:

> The tasks the individual must learn—the developmental tasks of life—are those things that constitute healthy and satisfactory growth in our society. They are the things a person must learn if he is to be judged and to judge himself to be a reasonably happy and successful person. A developmental task is a task which arises at or about a certain period in the life of the individual, successful achievement of which leads to his happiness and success with later tasks, while failure leads to unhap-

7. Gertrude Noar, *The Junior High School: Today & Tomorrow*, 2nd ed. (Englewood Cliffs, N.J.: Prentice-Hall, Inc., © 1961), p. 32. By permission of Prentice-Hall, Inc.

piness in the individual, disapproval by the society, and difficulty with later tasks.[8]

He then goes on to cite the three sources of developmental tasks: physical maturation, cultural pressure of the society, and the personal values and aspirations of the individual which are part of his personality. Havighurst gives two reasons why developmental tasks are important to educators: (1) they help in discovering and stating the purposes of education in schools, i.e., to help the individual to achieve certain of the tasks; and (2) the tasks affect the timing of educational efforts by determining the teachable moment when conditions are most favorable for learning the tasks.

Two of Havighurst's developmental periods are very important to the middle school: middle childhood and adolescence. Havighurst feels that the developmental tasks of middle childhood cover three areas. The first is the child's movement away from the home influence to that of the peer group. The second is the development of neuromuscular skills, and the third is an introduction to adult concepts. These are then broken down more specifically into the following areas:

1. Learning physical skills necessary for ordinary games.
2. Building wholesome attitudes toward oneself as a growing organism.
3. Learning to get along with age-mates.
4. Learning an appropriate masculine or feminine social role.
5. Developing fundamental skills in reading, writing, and calculating.
6. Developing concepts necessary for everyday living.
7. Developing conscience, morality, and a scale of values.
8. Achieving personal independence.
9. Developing attitudes toward social groups and institutions.

Havighurst sees the developmental tasks of adolescence as covering particularly the areas of physical and emotional maturing. They include the following:

1. Achieving new and more mature relations with age-mates of both sexes.
2. Achieving a masculine or feminine social role.
3. Accepting one's physique and using the body effectively.
4. Achieving emotional independence of parents and other adults.

---

8. Robert J. Havighurst, *Human Development and Education* (New York: Longman, Inc., 1953), p. 2.

5. Achieving assurance of economic independence.
6. Selecting and preparing for an occupation.
7. Preparing for marriage and family life.
8. Developing intellectual skills and concepts necessary for civic competence.
9. Desiring and achieving socially responsible behavior.
10. Acquiring a set of values and an ethical system as a guide to behavior.

As can be seen from the above, life tasks are also expectations. They represent not only what is expected of a human being at each stage of his development, but also what he expects of himself. These tasks help to give direction to his life. They must also be taken into consideration when structuring the curriculum so that the learning expected is at a level appropriate to the maturity and ability of the learners.

PROVISION FOR PERSONAL AND SOCIAL NEEDS   There are varying interpretations of the term *needs*, but, no matter how defined, needs fall into two categories: personal and social. Van Til, Vars, and Lounsbury define a personal need as any want or wish.[9] It may range from a deep-seated, long-established want to a passing, whimsical wish. It may be something demanded by the society in which an individual lives. A social demand may be one he recognizes and accepts, one he personally feels, or it may be a demand placed upon him by some outside force which he does not accept—a demand he does not personally feel.

As a rapidly changing and developing personality, the middle school child needs moral support and advice. He must be made to feel like an intelligent being, receive encouragement to find his own answers, and be treated like the individual he aspires to become. He must develop a competency to love, work, and play, and he must find healthy self-fulfillment through satisfaction of his personal needs. A positive view of himself will enable him to face new situations adequately.

The middle school program must provide its pupils with experiences that will foster satisfactory relationships among peers and mature relationships with adults. Students must be able to work harmoniously with others in the role of leader or follower. If a child receives effective guidance through his early middle school

---

9. William Van Til, Gordon F. Vars, and John H. Lounsbury, *Modern Education for the Junior High School Years*, rev. ed. (Indianapolis: Bobbs-Merrill Co., Inc., 1967), p. 149.

experiences, his social problems should decrease during his pubescent and early adolescent years. Interest and hobby groups, classroom group experiences, and activity programs all provide opportunities to achieve this goal.

Adjustment to relationships with the opposite sex is a problem that must be recognized. Boys and girls must be given opportunities to associate with one another if they are to derive maximum benefit from the academic program. Assignments that require boys and girls to work together in groups are an excellent means of achieving this goal. Five or six students may be required to plan and work together to develop and present a report in social studies. When groups of boys and girls were told to present current events in a unique manner, some very clever presentations resulted. Planning the menu and activities for a class picnic is another possibility.

PROVISION FOR PHYSICAL AND MENTAL DEVELOPMENT

Patterns of mental development and physical growth cannot be ignored in curriculum planning. They have a very definite effect upon school learning. Learning may decrease during periods of rapid physical growth as energy is depleted by the heavy physical demands upon it. The sequence and content of the curriculum and the methods of instruction must have the changing patterns of the child's mental development as their base. Energies and interests characteristic of middle school pupils at each stage of their development must be considered when planning the program. As the old saying goes, "You can lead a horse to water but you can't make him drink."

Krathwohl has defined education as "changing the behavior of a student so that he is able, when encountering a particular problem or situation, to display a behavior which he did not previously exhibit."[10] This should be the general objective of the total school program, particularly that portion described as general education. The preadolescent is beginning to awaken to certain goals which become more apparent as he approaches adolescence. These goals include the various aspects of maturity from physical through social–emotional to intellectual, and his education should be directed toward achievement of these goals in order to develop the desired self-actualizing, integrated personality.

Curricular provision for special interests is also influenced by

10. David R. Krathwohl, "Stating Objectives Appropriately for Program, for Curriculum, and for Instructional Materials Development," *Journal of Teacher Education*, 1965, p. 9.

growth patterns. An obvious example is a physical education activities program. Appropriate selection of sports activities will minimize the possibility of students injuring themselves through clumsiness, yet provide them with a feeling of achievement as they increase the effectiveness of their coordination.

The fact that girls tend to mature earlier than boys is another consideration, particularly when determining the kinds of social activities to provide. Shop and home economics experiences, music and art, and other areas must be available for exploration to meet developing special interests and capabilities. Availability of a variety of offerings should be the keynote for an effective middle school curriculum.

PROVISION FOR INDIVIDUALIZATION Teachers must recognize students as individuals: different individuals have different experiences when participating in the same learning activities.

Conformity and individuality each have a place, and the school must provide for the development of both. Each individual must have the opportunity to develop his potential to the fullest. This can be accomplished by curricular provision for both individualized and group learning situations.

The curriculum must be pupil-centered; it must provide opportunities for each child to exercise his desire for independence. He must be able to achieve his goals, learning in the process. Each student must be assisted in establishing realistic goals that will help him to move toward self-acceptance and acceptance of others. He must experience success as an individual, and the curriculum must lead him toward the understanding and acceptance of himself.

THE TEACHER'S ROLE

A prerequisite for development of a true middle school program is a team of teachers who are attuned to the nature of the students and who respond accordingly in both curricular planning and their relationships with students. The teachers must observe student characteristics and behaviors and be responsive to students' intellectual, personal, and social needs.

The teacher must see the school as a place that makes something possible for children, not as a place where the teacher does something to children. Teachers and pupils alike are working toward the same goal: the development of each individual self. Thus the teacher must see the learning situation as the learner sees it; he must put himself in the learner's place. He must respect the uniqueness of each individual while remaining aware of the common needs and interests of students.

DIFFERENCES IN GROWTH PATTERNS   Growth patterns differ tremendously between boys and girls.   As stated earlier, girls generally are ahead of boys in physical development by one and a half to two years.   The boys, however, are gaining over the girls in physical strength.   The teacher needs to realize that the growth spurts of the preadolescent and early adolescent periods consume much of the students' energy during this period.   Because boys develop at a slower rate and the changes are greater, the painful period of awkwardness seems to extend longer than it should.   This requires patience on the part of the teacher.   Boys' clumsiness and overactivity must be tolerated.   This is particularly difficult when they are compared to the quiet, more mature, and seemingly "settled" girls.   Boys and girls must not be compared; variations in growth must be accepted and provision made in curricular activities to accommodate their differences.

HEALTH PROBLEMS   Although children of middle school age are characteristically quite healthy since childhood illnesses have been left behind, the teacher must still be alert to health problems.   A seeming lack of interest could be the result of depleted energies stemming from very rapid growth.   Lack of sleep resulting from late hours and poor eating habits are not uncommon.   Some parents tend to become less watchful when their children reach this stage, since prepubescents and pubescents become more and more independent.

Late hours can be a particular problem, for the late-hour television programs become more attractive to the child.   Students have been known to fall asleep in school because they stayed up to watch the late show while their parents went to bed.   A healthy, rested child should be able to participate actively during the entire school day; if he appears unable to do so, this is a sign that bears investigating.   A certain amount of poor posture, lack of muscular coordination, and sluggishness are temporary reactions to spurts in physical growth.

ATTITUDES   A fully functioning, responsible individual will demonstrate positive attitudes toward school and his fellow human beings.   Stress will not take an undue toll on his abilities to respond, and there will be constant growth in his ability to cope with stress. The overanxiousness of a pupil is as much of a signal to the teacher that there is a problem as apathy or boisterousness. Consistent guidance and emotional support on the part of the teacher are essential. The teacher should avoid situations from which an emotional crisis might result.

During this period there are marked changes in the interests, aptitudes, and abilities of the maturing youngster. Healthy, normal human beings demonstrate a natural curiosity about the world around them. As they pass from childhood to adulthood through the adolescent period, this curiosity should become more apparent. It presents a challenge to the school and its teachers. Since children are not aware of everything around them nor of the particular needs they will face in the world, the teacher must assist them in extending their perceptions.

> Although spontaneous interest creates a most desirable atmosphere for learning, much school learning is not recognized by children as being directly satisfying to their needs. The teacher's task, therefore, often is to "motivate" the students. "Motivating" (getting learners to want the things the school hopes to teach them) can be carried out by: (a) awakening students to needs and to ways of satisfying them, (b) appealing to curiosity, (c) appealing to desire for adult or peer approval, and (d) capitalizing on the need to avoid disapproval or punishment.[11]

The teacher must realize that as the child approaches and enters adolescence, he is entering a period of growth in reflective thinking. By taking into consideration the nature and problems of the developing child, he should be able to provide an environment suitable for intellectual and social development. The needs of individuals are never completely satisfied, but tasks that can be accomplished must be provided if appropriate attitudes are to be fostered.

The attitudes of the teacher are important to the students, just as the attitudes of the students are important to the teachers. The teachers must reflect nonjudgmental attitudes and refrain from harsh, unnecessary judgments. If the teacher shows concern about the student, the student's attitudes will reflect this: "The teacher is interested in me." An attitude of rebellion and insubordination must be replaced by one of interest and eagerness to become involved.

---

11. R. Murray Thomas, "The Teacher Introduces Learning Tasks," *Learning and the Teacher,* 1959 Yearbook, Association for Supervision and Curriculum Development (Washington, D.C.: National Education Association, 1959), pp. 72–73. Copyright by the Association for Supervision and Curriculum Development.

VALUES AND CONFLICTS OF VALUES   As a child grows up, he seeks some value in the tasks assigned to him by teachers and parents. He needs a set of values to serve as his ideals and standards which will enable him to lead a healthy, happy, useful life. Current conflicts in our society between widely divergent social, economic, and political views make the development of such a set of values more difficult than ever. Much discussion and a wide range of reading are essential. Through these activities the teacher can gain greater insight into the values held by his students as individuals so that he can determine his strategies. The goals as defined by Kimball Wiles are the following:

> Each pupil will: (1) develop a set of values that will guide his behavior; (2) acquire the skills necessary to participate effectively in the culture; (3) gain understanding of the social, economic, political and scientific heritage; and (4) become able to make a specialized contribution to the society.[12]

Students must be asked questions that will help clarify their own beliefs and purposes. They must be helped to understand their own values and to evaluate how acceptable these values are to themselves, their peers, their parents, and the culture. Throughout this process, the teacher must serve as a nonjudgmental facilitator as each child attempts to develop his own system of values and resolve conflicts in values to his satisfaction. The teacher who senses that a student is having a particularly difficult time going through the process of value clarification can help by leading him to see himself clearly and then to identify his purposes and goals. The thinking required for this clarification of values will also help in development of the thinking process.

VARYING LEVELS OF SKILL DEVELOPMENT   Each child brings to school his own unique background and his own individual physical, mental, and social characteristics. One child may have a special aptitude for music, and another for art. It is not unusual for a sixth-grade teacher to find a variation of three or four years in the reading levels of her children. Tremendous differences are apparent in other basic skills such as mathematics. A truly homogeneous class does not exist.

By the time children enter the middle school, the diversity in their basic skill development is greater than it was in the lower

---

12. Kimball Wiles, "Education of Adolescents: 1985," *Educational Leadership*, Vol. 18, May, 1960, p. 489. Copyright by the Association for Supervision and Curriculum Development.

grades. This is normal and must be accepted by the middle school teacher. Middle schools must attempt to strengthen basic skill development where needed and encourage the child with well-developed skills to use these skills for further learning. It is not the time for the teacher to complain that the elementary school teachers did not do their job. Each teacher needs to determine the level of accomplishment of each child and then use that as a base from which to proceed. No child need be downgraded because his spelling skills leave something to be desired. Such a view weakens rather than strengthens his self-concept. The middle school is a place to further develop each child's basic skills; teachers should not expect the child to have mastered skills and to be ready for secondary school–type activities.

PEER RELATIONSHIPS   The teacher can learn much about his students from observing them as a group or in groups. Some students are members of many groups, whereas others seem to belong to none. Sometimes it is desirable to modify grouping patterns to improve the distribution of children with low peer status. The isolated child needs to be looked after carefully.

To many children, particularly as they approach adolescence, being "in the right crowd" is important. Efforts in this direction may divert too much of the child's attention from his learning activities. The teacher must recognize these situations and try to develop a positive, supportive classroom situation for all children so that they can use all their abilities.

The child of low peer status needs to be given tasks to improve his status, and all children must be encouraged to observe their own behavior in relationships with others. Teaching about individual differences and causes of behavior can be helpful. A child's membership in a group gives him a kind of strength which must be recognized by the teacher who is on the outside of that group. The teacher must also recognize that a child's peer status can be enhanced by open disagreement with the teacher.

❧ 3 ❧

LEARNING AND INTELLECTUAL DEVELOPMENT

It is the premise of the present volume and of all other works that deal with the middle school that the young person in his middle school years is different from the child he was before and the adolescent he will become. If the child's development is unique at this stage, then it follows that this period in his intellectual development is also unique. Further, it is quite likely that certain learning procedures or instructional strategies are more characteristic of or appropriate to this age group than to others. The present concern, then, is the development of a rationale to undergird curriculum planning and classroom instruction.

Waetjen has noted that, "Unfortunately, learning is not the simple act of taking over information that is made available, nor is teaching the simple act of organizing material in logical order and presenting it to learners."[1] Although it is possible to generalize about teaching groups of youngsters, the individual middle schooler remains an individual. Children and young adolescents grow according to generalized patterns of development, yet within the general pattern each has his own special pattern and his own particular rate of growth.

As Waetjen's remark makes abundantly clear, matters in the classroom are not simple. Individualized growth patterns are further complicated by the fact that children bring with them their

1. Walter B. Waetjen, "Curiosity and Exploration: Roles in Intellectual Development and Learning," in *Intellectual Development: Another Look*, A. H. Passow and R. R. Leeper, eds. (Washington, D.C.: Association for Supervision and Curriculum Development, 1964), p. 54.

own personal values, problems, drives, and incentives, most or all of which may be in conflict with the purposes of the school.

> Basic ability and cultural differences, reflected in that which boys and girls have learned previously, result in some who are younger in age than their peers in the grade groups, while still others, encrusted with years of failure and frustration in school, are one, two or even three years older than their grademates. . . . The more successful the schools are in meeting the needs of their clientele, the larger the differences that will exist between individual students; the longer boys and girls remain in school, the greater the differences will become.[2]

The foregoing constitutes a powerful argument for the individualization of instruction and underlines the difficulties created for students when each is expected to adapt to a single curriculum.

THEORIES OF LEARNING AND INTELLECTUAL DEVELOPMENT

No theory of learning or of intellectual development explains to the satisfaction of all either the manner in which learning occurs or the conditions that are essential for intellectual development. It is possible—with due regard for consistency—to be eclectic, drawing from the theorists those theoretical explanations and propositions that have relevance to the design of curriculum and the planning of instruction. Space prohibits a detailed examination, but it is possible to highlight the theories of learning and intellectual development that have aspects most pertinent to the middle school.

LEARNING DEFINED   Most educational psychologists accept as a working definition of learning the following: *learning is the modification or change of behavior.* Perhaps the preceding definition is an oversimplification, but it is useful in that it excludes those notions of learning that view the mind as a muscle to be exercised or a reservoir to be filled. A more precise definition is provided by Gagné, who defines learning as "a change in human disposition or capability, which can be retained, and which is not simply ascribable to the process of growth."[3]

---

2. John M. Mickelson, "Instructional Processes," in *The Intermediate Schools,* Leslie W. Kindred, ed., © 1968, Prentice-Hall, Inc., Englewood Cliffs, N.J.

3. Robert Gagné, *The Conditions of Learning,* 2nd ed. (New York: Holt, Rinehart and Winston, Inc., 1970), p. 5.

Some writers concerned with learning and intellectual development in the middle school extend the definition of learning as follows: learning is the modification or change of behavior *through experience*. Technically, a definition of something should not include the means by which that something is acquired, but the violation is deliberate and is intended to highlight the importance attached to the proposition that one learns through experiencing.

If the curriculum designer or instructional planner accepts the foregoing definition of learning, then he or she is face-to-face with the fact that major changes will be required in his own behavior and that of the classroom teacher. The function of instruction becomes one of promoting desirable behavior change, so, to various degrees and in varying ways, curriculum designers, instructional planners, and classroom teachers become change agents. This view of learning means that new and different problems must be faced in the selection of curricular content and the organization of instruction. The teacher functions in a new role. No longer can teaching be equated with telling; rather, it requires that the teacher or the teaching team create the type of situation in which learning can occur. This represents a major shift in the role formerly allotted the classroom teacher.

EXPERIENCING AND LEARNING It is important that the curriculum designer, the instructional planner, and the classroom teacher understand the relationship between experiencing and learning. This concept is basic to modern educational practice, particularly the increasingly popular open classroom system.

Experiencing (as contrasted with experience) is an active process which is often poorly understood. Clayton has described experiencing as follows:

> In any segment of time and space the learner is embedded in a situation. In this situation he responds to certain stimuli in particular ways. He acts and reacts to the situation. This interaction is what we call experiencing. The experience may be highly complex or relatively simple. It may involve the learner to a maximum degree and produce violent activity; it may be as simple as reading a book or as specific as making a check mark on a paper. At any rate, it involves the checker doing something under some condition of stimulation.[4]

In designing the curriculum and planning instruction for the classroom, then, experiences may be equated with the opportunities

4. Thomas E. Clayton, *Teaching & Learning: A Psychological Perspective,* © 1965, pp. 35–36. Reprinted by permission of Prentice-Hall, Inc.

for learning available to the learner. It is in the process of experiencing (acting and reacting in response to situations) that behavior change occurs. "To oversimplify, out of experience comes learning; out of many experiences comes understanding."[5]

The child is constantly experiencing in all types of places and under all kinds of circumstances. The circumstances under which the experiences occur may result in desirable learning or undesirable learning; controls may be limited or altogether lacking. In the school "the child's experiences can be selected, limited, complicated, simplified (varied), or timed as need may dictate, and, to a large degree, they may be controlled."[6]

In designing the curriculum it becomes the task of the curriculum designer and the instructional planner to specify the content and the conditions under which opportunities for learning will be provided.

Certain aspects of theory concerning learning and intellectual development that appear to have special meaning for the design and organization of middle school programs will be examined.

COGNITIVE DEVELOPMENT The term *cognitive processes* refers to the ways in which one perceives, interprets, forms judgments about, and reacts to his environment. From the child's reactions to the environment he develops the concepts, generalizations, and principles that aid him in making decisions, solving problems, and discovering and classifying new data. From his experiences the child obtains the data essential to the development and refinement of his cognitive processes.

Waetjen has compared the cognitive structure to a kind of private map which an individual gradually develops as a result of his experiences.[7] If Waetjen is correct, then the manner and order in which cognitive structures develop and the ways in which existing structures are modified or changed is of critical importance to those designing curricula and planning instruction. Knowledge of this sort helps to provide a rational basis for planning curricula consistent with the developmental stage of the middle school child and at the same time achieving the flexibility necessary if individualization is to occur.

Piaget and his colleagues at the Geneva Institute have engaged in extensive research and theory-building in the area of cognitive

5. Mickelson, *op. cit.*, p. 63.

6. *Ibid.*

7. Waetjen, *op. cit.*, p. 41.

development. Piaget differs from many American theorists in that he substitutes for the idea

> of an intelligence sufficiently fixed by heredity . . . that [a] child's position relative to his peers [remains] constant throughout the period of development, the notion of a natural ordinal scale of intelligence. The position a child [has] reached on such a scale would indicate the intellectual progress he [has] already made, but prediction of development from that point forward would have to be predicted on knowledge of the experiences in store for him.[8]

Piaget does not eliminate the organism as an important factor. As Hunt has indicated in discussing Piaget's theories,

> There is no question that somatic and cerebral structures with their functional properties are important, but it has become more and more clear that experience is required for the development of these behavioral patterns and capacities, and especially for the development of those central organizations for the processing of information that are required to solve problems.[9]

Although it is essential, a physical structure is insufficient in itself for optimum intellectual development. In other words, maturation alone is not enough. Wide and varied experiences are necessary to permit the individual to capitalize on the structures he has inherited.

No matter how rich and varied a child's experiences and no matter how unique he ultimately becomes, according to Piaget his intellectual development will proceed through four distinct but overlapping periods. Thus the problems inherent in meeting the individual needs of the child are somewhat alleviated by the fact that (1) there is a well-defined progression through the four major stages in intellectual development; and (2) large numbers of boys and girls are at similar stages at the same time. Although Piaget delimits the stages according to chronological age, the groupings must be perceived as ranges, not definitive rubrics.

Below the four stages in cognitive development as identified by Piaget are briefly summarized.

---

8. Millie Almy, "New Views on Intellectual Development in Early Childhood Education," in *Intellectual Development: Another Look*, A. H. Passow and R. R. Leeper, eds. (Washington, D.C.: Association for Supervision and Curriculum Development, 1964), p. 21.

9. J. McV. Hunt, *Intelligence & Experience*. Copyright © 1961 The Ronald Press Company, New York.

1. *The sensorimotor period,* which has little direct bearing on the middle school program, lasts roughly from birth through eighteen to twenty-four months of age. Initial cognitive development is obviously dependent upon whatever sensorimotor schemata exist at birth. During this period the elemental intellectual processes are developed as the infant interacts with his environment.
2. *The preoperational period* is characterized by intuitive thinking, much of which is illogical, and by egocentricity. Logical, reversible operations have yet to emerge. The preoperational stage is perceived by Piaget as a transitional period between the latter part of the sensorimotor stage and the earlier phases (ages seven to eight) of the stage of concrete operations.
3. *The period of concrete operations,* which encompasses children from age seven or eight to age eleven or twelve, is the stage during which cognitive systems of a sophisticated nature are beginning to develop, and the child becomes more autonomous as a thinker. Concrete operations based on concrete objects such as ordering, classification, seriation, and mathematical processes can be undertaken.
4. *The period of formal operations,* which is characterized by the development of formal operations or propositional thinking, takes place for most boys and girls between the ages of eleven or twelve and thirteen or fourteen. At this time the individual begins to systematize the concrete operations that were the chief characteristics of the previous level. He is now able to deal with all possible combinations in any situation without being limited to the empirical. As Hunt observes, "The child, [having] become essentially adult, can now operate with the *form* of an argument while ignoring its empirical content."[10]

To this point, the discussion has been focused mainly upon the various stages of cognitive development and their general characteristics. It is now time to examine the way in which the individual's cognitive structures are modified.

Earlier in the present chapter, attention was called to the importance of experience in cognitive development. It was noted that the mere possession of an appropriate physical structure is not enough to account for intellectual development as described by Piaget. It is in the process of experiencing that intellectual development occurs.

Experiencing involves two complementary processes referred

10. *Ibid.,* p. 115.

to by Piaget as *assimilation* and *accommodation*.[11] Assimilation is the process by which raw data are taken in from the environment and made a part of the cognitive structure. It is a continuing process. Cognitive structures are constantly being refined. For instance, to the possible embarrassment of his mother, the very small child may at first associate all men with "daddy" and address them as such. As his experiences with men increase, the child gradually comes to realize that "daddy" has a special meaning; he is able to distinguish between his daddy and other daddies. Although this is an oversimplification, it can be said that cognitive patterns are developing through the process of assimilation.

Accommodation—the other side of the adaptive coin—is involved whenever the individual is faced with a situation for which his previous experience has not prepared him, or for which his existing cognitive map is not adequate. "It is in the process of accommodation that existing cognitive structures (concepts, generalizations, etc.) are modified, reorganized, or even discarded in the light of the new information."[12] For instance, at a family reunion the small child discovers that all men are not either daddies, nondaddies, or possibly grandpas, but that some are called uncle, cousin, brother, or even mister. A further discrepancy (in terms of his previous experience) occurs when he discovers that daddies come in a variety of ages; they may be older or younger than his. These and similar new experiences, confusing though they may be in the beginning, ultimately result in the reorganization of existing cognitive patterns and the formation of a new perceptual structure to account for "daddy." Further experiences with men will involve the process of assimilation (as opposed to accommodation) and will tend to be increasingly less demanding. The new experiences that are most readily assimilated are those most like previous experiences. Existing cognitive patterns are adequate for managing the foregoing sort of new information, but

> As the experiences confronting the individual become more and more novel, assimilation increases in difficulty until the process becomes one of accommodation. It also follows that if new experiences are too far beyond the bounds of an individual's previous experience, they may simply be rejected, since he lacks the cognitive structures with which to deal with them.[13]

---

11. Piaget uses the term *adaptation* to encompass assimilation and accommodation.

12. Mickelson, *op. cit.*, p. 65.

13. *Ibid.*, p. 65.

It is through the interaction of assimilation and accommodation that previously developed cognitive patterns are discarded and modified or new ones developed.

In sum, intellectual development is a continuing process whose limits are not, for all practical purposes, fixed at birth; it takes place gradually as the child confronts new experiences and modifies his cognitive framework accordingly. It is clearly critical that the child have a wealth of carefully chosen experiences while he is developing; intellectual deficits will result from limitations of the child's experiences.

ATTITUDE AND SKILL DEVELOPMENT   The emphasis of the present chapter to this point has intentionally been on the cognitive development of the individual. Nothing has been said about the affective and psychomotor domains.

Much has been written concerning the development of attitudes and skills, but there is no body of research and theory to compare with that available in the fields of learning and developmental psychology. Nevertheless, helpful insights are available to those concerned with attitude formation and skill development in middle school youth.

Attitudes have been variously described as mental sets, predispositions to behavior, or acts waiting to happen. However they may be perceived, it is clear that attitudes are learned. Skills are defined as the application of intelligence to the solution of problems. Obviously, skills are also learned; they encompass many specific behaviors of a cognitive and/or manipulative nature.

The discussion of attitudes and skills in the same breath may seem puzzling, but there are valid reasons for doing so.

> First, they each involve learned behavior, and, as with cognitive development, the concepts and generalizations that form them are evolved from experience. Second, both skills and attitudes are difficult to define precisely, yet, despite their general fuzziness, any self-respecting list of objectives recognizes the necessity of teaching for skills and attitudes.[14]

For a long time schools apparently operated on the assumption that attitudes and nonmanipulative skills (that is, critical thinking) developed more or less spontaneously as the student gradually increased his storehouse of facts. Studies now show that, on the contrary, attitudes develop slowly out of shared cultural experiences. The title of a study of prejudice conducted about twenty

---

14. Mickelson, *op. cit.,* p. 85.

years ago puts the whole matter most succinctly: *They Learn What They Live*.[15] A child develops attitudes by becoming involved in his culture, by experiencing. It is this factor in the acquisition of attitudes that accounts in large part for the present efforts to integrate the public schools. Attitudes must be embedded in the individual's cognitive structures.

Psychomotor skills are also embedded in the cognitive structures, as the prefix to motor suggests. Except for certain rote manipulative behaviors (tying one's shoelaces, for instance), skilled behavior requires competency in problem-solving and the ability to generalize.

Also of concern to educators at this period in the children's lives is the development of social skills. Just as the development of attitudes and intellectual and motor skills is rooted in experience, so too is the development of the social skills. During the middle school years nearly all boys and girls will become pubescent, with all the developmental tasks—particularly heterosexual adjustment —that that particular period implies. Regardless of the position the school may wish to take, young people will attempt to master their tasks. Well conceived is the school whose curricula and teachers are geared to funnel this youthful energy into creative and socially useful channels.

IMPLICATIONS FOR THE MIDDLE SCHOOL

Throughout this summary of some of the more useful ideas concerning learning and intellectual development, the relationship of these ideas to the middle school has been kept in the forefront. Nevertheless, it seems worthwhile to summarize from a slightly different focus the implications of these ideas for curriculum and instruction in the middle school, especially since the two succeeding chapters will consider, respectively, curriculum design and program implementation.

SCOPE AND SEQUENCE If one accepts the middle school as serving a unique population in terms of its developmental characteristics, it is apparent that the scope and sequence of the curriculum must follow a developmental pattern. The direction and pace of the developing curriculum must follow the direction and pace of the intellectual growth of the child, and allow for his social, physi-

---

15. Helen G. Trager and Marian R. Yarrow, *They Learn What They Live: Prejudice in Young Children* (New York: Harper & Row Publishers, Inc., 1952).

cal, and emotional growth. When the child enters middle school he is probably near the end of Piaget's stage of concrete operations. While he is in the middle school, he enters the stage of formal operations.

The implications are twofold: (1) in the beginning the curriculum should emphasize the concrete, playing down highly verbal or highly abstract types of content; and (2) the scope (breadth) of the curriculum should be consistent with the child's growth stages, encompassing as many and as varied experiences as can realistically be managed by the child at his level of development within the school milieu. The content of those experiences should in the beginning place major emphasis on the concrete, with provisions for inferential thinking rooted in the concrete. Gradually experiences should move to the point where the young person, now an adolescent, not only performs formal operations, but thinks about them. In other words, he performs operations on the outcomes of his previous operations.

CURRICULAR EXPERIENCES   The point has been made that the child learns through his experiences. Experiencing involves both assimilation and accommodation. The implications for both curriculum and instruction are clear: (1) school experiences must be rooted in the child's past experiences, whether they are from school, the environment, or both; (2) school experiences must stretch the child sufficiently that he is required to make accommodations in his cognitive structures; and (3) school experiences must not be set beyond the limits of his experience nor be inconsistent with his developmental stage if frustration, rejection, and alienation are to be avoided.

There is little value in introducing into the content of the curriculum concepts for which *the child in terms of his intellectual development is not yet ready.* To do so can be both time-wasting and frustrating. Confronting children with concepts, ideas, principles, and information unsuited to or inconsistent with their stage of development is undoubtedly a major contributor to pupil learning difficulties, pupil failure, and pupil alienation.

The middle school overlaps the ending of the period of concrete operations and the beginning of the period of formal operations. (Note: Piaget uses the word *operations* to denote the activities of the mind as contrasted with the sensorimotor activities of the body.) At the stage of concrete operations the child thinks in terms of concrete objects, which may be people, things, or situations. Giving the child abstract concepts not rooted in the concrete and inconsistent with the limitations of the child's already developed cognitive structures is in all likelihood going to result in rejection and/or rote memorization. Rote memorization of the multiplication tables is an excellent case in point; it is not unlike learning nonsense syllables.

The author recalls the illuminating experience he had in his first year of teaching when he decided that his fifth-grade class, rather than simply reciting the "American Creed" in unison each morning, was going to understand its meaning. The whole project limped from the beginning, but foundered completely when the class came to the term "sovereign state." The coup de grace was administered by the class dictionaries in which sovereign was defined as a gold coin. To the children this definition suggested *Treasure Island*, a far cry from the abstract notion of sovereignty. The particular developmental stage of the students was firmly fixed at the level of concrete operations. The concept of a sovereign state was simply beyond their stage of development and experience.

The child entering the middle school in the fifth or sixth grade is likely to be in the stage of concrete operations and as such is yet unready for abstract notions. He can perceive sovereign as meaning a coin, for he has had previous experiences with coins, even though they may not have been gold or British, but sovereign as applied to a state is another thing. The cognitive structures needed to deal with the concepts inherent in the words sovereign and state have yet to be developed in most children.

It is important, then, that the design of both the middle school curriculum and the instructional program contain content consistent with the concrete stage of operations, and yet provide ever-increasing opportunities for those students moving into the period of formal operations to practice inferential reasoning.

INDIVIDUALIZATION   It follows that if we perceive the young middle schooler as a unique personality, much of his instruction must be individualized. It is patent that not all students will be at the same stage of intellectual development at the same time, so ways must be found to individualize or even, in some cases, personalize instruction. This can be accomplished through such programs as IPI (Individually Prescribed Instruction) or ISCS. (See the discussion of individualizing instruction in Chapter 6 and of instructional systems in Chapter 7.)

The ISCS program (Intermediate Science Curriculum Study) is an excellent example of a curriculum that attempts to provide for the shift from concrete operations to formal operations. It is designed for grades seven through nine. At the seventh- and eighth-grade levels the emphasis is on experiments in the area of the physical sciences. The kits include a wealth of objects upon which experiments are performed. These object-centered experiments permit the simple observation of what happens in given situations; they also provide opportunities for inferential thinking. Questions can be raised, such as the following: What happens when the model car runs down the inclined plane? What happens to the car when the angle of the plane is changed? What happens to the earth in the tray when water runs through it? What does this reveal about the process of erosion? What inferences can be drawn?

It must be reemphasized that not all children will be at the same developmental stage at the same time. Because of limited or different experimental backgrounds or because of lack of ability, some students will not have progressed as far as their fellows. Others will have forged ahead. The important thing is to design a curriculum that makes it possible to deal with the student where he is. The ISCS program is an example of a curriculum that permits the pupil to plug in at his own level of development and to proceed at his own rate.

THE ROLE OF THE TEACHER   To accommodate present views of learning and intellectual development, the role of the classroom teacher must shift dramatically. No longer is he or she solely the dispenser of wisdom. He now must function as a facilitator of behavior change. He must help students to grow and develop in ways consistent with their developmental patterns. In his new role he is diagnostician, guide, resource person, and evaluator. It is his responsibility to create a situation in which children can learn; he is no longer expected to beat learning into their heads.

❧ 4 ❧

CURRICULUM DESIGN

For many years the emphasis of those who designed educational programs, courses of study, curricula, units, or whatever they were called was upon method. Educational thinkers and planners were searching for a general method by which unity and order could be brought to the planning of instructional programs. They favored a consciously planned approach, as opposed to the prevailing practice of simply following a textbook. The methodological emphasis may account for the fact that many middle school curriculum planners still approach the problem of curriculum design from an instructional viewpoint. But within the last twenty years, "a conscious rationale or theory of design . . . has characterized most important curriculum proposals,"[1] however incomplete and simplistic they may be.

> The factors that influence the design of [a middle] school curriculum are the same as those that influence [or should influence] curriculum design at any level of the educational hierarchy. The differences lie in the complexity [of the needs] and maturity of the population to be served.[2]

Additional factors affecting the design of the curriculum include the school's expressed purposes, the underlying views of the nature of subject matter and learning held by the designer, the nature of the students, and the community from which the students come.

As was implied earlier, many currently accepted definitions of curriculum emphasize the instructional element: the curriculum consists of all the planned learning activities under the aegis of the

---

1. John M. Mickelson, "Curriculum Designs," in *The Intermediate Schools*, Leslie W. Kindred, ed. (New York: Prentice-Hall, Inc., 1968), p. 108.

2. *Ibid.*, p. 109.

school. Such definitions confuse curriculum with instruction. For present purposes, curriculum design will be perceived as placing primary emphasis on content, whereas instructional design gives first priority to the planned interaction between teachers and students. Neither can ignore the other. Thus the chief difference—and it is a major one—between curriculum and instruction is derived from the purposes of the designer, the level of generality at which he or she is working, and the resultant set of problems to be faced.

Curricula cannot be designed without concern for ultimate teacher–student interaction, nor can instructional systems be developed without a concern for content. Similarly, neither curricular nor instructional systems can be designed and implemented with total disregard for goals or objectives.

A curriculum design, then, constitutes the basic plan from which instructional systems are derived. The design of the curriculum precedes the development of the instructional design. Most curriculum designs permit the development of more than one instructional system. If only one sort of instructional system, such as programmed learning, can be developed from the curriculum design, then the design is much too narrow and probably inadequate for all except extremely limited purposes. The curriculum design should represent a higher level of generalization than the design for instruction, which is quite specific.

Any curriculum design must be concerned with the following components: objectives, content, and instructional strategy. These elements are interdependent, and in any curriculum design can be specified. (See Figure 4-1.) Unless there is a carefully developed design, the curriculum becomes a series of improvisations. Improvisation leads ultimately to chaos. The three essential compo-

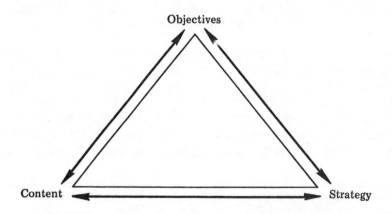

Figure 4-1. The Essential Elements of Curriculum Design

nents will be examined in detail, along with the related problems of scope, sequence, articulation, and evaluation.

PURPOSES AND OBJECTIVES

*If you don't know
where you are going
you are likely to end up
someplace else.*

Perhaps, as well as anyone, the student who produced this non sequitur in a final examination discussion of the role of objectives in curriculum planning identified their chief function—that of pointing a direction. Objectives are statements of ends or intent. As such, they are value statements. The goals and objectives of the middle school represent the educational ends to be achieved at the middle school level, and thus provide the ultimate criteria for the selection of curricular content and instructional strategies.

Little distinction has been made in the past between such words as purposes, goals, aims, and objectives. In fact, they have often been used synonymously. In recent years the terms goals, aims, and purposes have come to be applied to the grander, more global ends of education, whereas the word objective has been used to denote a much more specific and, in some instances, a much more limited statement of educational ends, particularly in the very restricted versions of behavioral objectives described by Gagné[3] and Mager.[4]

The chief function of the stated objectives of the middle school is to give direction to curriculum planning and instructional practice. Statements of objectives detail the answer to the question "Education for what?" Further, "educational objectives (constitute) the criteria by which materials are selected, content is outlined, instructional procedures are developed and tests and examinations are prepared."[5] Ends must be specified if an appropriate choice is to be made of the means to achieve those ends. The question to ask first is not "How?" but "What?" And we must not ask

---

3. Robert M. Gagné, "Curriculum Research and the Promotion of Learning," in *Perspectives of Curriculum Evaluation*, AERA Monograph Series on Curriculum Evaluation, No. 1 (Chicago: Rand McNally & Co., 1967), pp. 19–38.

4. R. F. Mager, *Preparing Instructional Objectives* (Belmont, Calif.: Fearon Publishers, 1962).

5. Ralph W. Tyler, *Basic Principles of Curriculum and Instruction* (Chicago: University of Chicago Press, 1950), p. 3.

"What are the means?" but "What are the ends?" When the ends become clear, so do potential means to the ends.

PURPOSES   The purposes of the middle school have already been discussed in Chapter 1. However, it seems wise to repeat them, since the purposes have important implications for program development, curriculum design, and instructional planning. The middle school does the following:

1. Serves young people in the age ranges of ten or eleven to fourteen or fifteen.
2. Facilitates self-development and self-actualization.
3. Provides for general education, including opportunities for the development of a sense of inquiry, curiosity, and commitment to learning.
4. Provides opportunities for exploration.
5. Provides for the individualization of instruction.
6. Improves articulation with elementary and high school programs.
7. Provides opportunities for racial integration.[6]

These purposes (with the possible exception of the last one, which is certainly open to serious question) point the direction for the middle school program and set the limits within which it functions. Thus, the middle school focuses upon a specific age group consisting of students who are moving from the concrete operations stage of intellectual development to the point where they will soon be ready for propositional thinking. At the same time they are undergoing major physical and psychological changes. All this has important implications for the content of curriculum and the selection of instructional procedures.

These purposes serve as criteria for the specification of programmatic and curricular objectives. The particular age range also represents a constraint. Let us examine the meaning of these purposes. The title of the middle school says something important. It is no longer a *junior* high school; it is now a school in the middle. It is, according to Alexander, a "school providing a program planned for a range of older children, preadolescents, and early adolescents that builds upon the elementary school program for earlier childhood and in turn is built upon by the high school's program for adolescence." Further, it is "a phase and program of schooling bridging but differing from the childhood and adolescent phases

6. Bernard M. Gross, "An Analysis of the Present and Perceived Purposes, Functions, and Characteristics of the Middle School," doctoral dissertation, Temple University, 1972.

and programs."[7] Quite obviously a program for kindergarten through twelfth grade is assumed. These statements should make it clear that the middle school has an integrity of its own and hence requires a program of its own. Constraints are also specified: (1) it is for a defined population; (2) it must build upon what has gone before; and (3) it must be articulated with the program for adolescents.

Further constraints are also specified in the stated purposes. It is the responsibility of the middle school to provide for the general education of its students. General education may be construed either as the subject matter all young people should study and the skills and attitudes they should develop, or it may be perceived as those needs, problems, and concerns that are common to all young people growing up in our society. Although in the first instance general education is conceived in terms of subject matter and in the second in terms of personal–societal problems, each view sees general education as meeting common needs, however such needs may be defined. Thus the middle school program has some sort of common core of subjects or experiences.

The middle school is also charged with the task of facilitating self-development, that is, of helping students to develop positive images of themselves and to become all that their talents and interests will permit them to become. A correlative task is that of providing opportunities for exploration. The implications here are twofold: (1) the middle school program and its curricula must provide opportunities for older children, preadolescents, and early adolescents to deal with areas relevant to their lives; and (2) in addition to those experiences that are required of all, a broad spectrum of experiences must be available for young people to sample and/or to pursue in depth as their interests may dictate.

Rather closely related to the foregoing task, yet with a further and most important implication, is the individualization of instruction. In addition to providing new and relevant experiences, individualizing instruction means giving the student an opportunity to move along at his own pace, not at the pace of classmates who may be faster or slower than he is. This may mean computer-assisted instruction or other types of programmed materials, or it may mean carefully selected experiences which permit the student to individualize for himself. Either way, the problems of curriculum design and implementation are exceedingly complex.

Finally, the middle school is perceived as a means of providing opportunities for desegregation. There is still a great deal of con-

---

7. William Alexander et al., *The Emergent Middle School* (New York: Holt, Rinehart and Winston, Inc., 1968), p. 5.

troversy as to whether or not integration—in the social sense—is an appropriate function of any school, however much one may feel that the cause is just. Integration as a purpose of the middle school is at least partially politically motivated. It receives its greatest emphasis in large urban areas, since large numbers of minority groups tend to congregate there.[8] Urban middle schools seek to achieve this purpose by increasing the geographical spread of the service area of a particular school (taking grades five and six from nearby elementary schools and adding them to the middle school), by busing, and by the inclusion of ethnic studies among the school's offerings.[9]

OBJECTIVES   Earlier in the chapter it was stated that the curriculum design is the basic plan from which instructional systems are generated and, further, that one of the essential elements of curricular design is the clearly specified objective. Curricular objectives are broad, yet they are not stated as generally as the purposes of the school (previously considered), nor specified in as narrow and limited a manner as are instructional objectives. They lie somewhere between the two extremes in terms of specificity. In a somewhat different context, Hough and Duncan use the term *intermediate objectives*.[10] Curricular objectives must, of course, be consistent with the purposes of the school and its program, just as instructional objectives must be consistent with curricular objectives.

Considerable controversy exists concerning the manner in which objectives should be stated. However, since the majority of writers believe that objectives should be stated as behaviors and since there are certain advantages to so stating them, the present discussion will be limited to behavioral objectives.[11]

Curricular objectives expressed in behavioral terms specify the desired changes in the action patterns of students, that is, the way the student should think, feel, and/or act after exposure to an educational experience. Statements of behavioral objectives at the curricular level are typically broad and include appropriate content limitations. Statements of curricular objectives do not specify

---

8. Gross, *op. cit.*, p. 119.

9. Thomas E. Gateswood, "What Research Says about the Middle School," *Educational Leadership*, Vol. 31, December, 1973, pp. 221–224.

10. John B. Hough and James K. Duncan, *Teaching: Description and Analysis* (Reading, Mass.: Addison-Wesley Publishing Co., Inc., 1970), p. 47.

11. For a contrary viewpoint see Elliot W. Eisner, "Instructional and Expressive Objectives: Their Formulation and Use in Curriculum," in *Instructional Objectives*, AERA Monograph Series on Curriculum Evaluation, No. 3 (Chicago: Rand McNally & Co., 1969), pp. 1–31.

teaching strategies, nor do they include criteria for success. Curricular objectives state in broad terms the kinds of ideas, skills, techniques of thinking, and feelings that planners desire the students to learn, utilize, and develop, such as thinking critically or writing and speaking clearly and coherently.

The problem of determining the degree of specificity required in stating an objective is a knotty one for many curriculum writers. The difficulty arises from two sources. First, confusion often comes from a failure to understand that there is a difference between curricular and instructional objectives. Second, curriculum writers tend to mistake specificity for clarity. The curriculum writer must state objectives clearly in terms of the generality of the behavior expected.

Curricular objectives must be consistent with the purposes of the school. The objectives that follow meet this criterion, for they fall very clearly under the broad middle school purpose of self-development. They are from one source unit of a series dealing with the personal–social problems of preadolescents and early adolescents. The unit was designed as a base from which teachers could plan instruction for and with particular groups of young people. These objectives are stated broadly in terms of student behavior. Although the example is problem-oriented, the same principles for stating behavioral objectives apply to the disciplines. Each statement should be limited to a single idea, should be stated in action terms (verbs are a must), should specify content limitations, and should avoid statements concerning teaching methodology and achievement criteria.

Getting Along with My Family

A. *Gaining independence at home.*
B. *Getting along with my brothers and sisters.*
C. *Sharing family possessions.*
D. *Earning and spending money.*
E. *Getting my family to accept my friends and dates.*
F. *Getting help from my family with my personal problems.*[12]

Since this chapter is concerned with curriculum design, space will not be devoted to a discussion of the specification of instructional objectives. For those interested in pursuing the subject further, many useful texts are available.[13]

---

12. John M. Mickelson, ed., *Getting Along with My Family* (Philadelphia: Curriculum Laboratory, Temple University, undated), pp. 2–4 (out of print).

13. See Robert F. Mager, *Preparing Instructional Objectives* (Belmont, Calif.: Fearon Publishers, 1962); Paul D. Plowman, *Behavioral Objectives* (Chicago: Science Research Associates, 1971).

In summation, statements of curricular objectives define intent, provide criteria for the selection of content and the determination of basic instructional strategies, and delimit that which is to be evaluated.

CONTENT

Once agreement has been reached concerning school purposes and curricular objectives, it is possible to determine curricular content. Even though the objectives of the curriculum may be stated in behavioral terms and with a high degree of precision, they are still broad. This is at once an advantage and a disadvantage. Broad objectives ultimately make possible a greater degree of individualization, but differences of opinion may arise concerning the exact content to be included in a particular instructional system to meet a particular set of objectives.

SCOPE   Scope refers to breadth or to the actual coverage of the curriculum. It should be readily apparent that any set of curricular objectives determined without some sort of organizing principles or rationale can only result in disorder. One part of the curriculum may be contravening another, and each may be contrary to the stated purposes of the school. In the case of the middle school, the purposes enunciated at the beginning of the present chapter provide a rationale and delimit the broad scope of the curriculum.

Subjects such as arithmetic, the language arts, and Spanish define the scope of the curriculum somewhat more precisely than do broad statements of purpose. Similarly, topics drawn from areas such as personal–social problems or based upon unifying themes such as the community, the school, or conservation also serve to delimit.

The specification of the scope of the curriculum depends upon the rationale; so does the selection of particular objectives. Tyler has stated that consistency and discrimination in the selection of objectives are provided for through the use of twin filters: a philosophy of education and a psychology of learning.[14] Certainly the rationale for the design of the middle school curriculum will depend upon what is conceived to be educationally "good" and what is believed concerning the way in which young people grow and learn. Rationale plus objectives equals scope. Scope is narrowed as objectives are refined.

---

14. Tyler, *op. cit.*, pp. 22–28.

SEQUENCE Sequence, which is related to scope much as curriculum is related to instruction, refers to the ordering of the content of the curriculum. Every curriculum must provide for some form of orderly, progressive arrangement of subject matter: this is sequence.

Determination of sequence is dependent upon three factors: objectives, content, and the learner. Obviously there can be no sequence without an objective, something to be learned, and a person to learn that something. This deceptively simple problem is often more difficult to solve than the question of scope.

In the past, sequence was usually determined by chronology or difficulty. For most of us American history began with the period of discovery and exploration, moved through colonization, then the Revolution, and so on. Arithmetic began with simple number combinations of addition and subtraction; then multiplication and division were introduced. Teachers assumed they were moving from the least difficult to the more difficult. Today curricular sequence is still based on chronology and difficulty, but with certain modifications. There are different views as to what constitutes difficulty and as to what children should learn at a given age, particularly in light of the writings of Bruner and Piaget. The work of Piaget in particular has much to offer the middle school curriculum designer (see Chapter 3) when it comes to planning sequence as well as selecting content.

The knowledge explosion has increased the need to be even more selective about what is to be included in the curriculum. At one time every United States history course, whether elementary, junior high school, or high school, included the period of discovery and exploration and the period of colonization. Because of the vast outpouring of knowledge, these historical periods are increasingly being left to the middle school; the high school course begins with the Revolutionary War.

Further shifts in sequence are no doubt on the way. For example, some experimentation is being carried on with introducing computer-assisted instruction in algebra at the middle school level rather than leaving it to the high school. Science, which formerly began with grade eight or nine, is included at all the levels of the middle school.

Among the modifications of the chronology–difficulty sequence is an approach known as *spiraling*. Spiraling is not a new concept, but was given new life by Bruner at the time he began his advocacy of basing curriculum content on the structure of subject matter. As Bruner perceives it, spiraling is a curriculum design in which basic concepts, principles, and generalizations are presented, ignored for a time, and then returned to; in this way the curricular plan progresses continuously toward a more sophisticated and deeper presentation of the subject matter.[15] The concept of spiraling may be applied just as readily to a needs- or problems-based curriculum.

The danger inherent in the spiral curriculum is that it can very easily become the repetitive curriculum.

> Essential to the success of a spiral curriculum is the clear-cut understanding . . . that spiraling is organized in terms of the structure of the subject matter . . . not in terms of the traditional view that subject matter is the continued incrementation of bits and pieces of information organized in some logical fashion to facilitate their mastery.[16]

Curricula that are supposed to spiral have not achieved notable success in actually spiraling. This is caused, more than anything else, by the failure of those who design and implement the curriculum to understand that spiraling must be based on constantly expanding and deepening presentations of concepts, principles, and generalizations, and not on increasing the quota of incremental bits and pieces of information to be covered.

Earlier, it was noted briefly that a problems- or needs-based curriculum might also spiral. An excellent example of such a design is to be found in *Developing a Curriculum for Modern Living*. The authors present "persistent life situations," which they define as "those situations that recur in the life of the individual in many different ways as he grows from infancy to maturity."[17] These life situations are classified according to four main stages in life: early childhood, later childhood, youth, and adulthood. The various categories of life situations include such things as maintaining both physical and mental health, meeting social needs, developing the intellect, making moral choices, developing aesthetic appreciation, and maintaining good group relations. All areas of living are included.

It is obvious from the two examples of spiraling just described —spiraling by subject matter and spiraling by needs—that any long-range curriculum plan involving spiraling must be on a kindergarten-through-twelfth-grade basis; otherwise there can be no spiral. All long-range curriculum plans should be kindergarten through twelfth grade in scope. When the concept of spiraling is

---

15. Jerome S. Bruner, *The Process of Education* (Cambridge, Mass.: Harvard University Press, 1960), pp. 12–13.

16. Mickelson, "Curriculum Designs," p. 113.

17. Florence B. Stratemeyer, Hamden L. Forkner, Margaret G. McKim, and A. Harry Passow, *Developing a Curriculum for Modern Living*, 2nd ed. (New York: Teachers College Press, 1957), p. 115.

explored, it becomes most apparent that no respectable middle school curriculum can be designed and planned without concern for what has gone before at the elementary level and what is to come after in the high school.

In summation, it is the responsibility of the middle school to make curricular provisions for the development of concepts and skills introduced at the elementary school level, to introduce appropriate new content, and to assure the interlocking and blending of the middle school curriculum with that of the high school.

SUBJECT MATTER   Although the middle school represents a new approach to education for the "middle years," Gross determined that approximately 55 percent of the middle schools queried in a study had what was apparently some sort of subject matter–based curriculum.[18]   In any case, they did not utilize a block-of-time program, which the remaining 45 percent acknowledged.   Of additional interest is the fact that sixty-seven (almost 42 percent) of the 160 schools reporting block-of-time programs stated that the subjects maintained their identity within the block.   (The self-contained classroom seems a likely explanation.)   Thus, it appears that conventional subject matter areas not only provide the content for most middle school curricula, but also help to define scope. This tendency to cling to the old and to disregard the opportunities for experimentation and innovation is indeed unfortunate.   It appears that the middle school in the majority of instances is simply perpetuating at least some of the less desirable practices of the junior high school.

Definitive data are unavailable, but it does seem likely that the majority of the 75 percent of the schools designing curricula based on conventional subject matter areas may have utilized recent approaches to curriculum design within subject matter areas.   In the last fifteen years the emphasis has been on designing the curriculum in terms of the structure of the subject matter.   Jerome Bruner, who is generally credited with bringing national prominence to this approach, uses the term structure to mean the basic concepts, principles, generalizations, and the like that are peculiar to a specific discipline.[19]   For example, the emphasis in mathematics has shifted from computational skills to sets, and those who attended school some years ago find themselves in classes in modern mathematics for parents!   Computational skills are not ignored by the curriculum planners; mathematics curricula have simply

---

18.   Gross, *op. cit.*, pp. 132–146. See also Gateswood, *op. cit.*, p. 222.

19.   Bruner, *op. cit.*, pp. 6–8.

been cast in a different context. A similar emphasis on the structure of subject matter may be found in programs developed or proposed in English, science, and social studies. The emphasis is on the cognitive.

STUDENT NEEDS   Recently Bruner noted that the "rationale is not enough," and he publicly called for greater emphasis on the affective in curriculum building.[20]   Interesting in connection with Bruner's remarks concerning the need for a greater emphasis on the affective in education is the fact that about one-fourth of the middle school programs surveyed by Gross are based on some sort of personal–social needs or problems approach.[21]   Needs are usually assumed to be common to the students for whom the curriculum is planned.   Unfortunately, the concept of needs is extremely ambiguous, a characteristic that led Havighurst to develop his well-known list of developmental tasks[22] and that led Stratemeyer, Forkner, McKim, and Passow to develop their list of persistent life problems.[23]   In reality, however, although the notion may have hit Bruner recently, the desirability of emphasizing the affective in one way or another has permeated the thinking of curriculum specialists for many years.   This has been particularly true of those concerned with the middle years of schooling.

The necessity of the middle school meeting the needs of the students it serves is clearly stated in the list of purposes at the beginning of this chapter.   The notion of needs implies a concomitant lack or weakness in the student or society.   Just what these needs are and which ones the middle school should seek to meet are prickly questions.

Needs can be roughly divided into two categories: personal (including social) and societal.   The personal–social needs of middle youth are those any boy or girl must face while growing up in our society.   The complexity, difficulty, and impact of the problem of meeting these needs will vary with the individual.   Havighurst called these needs developmental tasks; for him a developmental task is one "which arises at or about a certain period in the life of an individual, successful achievement of which leads to his happi-

---

20. Jerome S. Bruner, "The Process of Education Revisited," address given at the Annual Conference of the Association for Supervision and Curriculum Development, St. Louis, Mo., March 9, 1971.

21. Gross, *op. cit.*, pp. 132–146.

22. Robert J. Havighurst, *Human Development and Education* (New York: Longman, Inc., 1953).

23. Stratemeyer et al., *op. cit.*

ness and to success with the later tasks, while failure leads to unhappiness in the individual, disapproval by society, and difficulty with later tasks."[24] Examples of developmental tasks at the middle school level would include getting along with peers, achieving a satisfactory heterosexual adjustment, laying the basis for a career choice, and becoming less dependent upon one's parents.

At the opposite pole of the needs concept lie the needs perceived as the needs of society. Any society makes certain demands upon its citizens; these are perceived by the curriculum designer as student needs even though the student may not share the precept. "Society-based needs can be construed in many ways, such as the 'need' to be a good citizen, the 'need' to understand the American heritage, the 'need' to support the 'American way of life,' and so on."[25]

Designing a curriculum plan based solely upon either of the extremes is not really satisfactory for middle school students. As a result, curricula that are designed to "meet needs" generally reflect some sort of personal–social/societal compromise which takes into consideration the needs of both youngster and society. The determination of which needs to select at a particular time, which to reject, and which merely to postpone to a later date depends upon the children and the communities to be served.

STRATEGY

In the lower right-hand corner of Figure 4-1 appears the word *strategy*. Strategy refers to planning for instruction at the curricular level. It is used in the broad military sense; that is, the planning and directing of projects involving the movement of forces (for our purpose we substitute the broad planning of programs of instruction). This is in contrast to *tactics*, which refers to the actual processes or procedures for moving or handling forces (for present purposes we substitute classroom methodology for tactics). This phase of the discussion of curriculum design will be concerned with instructional strategy at the broad planning level.

We have noted several times that objectives, content, and strategy are interrelated and that no one part can be emphasized at the expense of the others if a complete design is to be the outcome. Like content, strategies are determined by the objectives to be reached.

24. Havighurst, *op. cit.*, p. 2.
25. Mickelson, "Curriculum Designs," p. 112.

METHOD OF INQUIRY   New strategies that are commonly used include critical thinking, discovery, the method of inquiry, and problem-solving.   In practice there is not a great deal of difference between them, and it seems likely that the basic cognitive abilities required in their performance are not substantially different, no matter what the strategy is called.[26]   Consequently, only one of the strategies will be illustrated here.

The great majority of middle school curricula include science; unquestionably all should contain it.   One of the broad objectives commonly assigned to science courses is that "the student shall act in the manner of a scientist," even though it is clearly understood that the degree of scientific expertise expected of or achieved by the student is far below that expected of a professional.   This new curricular objective has meant not only new subject matter and new ways of organizing subject matter, but also new ways of organizing for instruction.   The instructional strategy most often selected to achieve this objective is the method of inquiry.

Inquiry is a fundamental process in basic science, for the scientist is engaged in an unending quest for knowledge.   "The method of inquiry" provides a handy label for describing what the scientist does to discover what he wants to know.   Although it is true that the method of inquiry is usually associated with new science programs, "It has application wherever there is a need for the development of understanding, for generalizations, or for new knowledge.   Inquiry procedures are essential to critical thinking, to problem solving and . . . to the discovery method."[27]   It is, therefore, a useful example for present purposes.

The method of inquiry is not something that proceeds by numbers or has a set procedure.   However, it does possess identifiable elements which it will be helpful to examine.   One of the ways in which the method of inquiry can be represented is shown in Figure 4-2.

It cannot be emphasized too much that if curricular objectives require that the method of inquiry be the instructional strategy, then a major shift in the usual instructional practice will have to take place.   Over the years the emphasis has been on learner intake, storage, and retrieval of information, accompanied by instructional strategies appropriate to these demands.   The inquiry method as represented in Figure 4-2 requires first some kind of blocking. The inquirer then needs opportunities to secure what are for the

26.   J. P. Guilford, "Intellectual Factors in Productive Thinking," in *Productive Thinking in Education*, rev. ed. M. J. Ashner and C. E. Bish, eds. (Washington, D.C.: National Education Association, 1968).

27.   John M. Mickelson, "Instructional Processes," in *The Intermediate Schools*, Leslie W. Kindred, ed., © 1968, Prentice-Hall, Inc., Englewood Cliffs, N.J.

General direction of flow of inquiry

→

Questioning	Data	Hypothesis	Testing	Concepts
Discrepancies	collection	production		Generalizations
Blocking	Analysis			Theories
	Synthesis			Solutions

←   →

Ebb and flow

Figure 4-2.   The Inquiry Process (Source: Adapted from Mickelson, "Instructional Processes," Figure 4-1.)

learner the essential raw data, the freedom to hypothesize, the chance to test his hypotheses, and, ultimately, the ability to develop concepts and generalizations.   This is a slow process, and there is much ebb and flow among data analysis, hypothesis production, and testing.   The implications for content selection and organization are enormous.   The importance of the choice of the method of inquiry (or a similar approach) as the broad instructional strategy to be used in planning a curriculum for middle schoolers who are just moving into the formal operations stage of intellectual development should be readily apparent.

SIMULATIONS   The technique of using simulations has been largely untested and little used in middle grades classrooms.   For the purpose of definition, simulations can be defined as a teaching technique that uses or creates "real-life" situations through games, role playing, or sociodramas, generally with decision-making involvement of the participants during and at the end of the program.

Many claims have been made for the effectiveness of simulations as a teaching tool.   Among the values are the high-level interest of students, large individual involvement of participants, the ability to develop higher-level thinking skills such as observation, classification, and defining.   All of these lead to greater motivation by students.   Research to date has neither supported nor refuted these claims.

The greatest emphasis on simulations has been at the postsecondary or high school levels.   Simulations began to appear in large numbers in the middle 1960s, but very little new games material has appeared since the zenith of the 1960s.

The most probable direction for simulations lies less in the occasional use of games than in the area of role playing.   Through the techniques of role playing, students can be helped to better understand both themselves and their classmates, to comprehend their own attitudes toward issues and the probable causes of the issues, as well as, hopefully, to develop new directions for rethinking a problem. As more teachers receive training in human development, interaction through simulations should receive even greater impetus than at present.

With this brief account of instruction as it relates to curriculum design (brief because the major focus in curriculum design is on content) our discussion has come a full circle.

PUTTING IT ALL TOGETHER

Curriculum design must be concerned with objectives, content, and strategy. Along with these basic elements go related problems of determining scope and sequence.

The Social Science Studies Curriculum Project has developed a curriculum called *Man and Politics,* designed for use at the upper middle school level.[28] One of its units is "From Subject to Citizen." A major objective of the unit is to have the student function as a historian functions; content selection is based on the structures-of-knowledge notion, and the broad instructional strategy is the discovery approach. The case study provides the format. In the following quotation Patterson describes the implementation of the curriculum in the classroom. "Sudbury: A Case Study in New England Land Settlement" follows a young Englishman, Peter Noyes, who leaves his home in Weyhill, England, in 1637, to go first to Watertown, Massachusetts, and finally to Sudbury. There he remained, as do his descendants today.

> (As Peter Noyes) moves from Weyhill to Watertown to Sudbury—and as others move farther to Marlborough—relevant records of the time are used. These include land distribution lists, maps, town records, and the like. Students work through these materials, formulating hypotheses step by step as they go. In the process, they encounter an evident breakdown of medieval concepts of social status and land rights. Common land ownership in a ranked society gives way to individually owned land in a much more equalitarian and mobile society. "Sudbury" involves students in speculating about factors that conditioned the distribution of land, and has them try their own hands at dividing up land and comparing their own decisions with decisions that were actually made by colonial settlers. They generalize about the causes of change and the

---

28. Educational Development Center, Newton, Massachusetts.

democratization of land ownership; in addition they hypothe-size about the relationship between increasing equality of land ownership and political attitudes and behavior.[29]

This quick summary by Patterson reveals the careful curricu-lar planning underlying the implementation of the unit. The broad objective was clear, and it was accurately reflected in the choice of curriculum content and basic instructional strategy. There were no dry-as-dust facts to be memorized; there were only primary ma-terials of the type with which historians themselves work. There was the challenge to develop hypotheses, to test them, and, ulti-mately, to develop generalizations with implications far beyond seventeenth-century Sudbury.

EVALUATION

At the start of the present discussion we noted that a factor *related* to the design of curricula is evaluation. The Eight Year Study pre-sents a contrary point of view in which evaluation is perceived as an integral part of the basic curriculum design.[30] There is no question of the importance of evaluation. The question concerns the func-tion of evaluation. There appear to be several functions:

1. Diagnosis of student strengths and weaknesses.
2. Assessment of student achievement.
3. Assessment of teacher effectiveness.
4. Assessment of the curriculum.

None of these are really a part of the curriculum. The first two represent something carried out upon the student, the third something done to the teacher, and the fourth judgments concern-ing the curriculum itself. The confusion arises from an inability to distinguish between curriculum and instruction. Item one is unquestionably a part of instructional tactics; item two could either be an effort to assess a student's level of achievement for guidance purposes or an attempt to assess the effectiveness of instruction. Item two might also provide data for item three. Item four repre-sents a very complex problem that certainly cannot be a part of a curriculum design without disarranging the basic design itself.

---

29. F. K. Patterson, *Man and Politics*, Occasional Paper No. 4, The Social Sciences Cur-riculum Study Program (Cambridge, Mass.: Educational Development Laboratory, 1965).

30. See Hilda Taba, *Curriculum Development: Theory and Practice* (New York: Harcourt Brace Jovanovich, Inc., 1962), pp. 424–425; or Virgil E. Herrick, in *Strategies of Curriculum Development*, James B. MacDonald, Dan W. Anderson, and Frank B. May, eds. (Columbus, Ohio: Charles E. Merrill Books, Inc., 1965), p. 24.

The design for a bridge does not include within the design provisions for evaluating the bridge. The design is first conceived and then ways of testing the design are conceived.

Thus evaluation of curriculum design may be part of instruction on the tactical level, it may be used to assess the teacher, or, more broadly, it may be used to assess the curriculum itself. *In any event, evaluation requires its own designs and models,* which must be consistent with its own purposes. It is not and cannot be a part of the basic design of the curriculum. For a discussion of evaluation see Chapter 10.

⪦ 5 ⪧

MIDDLE SCHOOL ORGANIZATION AND PROGRAMS

As important as it is to examine the basic elements of curriculum, it is equally as important to examine actual curricular practice. This task is accomplished in two ways in this chapter. First we look at the curricular practices of middle schools in general. Then we examine several selected programs in particular and judge the programs against the criteria developed in Chapter 4.

ASPECTS OF THE MIDDLE SCHOOL CURRICULUM

The mere fact that "everybody's doing it" does not of necessity mean that a particular curriculum or curriculum-related practice is right or desirable. Data concerning the trends in middle school curriculum design and development make possible the comparison of specific programs with general practice, provide a reservoir of ideas and experience upon which persons contemplating the organization of a middle school program may draw, and constitute a basis for ascertaining whether or not middle school programs are fulfilling the purposes for which they were developed.

Four aspects of general middle school practices have been selected as having particular relevance to present purposes: grade-level organization, school size, curricular provisions, and program implementation. The data cited in this section of Chapter 5 are drawn primarily from a study by Gross, "An Analysis of the Present and Perceived Purposes, Functions, and Characteristics of the Middle School."[1]

GRADE-LEVEL ORGANIZATION Differences of opinion exist concerning the grade levels that ought to be included in the middle school. A variety of practices have evolved, but little solid evidence is available concerning the extent of particular practices. Gross's findings, to the extent that they are representative, do reveal the emergence of several clear patterns of practice.

Of 1,337 middle schools identified by Gross, 64 percent included grades six through eight, whereas slightly less than one-third (32.9 percent) encompassed grades five through eight. Three years earlier Alexander uncovered the same proportions in his survey of 1,101 middle schools.[2] Middle school program planners, it seems clear, are adopting, at a ratio of nearly two to one, the five-three-four pattern of grade organization over the four-four-four plan. The occurrence of other grade arrangements is negligible. Gross's findings were later confirmed by Raymer.[3]

Nearly two out of three schools have resolved the question of the point between the lower and middle schools in favor of beginning with grade six. The majority of those middle schools that begin with grade five appear to be in large urban areas. These figures suggest that attempts to resolve the twin problems of housing and de facto segregation may have exercised the greatest influence on the decision to begin schools at grade five.

In the minds of some middle school advocates, the ninth grader is not yet ready to enter the specialized academic situation found in the senior high school. Placement of the ninth grade is being debated by an increasing number of educators. Should it be in a separate unit like the junior high school, or does it really belong in the senior high school where a continuous, integrated four-year sequence would then be possible? An increasing emphasis on post–high school education, of which the growing numbers of com-

---

1. Grateful acknowledgment is made to Bernard M. Gross, for permission to draw extensively upon his dissertation, "An Analysis of the Present and Perceived Purposes, Functions, and Characteristics of the Middle School," doctoral dissertation, Temple University, 1972.

2. William M. Alexander, *A Survey of Organizational Patterns of Reorganized Middle Schools* (Washington, D.C.: U.S. Dept. of Health, Education, and Welfare, 1968). See also Ronald D. Kealy, "The Middle Schools Movement, 1969–70," *The National Elementary School Principal*, Vol. 51, November, 1971, pp. 20–25.

3. Joe T. Raymer, "A Study to Identify Middle Schools and to Determine the Current Level of Implementation of Eighteen Basic Middle School Characteristics in Selected United States and Michigan Schools," doctoral dissertation, Michigan State University, 1974.

munity colleges are evidence, is causing school people to look again at the desirability of a four-year college preparatory sequence. With this sequence, basic subjects can be pursued with increased articulation. The feeling is returning (actually it never completely disappeared) that the ninth grade is more closely related to the grades above than to those immediately below.

It cannot be said that one particular organizational pattern is better than the others. Each school district must determine for itself the pattern best suited to helping its student population meet the specific educational objectives established for the projected unit. Certainly the overwhelming employment of the five-three-four and four-four-four patterns of grade organization means that the majority of public middle schools are serving the children who are in the developmental stages for which the schools were designed.

SCHOOL SIZE   In addition to grade-level patterns, another important factor is the number of students a school accommodates. Extremely large schools may defeat the purposes of the middle school simply because of sheer numbers; on the other hand, schools with small enrollments may be uneconomical. Obviously, neither extreme is desirable.

The figures developed by Gross in his analysis of middle school trends reveal that most middle school enrollments are somewhere between the extremes. Of the 363 schools reporting enrollment figures, approximately 65 percent listed 700 or fewer students. An additional 16.5 percent were in the 700–900 range, and 8.8 percent enrolled between 900 and 1,100 students. Slightly more than 8.0 percent reported enrollments in the 1,100–1,500 range. Only nine schools acknowledged total enrollments beyond 1,500.

Although the history of the middle school is brief and schools have a way of increasing their enrollments unexpectedly, it seems reasonable to infer that a serious effort is being made to keep the size of the middle school in line with its purposes. What is the optimum size for a middle school? The school must be large enough to provide the services and curricular alternatives needed by middle school children economically, but it must not be so large that regimentation and depersonalization become the order of the day. This suggests a school with an enrollment of 750–1,000. Certainly it is desirable to have no more than 1,200 students.

CURRICULAR PROVISIONS   The middle school may very well be enrolling within its parameters the older children, preadolescents, and early adolescents for whom it is intended, but if the program provided is irrelevant to their needs, then the whole is wasted effort. Caught in the midst of such a program, any teacher, no matter how competent, will find it extremely difficult to meet the needs of the students in his or her charge. In short, a school may be in the paradoxical position of actually creating a great many of the problems with which it then must contend.

Curricular provisions may be divided into three segments for convenient analysis: the part of the curriculum that is required of all, elective offerings, and cocurricular activities. We will then look briefly at the new concept of mini-courses.

Required Curriculum. What curricular experiences are required of all students? It certainly comes as no great surprise to find, upon examining Table 5-1, that four major academic subjects are required of all students at all grade levels: English or language arts, mathematics, science, and social studies. English and social studies are sometimes offered in some sort of block-of-time combina-

Table 5-1 REQUIRED SUBJECTS IN FIFTH, SIXTH, SEVENTH, AND EIGHTH GRADES*

	5TH GRADE		6TH GRADE		7TH GRADE		8TH GRADE	
	NO.	%	NO.	%	NO.	%	NO.	%
Language Arts	369	100.0	369	100.0	369	100.0	369	100.0
Social Studies	369	100.0	369	100.0	369	100.0	369	100.0
Science	369	100.0	369	100.0	369	100.0	369	100.0
Mathematics	369	100.0	369	100.0	369	100.0	369	100.0
Health and Physical Education	369	100.0	369	100.0	369	100.0	369	100.0
Foreign Language	25	6.7	52	14.0	61	16.5	48	13.0
Arts and Crafts	72	19.5	168	45.5	166	44.9	133	36.0
Shop and Home Economics	32	8.6	51	13.8	141	38.2	144	39.0
Typing	8	2.1	11	2.9	21	5.6	17	14.6
Vocal Music	109	29.5	218	59.0	183	49.5	149	40.3
Instrumental Music	34	9.2	70	18.9	72	19.5	63	17.0

* Table indicates number of schools requiring courses listed and what percentage of the total sample of 369 it constitutes.

tion. The only other across-the-board requirements are health and physical education.

Other subjects familiar to junior high school programs, such as industrial arts, vocal music, foreign languages, arts and crafts, and home economics, are regularly required in the middle school. But in only one instance and at one grade level—sixth-grade vocal music—is one of these subjects required of more than half the students at a single point in the middle school program.

Two conclusions may be drawn from the preceding data; one is certainly positive, the other may possibly be negative. The first conclusion is that the middle school takes its responsibility to provide for the general education of its students quite seriously. The second conclusion, which requires a familiarity with the curricular offerings of the junior high school, is that the majority of middle schools do not differ significantly from their predecessor, the junior high school.

Electives. In addition to the general education of its clientele, another commonly accepted purpose of the middle school is to provide opportunities for exploration, both to enhance the richness of the student's experiential background and to provide him with a broader base of knowledge from which to make academic and career decisions. If this is indeed an accepted purpose, and there seems little

Table 5-2 ELECTIVE SUBJECTS IN FIFTH, SIXTH, SEVENTH, AND EIGHTH GRADES*

	5TH GRADE		6TH GRADE		7TH GRADE		8TH GRADE	
	NO.	%	NO.	%	NO.	%	NO.	%
Speech	3	0.8	12	3.2	38	10.2	47	12.7
Foreign Language	8	2.1	13	3.5	79	21.4	100	27.1
Arts and Crafts	10	2.7	25	6.7	70	18.9	81	21.9
Shop and Home Economics	6	1.6	11	2.9	43	11.6	74	20.0
Typing	3	0.8	7	1.8	15	4.0	24	6.5
Vocal Music	26	7.0	58	15.7	114	30.8	131	35.5
Instrumental Music	7	1.8	0	0.0	194	52.5	185	50.1
Modern Math	6	1.6	15	4.0	17	4.6	18	4.8

* Table indicates number of schools providing courses listed and what percentage of the total sample of 369 it constitutes.

disagreement, then it follows that a wide range of alternatives should be available to the student.

The subjects most often offered as electives are instrumental music, vocal music, and foreign languages, in that order. Arts and crafts, shop, and home economics are also available, although not as often as music and languages. The remaining electives are offered even less frequently.

The findings concerning elective offerings, especially when compared with the required courses described earlier, lead to several conclusions. First, unless a great deal is hidden behind the titles of the various categories, there is little to suggest that the formal elements of the curriculum are contributing much to the exploratory function of the middle school. The program does not generally appear to be different from that of the junior high school.

There are a few signs, which we will describe later, that a transition is beginning to occur. Hopefully Alexander and his colleagues were correct in applying the term "emergent" to the middle school.[4]

Cocurricular Activities. The middle school without a cocurricular program must be a rarity if it exists at all. One hundred percent of

Table 5-3   COCURRICULAR PROGRAMS*

ACTIVITY	NUMBER OF SCHOOLS	PERCENTAGE OF SCHOOLS
Band	306	82.9
Orchestra	115	31.1
Chorus	270	73.1
Glee Club	75	20.3
A Capella Choir	13	3.5
Student Government	239	64.7
Student Publications	193	52.3
Intramural Athletics (Girls)	232	62.8
Intramural Athletics (Boys)	253	68.5
Speech, Debating, etc.	96	26.0
Dramatics	149	40.3
Clubs	185	50.1

* Table indicates number of schools offering programs listed and what percentage of the total sample of 369 it constitutes.

4. William Alexander et al., *The Emergent Middle School* (New York: Holt, Rinehart and Winston, Inc., 1968).

the middle schools surveyed by Gross reported cocurricular programs, although the nature of the programs varied from school to school. A glance at Table 5-3 reveals that band is the activity most often provided, followed in descending order by chorus, intramural athletics for boys, student government, intramural athletics for girls, student publications, and clubs. No other type of activity is found in 50 percent of the schools.

A further examination of Table 5-3 reveals that five activities are overlapping musical activities, and two involve athletics. Only 50.1 percent of the schools offered a club program. A diversified musical program and a well-run intramural athletics program are important, but the findings suggest an imbalance, especially since many schools limit student participation. These findings suggest that club programs, which are available in only half the schools and are often of questionable value, are being required to carry a disproportionate share of the burden of providing a variety of alternatives for broadening the experiences of boys and girls.

Once again the question must be raised: Are most middle schools really providing for self-development, for exploration, and for individualization? Here is a real challenge to the designers of middle school programs. See Chapter 8 for a detailed discussion of the activity program.

Mini-courses. Far-sighted middle school principals have recognized that the ten- to fourteen-year-old student has the capability to be more responsible for his own learnings. As a result, innovative middle schools have allowed students to choose short-term courses geared to their own interests. These mini-courses are generally planned cooperatively by teachers and students, ensuring maximum involvement of all parties concerned.

The Wilmer E. Shue Middle School, Newark, Delaware, offers a large variety of short-term electives geared to the interests and needs of middle school students. These non-credit courses vary in length from two, three, or four weeks to six weeks.

Among the mini-course subjects offered within the major disciplines are the following:

HUMANITIES (LANGUAGE ARTS)

Cultural Anthropology
Newspaper Production
Poetry
Let's Express Ourselves

Myths and Legends
Monologues and Radio
Plays
Playwriters' Forum
Writing Lab

HUMANITIES (SOCIAL STUDIES)

Cartography

Holidays around the
World

African Music and Dance

Imaginary Field Trip

Current Events

Forms of Government

Gandhi Passive Resistance

Great Men of European
History

Hawaii, A Racial Study

History of European
Sports

History of Law

Major Religions of the
World

Mystery of Easter Island

Blacks in American
History (1400–1865)

The Opium War

Tax

MATHEMATICS

CSP (Compass, Straight-
edge, and Pencil)

Base Systems (Numera-
tion Systems)

Probability

Math Catch-Up

Chess

Architecture around Us

Logic

Map Reading

Math in Music

Sea-Saw Arithmetic
(Ratio and Proportion)

Of Men and Numbers

Candy-Store Arithmetic

SCIENCE

Ornithology (Bird Study)

The Laser

Oceanography

Man versus Nature

Photography

The Pond Community

Suburban Conservation

Radiation Biology

Space Biology

Animal Behavior

Scientific Fiction

Basic Electricity

Learning about Trees

Atomic and Nuclear
Energy

Current Topics in
Medicine

Drug Seminar

Fossil Collecting

Rocks and Minerals

Raising Houseflies

In addition to those offered by the major disciplines or departments, the teaching teams also offer a variety of mini-courses extending from a minimum of two weeks to a maximum of four weeks. Sample electives by grades include the following:

GRADE SIX

Butterfly Metamorphosis | Fun with Words
Storytelling | Folk Dancing
TV News and Production | Chess
Map Making | Creating a Puppet
Basic Rocketry | America, A Melting Pot
Creative Stitchery | Oceanography

GRADE SEVEN

Cartography | Handwriting
Tours Abroad | Science Fiction
Science Illustrations | Creating Flowers
Speed Reading | Scrabble
Christmas Literature | Parlor Games

GRADE EIGHT

Physical Anthropology | The Laser
Scrabble | Stock Market
Ancient Egypt | Glass Bending
Public Speaking | Photography
Free Reading | Industrial Science Projects

Many mini-courses cross grade lines, as would be expected, and many are reoffered during the year according to student interest.

A comparison of the mini-course idea with the old club program of the junior high school clearly demonstrates the improvement. The topics, selected frequently, are geared to current interests rather than being static year-long choices. Obviously, these short-term programs related to immediate student interests accord better with what we have long known about the unpredictable ten- to fourteen-year-old student.

IMPLEMENTATION The manner of implementation of any curriculum is of critical importance. The way in which the curriculum is organized and staffed has much to do with whether or not the school's mission is achieved. Consequently, a brief examination of selected aspects of implementation may yield additional valuable insights into the degree to which the middle school is achieving its purpose.

Block-of-Time Classes.   Classes utilizing two or more consecutive periods and classes operating as self-contained units are not new. Both types were reported by approximately one-half of the respondees to Gross's questionnaire.   Of the two types, the two-or-more-consecutive-periods type probably represents the nearest thing to a minor crack in the shell of conventional curriculum design in most middle schools.   Self-contained classes, generally operative at the fifth- and sixth-grade levels, are mainly holdovers from former elementary programs.   The purpose of the self-contained classroom in this instance is to facilitate the articulation of programs and to ameliorate student adjustment problems in a new situation.

More than 90 percent of the block-of-time classes identified included English and/or social studies in combination with each other or some other subject(s).   Further, in actual practice, the block-of-time arrangement represents a minimal change from the conventional system, since each subject retains its identity within the block (in 36 percent of the cases reported), or, if the subjects remain separate, there is a planned effort at correlation within the block (an additional 30 percent of cases reported). Although these figures suggest that about one-third of the schools may be doing something different within the block of time, other factors reduce this proportion further.   Thus evidence indicates that about one-fourth of the schools are developing programs that go beyond the conventional programs which have been so often tried and so often found wanting.

Our earlier conclusion that the middle school program reflects a serious effort to provide for the general education of its students is not rendered invalid by the apparent deficiencies in the implementation of the block-of-time program.   What is questionable is whether the middle school is in reality meeting the closely related purposes of individual self-development and self-actualization when the bulk of the students' school day is occupied by a mandated curriculum which appears to be little different from that which it is supposed to supplant.   It is to be devoutly hoped that the situation is merely transitional.

Modular Scheduling.   Reams of paper have been devoted to the desirability of modular scheduling, but apparently the designers of middle school programs have as yet been little influenced by this movement.   The modal school day in the schools surveyed by Gross consisted of seven periods of 40–45 minutes in a six-hour school day exclusive of lunch.   Although a number of the schools scheduled fewer periods and larger blocks of time, only five of the 327 stated that they used a modular schedule.   The time range of the school day for most schools was five and one-half to six and one-half hours, and the number of periods was six to eight. It is apparent that middle schools are approaching cautiously the notion of dividing the school day into many short time blocks, or modules, which are then combined according to need.

Another factor accounting for the apparent reluctance to employ modules is that many middle schools use the self-contained classroom in grades five and six. It is also possible that a sort of modular scheduling takes place within the longer blocks of time, especially if a team is involved. In any event, data presently available do not suggest any major change in the patterning of the middle school day.

ORGANIZATION FOR INSTRUCTION   Previously we noted that the middle school curriculum was generally conventional in its organization, although the block-of-time approach appears as an innovation in a number of schools. There is more to organizing for instruction, however, than simply setting the limits within which one plans for learning to occur. Careful attention must be given to what will happen within those limits.

Team Teaching.   The most frequently reported pattern of instructional organization is team teaching. Almost 85 percent (313 schools) in Gross's study reported team teaching in some form and to some extent. Further, it seems likely that the use of paraprofessionals as team members was limited since only 52 percent (192) of the schools reported employing them. The number of teams not including paraprofessionals is actually greater than the difference between the immediately preceding figures, because many schools limit the assignment of paraprofessionals to such duties as playground, lunchroom, or study-hall supervision. Most teaching teams, then, are completely staffed by certified personnel.

Large-group instruction is usually thought of in connection with team teaching, possibly because of the Trump recommendations, so it is surprising to find that less than half the schools reported the use of large-group instruction. Possibly large-group instruction was perceived as a part of team teaching and hence it was not reported separately. More likely, however, team teaching referred to the manner in which teachers functioned in relation to each other and not to the way in which pupils were organized for instructional purposes. This could account for the fact that many schools apparently did not include the paraprofessionals as team members. See Chapter 9 for a full discussion of team teaching.

Individualization. Along with other changes in the organization for instruction has come increased emphasis on independent study as a means of individualization. Independent study may range all the way from a project carried on within the confines of the conventional class to a student working on his own under the supervision of a teacher. Although it is not possible to determine from Gross's findings just what kind of independent study is involved, slightly more than 84 percent of 369 schools reported provisions for individual work by students; 46 percent provided special facilities for students working alone. Of most interest is the provision of special facilities, for this suggests a commitment to the idea of independent study even if present performance leaves something to be desired.

Class Size. Consistent with the goal of individualization are efforts to place limitations on class size. Even though it is a crude and insufficient measure, it is nevertheless one of the few gauges available. Gross found the average class size among those reporting to be in the range of twenty-five to twenty-nine students. More than 71 percent of the schools averaged fewer than twenty-nine students per class, and the great majority of the rest averaged thirty to thirty-four students. None of the schools reported more than forty.

Obviously, some classes in schools where the average size was in the range of twenty-five to twenty-nine enrolled more than thirty students in some classes. However, in view of the pressures on the schools to increase class size, it would appear that a definite attempt is being made to keep the student–teacher ratio at a reasonable level. This will, of course, be helpful in increasing opportunities for individualization in the conventional classroom setting. Perhaps what is most needed is for the middle school to develop new strategies for instruction and new patterns for staffing in the face of the economic and other pressures operating on today's schools. See Chapter 6 on individualizing instruction for a discussion of strategies.

TRENDS   In summarizing the chapter this far, several trends may be discerned in the middle school.

1. Nearly two out of every three middle schools include grades six, seven, and eight, and most of the remainder are accounted for by the five-six-seven-eight combination.
2. Ninety percent of the middle schools enroll 1,100 or fewer students; 83 percent enroll 900 or fewer.

3. All schools require English, mathematics, science, social studies, health, and physical education at all grade levels. Other required subjects include industrial arts, vocal music, a foreign language, arts and crafts, and home economics.
4. Only about 25 percent of the schools appear to have block-of-time programs, most of which are not innovative.
5. The most commonly offered electives are instrumental music, vocal music, and foreign languages, in that order.
6. The majority of cocurricular activities are centered around music and athletics. Other major activities include student government, publications, and clubs.
7. Team teaching and provisions for independent study are the instructional innovations most frequently reported. The use of paraprofessionals is to be found in less than half the schools.
8. Average class size is twenty-five to twenty-nine.
9. The modal school day is six hours long and includes seven periods of 40–45 minutes including lunch.
10. Very few schools report modular scheduling.

It is possible to draw a number of conclusions about the middle school. Since these have already been discussed, they will only be summarized here.

1. The middle school is serving the population for which it was designed.
2. An attempt is being made to make individualization possible through organizational means.
3. The middle school is attempting to provide for the general education of its clientele, although questions must be raised concerning its relevancy.
4. A serious question must be raised as to whether or not the middle school is meeting its obligations in terms of exploration, self-development, and self-actualization.
5. Questions must also be raised as to whether or not the instructional strategies vary greatly from the conventional procedures they were supposed to replace.

SELECTED MIDDLE SCHOOL PROGRAMS

The preceding survey of general practices provides a useful gestalt of the way in which curriculum and its implementation are developing at the middle school level. It is also worthwhile to engage in some "post-holing" and dig a little deeper than a survey permits.

In the pages that follow several actual middle school programs are described. These are only a few of the many fine programs that might have been chosen. The following examples reflect both imaginative and practical approaches to the development of the middle school program.

DEL MAR COMMUNITY INTERMEDIATE MIDDLE SCHOOL

The Del Mar Middle School is in the Reed Union School District, which lies north of San Francisco, just across the Golden Gate Bridge in Marin County. The district serves children from kindergarten through grade eight. The parents are generally well-educated professional people who expect a great deal from their schools and have high aspirations for their children. Per-pupil expenditures are above the state average and among the highest in Marin County. Although careful professional attention is apparent in the program development in the Reed District, "Parent participation has had a large part in the development."[5]

The Rationale. The faculty and the administration of the Del Mar School perceive a difference between the goals of the middle school and of other kinds of schools-in-the-middle. The difference, as they see it, lies not so much in the organization, grouping, courses, schedules, or staffing, but, rather, in terms of the attitudes, expectations, feelings, and perceptions of the faculty. The middle school is perceived as placing a particular value on "*the differences of students* and has the ability to accommodate children whose chronological ages are dominated by problems of coping with change —changing psychological structure, interests and personal relationships."[6]

Other prominent features of the rationale underlying the Del Mar program include the belief that the uses of subject matter should be taught (applications as opposed simply to mastery as an end in itself), that diagnosis of individual pupil needs forms the basis for individualized instruction, and that the pupil must be helped to direct his own learning.

Purposes. The purposes of the Del Mar Middle School are not unlike those of other schools-in-the-middle. Nevertheless, the middle school is perceived as being better able to achieve these goals. Del Mar firmly believes that the middle school should do the following:

---

5. "What's Happening to Schools and Children in the Middle?" Reed Union School District, Tiburon, Calif., 1970, p. i.

6. "Questions Asked about Del Mar Middle School, 1969," Reed Union School District, Tiburon, Calif., 1969, mimeo, p. 1.

1. Provide for the "intellectual training and education of each individual."
2. Aid the student "to move from dependence to independence as a learner."
3. Help to strengthen the student's self-concepts.
4. Try to preserve (or recapture) the sense of inquiry, curiosity, and commitment to learning and values through choosing from responsible alternatives of action.[7]

Organization and Program. School organization and program are usually interwoven to a degree that makes it difficult to discuss one without the other. This is particularly true of the Del Mar Community Intermediate Middle School.

Although the Del Mar School is an administrative unit, it is really two schools: an intermediate school and a middle school. The intermediate program, which was originally departmentalized, has evolved into a program for grades seven and eight "with three integrated subject areas: (1) humanities, (2) math–science, and (3) creative arts, Spanish, physical education and exploratory areas, with some nongradedness, interdisciplinary training and flexible modular scheduling."[8]

Side by side with the intermediate school functions a smaller middle school program for students in grades six, seven, and eight. The middle school is ungraded. Its total population of 110–125 is the responsibility of a team consisting of four teachers representing the major subject areas, one reading teacher, and one guidance counselor. Supporting the team are specialists in physical education, foreign languages, and the unified arts who serve as consultant instructors for the team. Only the middle school segment of the program will be described here.

As indicated, a team of six supplemented by appropriate specialists is responsible for a basic group of 110–125 children. The basic group contains all three grade levels. One team is responsible for the same group of children for all three years they are in the middle school, although there is some annual turnover in the class enrollment. This arrangement is believed to increase greatly the opportunities to individualize instruction and to improve the quality of guidance. "Students are able to progress on a continuous learning basis (in terms of) their individual needs and the teaching team's abilities to assess these needs and provide for them. Whether or not grade assignments are used as designated or the

---

7. *Ibid.*, p. 1.
8. "What's Happening?" *op. cit.*, p. 9.

program is 'ungraded' is immaterial."[9]   What is important is that teachers are attempting, in an atmosphere conducive to success, to individualize instruction.

The school day is flexibly organized.   Period length is determined by the objectives to be met and the needs of the students. Organizational strategies include large-group instruction, small-group instruction, and independent study.   There are times when the total group is involved in the same subject, such as social studies or science; at other times different students are pursuing different subjects.

The particular emphasis of the Del Mar Middle School is on the individualization of instruction.   It appears that this goal is being reached, although the basic curricular content seems to be rather conventional.   There is little apparent emphasis on personalization (as opposed to simple individualization).   It is very definitely a teacher-directed program.   The opportunities for the children to participate in the planning appear minimal, if they exist at all.   Del Mar is without question organized and equipped to meet the twin goals of intellectual training and developing student independence in learning.   The content and general strategies of instruction are consistent with the goals.   The degree to which the program strengthens the student's self-concepts and preserves his sense of curiosity and inquiry, however, is open to question.

LEXINGTON MIDDLE SCHOOL   The Lexington Middle School serves a small rural town and its surroundings in north-central North Carolina.   The school itself represents a happy combination of the local desire to improve educational opportunities for older children, preadolescents, and early adolescents and a substantial grant from the United States Office of Education under the PACE Project.

Rationale.   Lexington has set forth the rationale for its middle school succinctly and clearly.

> There are certain things we seek for the child who progresses through the Middle School, the most outstanding being that he learn to function usefully and thus happily in his environment.   With this in mind, we try to provide as many roads and vehicles as possible in order to achieve this end.   We believe that education cannot be conferred upon an individual but that education is a do-it-yourself process   The workmanship depends upon the individual child.[10]

---

9.   *Ibid.*, p. 9.

10.   R. Jack Davis and Daniel E. Todd, Jr., "Lexington Middle School," The City Schools, Lexington, N.C., undated.

Purposes. The purposes identified as appropriate for the Lexington Middle School are expressed as general objectives. When these objectives are analyzed in conjunction with what the school perceives to be the significant features of its program, it is clear that a sincere effort is being made to implement the commonly accepted purposes of the middle school.

Briefly, the general objectives are as follows: (1) to augment areas of instruction; (2) to improve pupil personnel services; (3) to improve evaluation procedures and reporting; (4) to improve school–community relations; (5) to increase the diversification of course offerings; and (6) to increase the holding power of the schools.

Program. Lexington has made certain assumptions concerning the nature of an educational program appropriate for middle school students. These assumptions are that the student should be able to progress at his own rate; that he should compete with himself, not others; that he should assume a reasonable amount of responsibility for his own learning; and that he should not fail a subject or grade. The foregoing assumptions in no way imply ability grouping or phasing.

The Lexington Middle School accepts the child "where he is in terms of his own academic achievement; it then permits him to proceed at his own rate and to the extent possible in each of the subject matter areas."[11] Thus, both the design of the curriculum and its implementation are firmly rooted in the needs of the child.

Within some subject areas, instruction is organized along continuous progress lines. The objectives are carefully defined. For instance, in seventh-grade mathematics the learning objectives are divided among the thirty-six weeks of school, with particular objectives assigned to a particular week. A plan of behavioral objectives for each work week is devised by a team of mathematics teachers working together.

The plan for the work week includes a precise statement in behavioral language of the objectives for the week, minimum criteria for student achievement at the week's end, the means and conditions for evaluating achievement, and the resources available for accomplishing the objectives.

The student moves from one work-week plan to another as he satisfies the achievement criteria for each plan. It is possible for some students to complete the thirty-six plans in less than thirty-six weeks; others may take longer than thirty-six weeks. The student who completes the work-week plan ahead of schedule may continue

---

11. *Ibid.*

on to the first work week of the next level of work-week plans, undertake supervised independent study, or participate in special seminars. Presumably, a combination of the available options is also possible.

The student who does not complete the work-week plans in the allotted time is expected to complete the remaining plans before he moves on to the first work-week plan at the next higher level.

Organization. A program that permits students to pursue lessons at their own rates, to engage in independent study, and to participate in seminars and other enriching experiences based on their needs and interests is difficult to schedule. Neither the self-contained classroom nor the six-period day provides sufficient flexibility. Consequently, the school day at Lexington is divided into fifteen 26-minute modules with provisions for four different types of learning experiences. These include basic time, probe or help time, IDLE (individually directed learning experiences), and discussion topic seminars. Figure 5-1 is a sample student schedule.

Briefly, basic time involves direct instruction in large or small groups in the fundamentals. Probe or help time permits the student to research a matter of personal interest, read a paper, go on to the next work-week plan, or obtain individual assistance from a teacher. IDLE is independent study under supervision. Discussion topic seminars yield the opportunity to study in depth, during a nine-week block, a personally and socially relevant topic. Each discussion topic seminar is limited to a maximum of twelve students.

No age or grade barriers exist in the Lexington Middle School program, and the conventional emphasis on a single text has been scrapped for a multi-media approach. Provisions are made for those students hoping to enter college or undertake some other form of post–high school education. It is also possible for an interested student to begin some form of career training in grade seven.

The Learning Center. Essential to whatever success the Lexington Middle School may have achieved is its learning center. It is, literally, the hub of the school, with four spokes radiating outward from it. It is extremely well equipped. Sixteen-millimeter film projectors and a collection of more than 700 color films with sound are available for the students themselves to project in "small theaters constructed with seating, writing surfaces, and earphones for six to ten students."[12]

Filmstrip projectors, tape recorders, controlled readers, language masters, and overhead projectors are available for student

---

12. *Ibid.*

MODS	MONDAY	TUESDAY	WEDNESDAY	THURSDAY	FRIDAY
1	French 908 Help LC	French 908 Help LC	French 908 Help LC	French 908 Help LC	French 908 Help LC
2	TV Sci.	TV Sci.	TV Sci.	TV Sci.	TV Sci.
3	TV Sci.	TV Sci.	TV Sci.	TV Sci.	TV Sci.
4	Help 809	Help 809	Help 809	Help 809	Help 809
5	Guid. 2C	P. E. Fall	Help 2C	Help 2C	P. E.
6	Guid. 2C	P. E. Fall	Help 2C	Help 2C	P. E.
7	Math 804	Math 804	Math 804	Math 804	Math 804
8	Math 804	Math 804	Math 804	Math 804	Math 804
9	Lunch	Lunch	Lunch	Lunch	Lunch
10	Lang. 807	Lang. 807	Lang. 807	Lang. 807	Lang. 807
11	Lang. 807	Lang. 807	Lang. 807	Lang. 807	Lang. 807
12	S. S. 1C	S. S. 1C	S. S. 1C	S. S. 1C	S. S. 1C
13	S. S. 1C	S. S. 1C	S. S. 1C	S. S. 1C	S. S. 1C
14	Help LC H Ec 1 Sem	Help LC H Ec 1 Sem	Help LC H Ec 1 Sem	Help LC H Ec 1 Sem	Help LC H Ec 1 Sem
15	Shop 1 Sem Help LC	Shop 1 Sem Help LC	Shop 1 Sem Help LC	Shop 1 Sem Help LC	Shop 1 Sem Help LC

Figure 5-1. Sample Student Schedule from Lexington Middle School

use. Standard reference works and diverse books and periodicals are also housed in the center. The center operates a paperback bookstore where students may purchase inexpensive copies of good books for their personal libraries.

Lexington places great emphasis on the provision and use of a wide variety of instructional materials. This, coupled with the continuous progress plan, makes possible the individualization of instruction, a major goal.

CENTERVILLE MIDDLE SCHOOLS The last example is from Washington Township, Ohio, which occupies a rapidly growing section of the fertile Miami Valley. It lies within easy commuting distance of Dayton, and a high proportion of its residents are either professional or self-employed. The educational preparation of its people is high; one-third are college graduates, and slightly more than nine out of ten are high school graduates. Three middle schools serve the district, each designed to accommodate 600 students in grades six, seven, and eight.

Rationale. Centerville state unequivocally, "We believe the ninth grader of today belongs with older high school students. At the same time research indicates the earlier maturation of children dictates a regrouping of upper elementary grades."[13] Thus, the middle school is perceived as serving a unique population of students who are rapidly changing physically, psychologically, and socially.

Purpose. Centerville middle schools are not at all unlike other middle schools in the purposes they espouse. Briefly, their expressed purposes are to help boys and girls become self-actualizing persons, to help them refine the basic skills initially acquired in elementary school, and to individualize instruction. Although general education is not explicitly stated as a purpose, a review of their curricular offerings reveals that Centerville Middle Schools take seriously the responsibility of providing for the general education of their young charges.

Program and Organization. In each of the three middle schools the teachers are organized into teams. The precise way in which the teams are structured varies with each school and within the same school. Some teams are interdisciplinary, whereas others are organized within the limits of a single discipline. Each team is assisted by teacher-aides who perform clerical tasks and various other nonprofessional duties.

In addition to the teams, which are responsible for instruction in the areas of language arts, social studies, mathematics, and science, educational specialists are also available. These specialists provide physical education, typing, music, foreign languages (French, German, and Spanish in each building), and unified arts. Unified arts, handled on an interdisciplinary basis by a team of three, include art, home economics, and industrial arts. Subject matter serves as the medium for individual expression.

The curriculum is organized in most instances in terms of a theme; for example, themes in English might include animals, folklore, the sea, semantics, or careers. Unipacs based on a particular theme are written by team members for use by each child. Then minipacs are prepared to supplement the basic packets.

---

13. "A Guide to the Middle Schools of Centerville," Centerville City School District, Centerville, Ohio, undated.

The daily schedule provides both for blocks of time (teacher-scheduled) and unstructured time (student-scheduled). The blocks permit a great deal of flexibility in grouping and organizing the school day; teachers may lecture, use small groups, assign students to work individually, and so on. During the unstructured time, which is scheduled as a part of the common sixty-minute noon hour, students eat their lunches and then take part in activities in the gymnasium or outside the building, work on projects in the unified arts, or relax in the instructional materials center.

Each team of teachers is responsible for 120 students (approximately half of one grade level) for each block of time. Grouping within the block is determined by the team in light of student needs and interests. The class facilities are open and are distributed around a well-equipped instructional materials center. To the degree possible and appropriate, instruction is individualized.

A unique aspect of the Centerville Middle School program is that nearly all the sixth-grade students spend the better part of a week in a school camping experience at the Grant Life Science Center, a sixty-acre park operated jointly by the school district and the township. The usual practice is for about thirty students and one of the middle school science teachers to arrive at the center on Tuesday and remain for the remainder of the week. While at the center, the students investigate a variety of topics pertinent to environmental science.

Special Emphasis: Learning Packages. The unipac is the Centerville name for the learning activity package, a design for learning that places greater responsibilities and opportunities for learning squarely on the student. The unipac is not an end in itself but the means to an end—individualization of instruction.

Each unipac contains a common core of knowledge and skills through which all students are expected to progress. Within the unipac a student works at his own unique level of ability; he proceeds through a carefully "programmed" set of experiences at his own speed to reach the goals of any given package. The goals are usually expressed in behavioral terms. Because not all students learn equally well in a particular way, variety is provided in the modes of instruction, media, activities, and content, although the objectives remain the same. The minipac is designed in the same manner as the unipac, but instead of dealing with the core aspects of the theme, it is supplementary in nature.

Quite clearly the Centerville Middle Schools are seeking to individualize instruction. In addition, by providing flexibility in instructional modes, media, activities, and content, they are taking a long stride toward personalizing the program.

❧ 6 ❧

INDIVIDUALIZING INSTRUCTION

The consideration of instructional practice takes a teaching staff to the pinnacle of its professional concerns, because it is through the vehicle of instruction that the program of studies is applied to serve the needs of students. The success of this application is directly related to the understanding a faculty displays of human individuality. The material in this chapter will be helpful in adapting instruction to the diverse needs of middle school students.

DEVELOPING STRATEGIES

Given a goal, the plan by which the goal is to be achieved is the strategy. In education, the achievement of objectives is a complex task involving the consideration of many variables; therefore, the development of a teaching strategy is a complicated matter. Before we can proceed to consider strategies for individualization, we must first agree upon what individualizing instruction means. Is it setting students off on their own and making them responsible for what they learn? Is it plugging them into computers which then manage programs, instruct, evaluate, and reward with advancement to the next learning stage? Is it a teacher in a classroom with thirty students trying to go in thirty different directions in five or six subject areas all at the same time? According to Madeline Hunter, it is none of these things; it is the "process of custom-tailoring instruction so it fits a particular learner."[1] This definition will serve well for the present discussion.

---

1. M. Hunter, "Individualized Instruction," *Instructor*, Vol. 79, No. 7, March, 1970, pp. 53–63.

In developing strategies for individualized learning, our first concern must be the students. Since strategy is a planned design for achieving particular goals, we must look at learning objectives. Program is the vehicle through which we work so it must also be considered. And since we are concerned with instruction, we must look at the teacher and what he or she does to make learning appropriate for each student. Our strategy, then, develops on the basis of answers to the following questions: Who are my students? What are the learning goals? What is the program with which we will work? What will I, the teacher, do? Following is an outline of illustrative questions that could be considered in each of these areas.

WHO ARE MY STUDENTS? (Looking at them individually)
1. Where is he or she developmentally?
   a. How emotionally and socially mature is he for his age group?
   b. What is his apparent physical condition?
   c. What learning achievements has he mastered?
2. What are his unique attributes as a person?
   a. What are his attitudes, biases, and values?
   b. What interests him?
   c. What are his particular skill abilities?
   d. What is his style of learning?
   e. What particular personality traits does he exhibit?
   f. What is he ready for next?
3. Where is he in the group?
   a. Who are his friends?
   b. Is he accepted or rejected by his peers?
   c. When is he a leader? When does he follow?

WHAT ARE THE LEARNING GOALS?
1. What are the specific behaviors that are to be developed? Are they cognitive, affective, or psychomotor?
2. How are they best ordered?
   a. Are the learning accomplishments sequential and developmental?
   b. Is there a hierarchy of easy to difficult or simple to complex?
   c. Are alternative ordering arrangements possible?
3. How can these goals be differentiated?
   a. Are there basic goals all should achieve?
   b. Are there goals that only some students will achieve?
4. How will achievement of these goals manifest itself?

WHAT IS THE PROGRAM WITH WHICH WE WILL WORK?
1. What are the concepts that are involved in this program?

2. How can the material be sequenced?
    a. Is it chronological?
    b. Is it topical?
    c. Is it thematic?
3. At what points can the material be approached?
    a. What understandings must precede its study?
    b. What skills are necessary to cope with it successfully?
4. What kinds of learning resources are pertinent to this material?
5. To what activities does the material lend itself?

WHAT WILL I, THE TEACHER, DO?
1. How will I organize students for this learning?
    a. Is this best approached on an individual basis?
    b. Will student work groups help in the achievement of goals?
    c. Are there certain activities that lend themselves to large-group situations? seminar situations?
    d. By what methods can I generate compatible groups when groups are desirable?
2. How can I adapt the learning tasks?
    a. What various activities are associated with the learning tasks?
    b. What children are ready for each kind of activity?
    c. Are there learning activities to serve the needs and interests of each student?
    d. How can I provide for multiple activities?
3. What must I do to make each student's learning more efficient and successful? (Considering the students individually)
    a. What can I do to stimulate interest and desire?
    b. What special instructional help does he need?
    c. How can I help take the sting out of his unsuccessful attempts?
    d. How can I reinforce his successes?
    e. Does he react better to praise or prodding?
    f. Does he need frequent attention?

By raising such questions, developing the most accurate answers possible, and adding to the mix the professional talents of the teacher, a strategy for achieving specific goals with particular learners is formulated. Strategy is the day-by-day plan of operation by which the teacher attempts to help learning to take place, and it grows out of his attention to concerns like those above. In this respect each teacher's strategy is unique; it is based on his professional talents and understandings, his students, and his teaching situation.

Lesson planning is strategy building. The process described above is applied over and over again each day. Each daily session

Table 6-1

Opportunities for individualized learning are being afforded	Opportunities for individualized learning are not being afforded
If subgroups formed include only those children ready for the specific learning task to be undertaken.	If subgroups formed include children for whom the specific learning task will be too easy or too difficult.
If learning tasks provide for the expression of individual interests, for obtaining information particular students require, or for activities that individual students need for specific reasons.	If learning tasks require that all students do the same things in the same way.
If learning expectations are varied according to the student's ability and previous acquaintance with the learning task.	If learning expectations are the same for all students.
If time schedules vary according to the needs of each student.	If all students are expected to complete tasks in the same amount of time.
If provision is made for the expression of each student's ideas and creative contributions.	If all students are expected to emerge with the same ideas and conclusions.

builds toward the overall objective of actualizing more fully the potential of each student. How can the teacher determine if the instructional strategies being planned and implemented are indeed promoting individualized educational experiences? What are the characteristics of individualized learning situations? The examples in Table 6-1 help answer such questions.

THE LEARNING ENVIRONMENT

Schools should be happy places where people are comfortable, where success abounds, and where failures are viewed only in relation to their potential for further understanding. Schools should be places where students and teachers come together in an effort to seek truth, develop potential, and extend human abilities. Schools should be places where the most important considerations concern people and where students feel wanted, respected, and competent as human beings. Only if schools are such places can they contribute to the development of positive, healthy self-images. Only then can they capitalize on the individual's natural desire to grow, to become, and to direct his motivation into desirable avenues. Only if such an environment exists can each young person continue to develop the faith and belief in himself that is necessary to tackle the tasks of intellectual, social, and psychological development that are a part of growing up.

The importance of interpersonal relationships and the influence that these have on behavior change and growth are evident. Education can only take place in an environment where teachers and students are free to share their own humanity with each other, where a mutual feeling of respect exists, and where there is a deep bond of understanding. Paul McClendon quotes a succinct description of such a relationship by Rogers.

> If I can create a relationship characterized on my part: (a) by a genuineness of transparency in which I am my own real feelings; (b) by a warm acceptance of and a genuine liking for the other person as a completely separate individual; and (c) by a sensitive ability to see his world and himself as he sees them; then the other individual in the relationship: (a) will experience and understand aspects of himself which previously he repressed; (b) will find himself becoming better integrated, more able to function effectively; (c) will become more unique, more self-expressive; and (d) will be able to deal with the problems of life more adequately and more comfortably.[2]

This is the ultimate step in individualizing instruction, but a step without which all other attempts at individualization become mere educational rituals that hold little hope for real efficacy because they lack the human ingredient. The first step in individualizing instruction is the attempt to develop such a relationship between the teacher and each of his students.

Recent insights into the relationship between teachers' attitudes and student learning show that there are very real and significant implications for educational success or failure in this relationship. As pointed out by Robert Rosenthal, teacher attitudes have been shown to affect intellectual and psychomotor development, as well as student behavior.[3] Significant positive development in IQ test achievement, scholastic performance, and

---

2. Paul E. McClendon, "Teacher Perception and Working Climate," *Educational Leadership,* Vol. 20, No. 2, November, 1962, p. 105.

3. Robert Rosenthal, "Teacher Expectations and Pupil Learning," in *The Unstudied Curriculum: Its Impact on Children,* Norman Overly, ed. (Washington, D.C.: Association for Supervision and Curriculum Development, 1970), pp. 71–78.

swimming ability has been reported when teachers were led to believe, even when there was no actual basis for such beliefs, that certain individuals were potential bloomers or that they had an unusual potential for learning. These expectations also have significant effects upon the attitudes of teachers concerning students. As Rosenthal further indicates, when students perform in line with expectations that teachers hold for them, they are viewed more favorably by teachers regardless of whether the expectation is for potentially high or low performance. When students who were considered to have less intellectual potential showed good development, teachers generally perceived their behavior as being undesirable, and "the greater their IQ gains the more unfavorably were they rated both as to mental health and as to intellectual vitality."

Rosenthal notes that there is also evidence that the effect of such attitudes on the part of the teachers can include overt changes in teaching styles. More content and faster learning paces can be established when the teacher has favorable expectations regarding the potential of students. Thus the attitudes that teachers hold about students not only affect learning though affecting the self-concept and the attendant motivational aspects of self-feelings, but they also affect the actual performance and development of students directly in a dramatic way.

The attitudes and policies of administration are also important effectors of the school environment. These attitudes and policies affect staff and students alike; they either promote openness to experience and the growth potential that this holds, or they cause people to become closed to their experiences. As people become more open or closed to experience, their potential to learn and to grow as a person is either increased or decreased. Bills reports that "teachers with qualities of openness can be closed to their experience by the nature of the administrative and supervisory relationships they encounter."[4] Data are available to show that "the more open the teacher, the more positive were the attitudes boys and girls held toward themselves." The series of studies summarized by Brogman and reported by Bills concluded among other things that

> The more democratic the method of operation of the principal, the more accepting of self and others were the teachers and pupils, the more favorable were the attitudes of parents toward the school, the more democratic was the behavior of teachers, and the more the teachers interacted with the community.

---

4. R. E. Bills, "Education Is Human Relations" in *New Insights and the Curriculum* (Washington, D.C.: Association for Supervision and Curriculum Development, 1963), p. 181.

Clearly, administrators, without ever entering a classroom, increase or diminish the possibilities for educational growth by the effects on the school environment of the policies they institute and the attitudes they convey.

The learning environment, then, is a complex function of many factors within each school which combine to create a climate that either inhibits or promotes desirable human development.

GROUPING PRACTICES

Since the middle school staff deals with large numbers of students, organization for instruction is very important. Grouping practices must enhance learning opportunities.

A learning group is an organizational device, a means to an end. Experience and research have shown that there is nothing magic about any one grouping philosophy when it comes to guaranteeing results. Just as no one method of teaching reading can be applied with equal success to all learners, neither can one grouping arrangement serve equally well in all learning situations.

Learning groups should be designed around specific purposes. If, for example, a staff is concerned with forming a group of students of age thirteen or fourteen who are ready to study algebra, they had better be very similar in mathematics background and their ability to think abstractly. On the other hand, a learning group that is studying the development of the United States and examining various aspects of its social, economic, and political background can well be composed of students with a range of developmental levels, interests, and skills. This diversity can help to promote outcomes such as the following:

1. More insightful students opening up ideas that would not occur in the group if they were not there.
2. Students of various talents recognizing the differences among the group members and coming to respect each for his uniqueness.
3. Individuals of different intellectual levels learning to work with each other.
4. Students experiencing the social problems that arise in diverse groups and learning the conditions that lead to movement toward or away from the group objectives.

The school setting should maintain as many options as possible. If flexibility in grouping students for learning can be maintained, group composition can be varied to fit instructional objectives. The more rigid the organizational structure, the less able the staff will be to capitalize on unique arrangements to promote specific outcomes. Flexibility implies the option to change when change is desirable, but also the ability to maintain a given structure when that is best.

GROUPING PROCEDURES   A recent sampling of grouping procedures in middle schools reveals a wide range of practices extending from various forms of homogeneous and heterogeneous groups through procedures that allow students to work individually.   In many cases, however, there is a discriminating application of grouping techniques that avoid gross generalizations about learners in groups, provide for flexibility in grouping according to instructional purposes, and take into account current knowledge regarding individual differences among learners.

Homogeneous grouping, for example, is moving away from the practice of forming groups on the basis of generalized measures of ability and achievement and toward grouping students who are similar with respect to specific traits.   At the Boyce Middle School in Upper St. Clair, Pennsylvania, there are two separate but related dimensions involved in forming learning groups—the rate of mental growth and the rate of student growth physically, socially, and emotionally.   Table 6-2 is a distribution chart for 600 students.

Using this approach, students are located on the vertical axis according to their mental achievement and along the horizontal axis according to their physical, social, and emotional maturity. Relatively immature students whose mental development is slow would be placed in Unit I; the mature individual who is also developing fast mentally would be assigned to Unit V.

Table 6-2   DISTRIBUTION OF STUDENTS BY GROWTH CLASSIFICATIONS

	UNIT I	UNIT II	UNIT III	UNIT IV	UNIT V
J					30
I				30	60
H			30	60	30
G		30	60	30	
F	60	60	30		
E	30	30			
D	30				

Source: "Current Status of Middle School Model," Boyce Middle School, Upper St. Clair, Pa., July, 1969, unpublished.

Grouping procedures used in the intermediate schools in the Council Rock School District in Pennsylvania reflect a flexible policy which attempts to match the grouping procedure to the learning situation. Students are assigned to classes in academic learning areas according to their developmental level in each individual subject. In other learning areas a deliberate attempt is made to compose heterogeneous groups. Heterogeneous grouping is used where there is a desire to bring together learners reflecting a range of differences because the learning situation can be enhanced by this divergence of backgrounds.

The unit school represents another current arrangement for organizing for instruction. The Shikellamy Middle School in Shikellamy, Pennsylvania, is representative of schools organized on a unit basis. In this middle school learners are assigned to teaching teams in units of from 120 to 150 students. A team of professionals working with a given unit then assigns students to specific learning situations on the basis of their particular developmental levels. Such an arrangement provides for the flexible adaptation of learning groups to reflect the day-by-day developmental patterns of learners.

The multi-unit organization is employed by the individually guided instruction (IGE) system, which is a product of the Wisconsin Research and Development Center for Cognitive Learning. (See the discussion of IGE in Chapter 7.) The National Commission on Teacher Education and Professional Standards (TEPS) in collaboration with the Center for the Study of Education has discussed unit schools in a publication entitled *The Teacher & His Staff: Man, Media, & Machines*.[5]

A few middle schools have begun to institute individual progress programs which permit students to pursue certain learning goals independently. The Boyce Middle School, which is employing such learning programs, reports the development of content units through which students can progress at their own rate of development. Progress is based on mastery rather than on allotted units of study time and varies among students. Learning groups can be formed with a great deal of flexibility, since common learning development is not an imposed criterion for the formation of classes. Factors like student–teacher compatibility, friendship groups, and individual physical, social, and emotional needs can receive a new priority when organizing students for learning. Teachers working with such class groups do little large-group instruction; they prescribe instructional tasks for individuals, assist students in their

5. Bruce R. Joyce, *The Teacher & His Staff: Man, Media & Machines* (Washington, D.C.: National Education Association, 1967).

progress toward their learning goals, identify areas of difficulty, and evaluate student progress. Small subgroups of learners within the class who need help with particular skills or insights can be formed quite easily and disbanded when these special purposes have been served. Thus the working groups in such situations can and do change almost daily.

Although we have been stressing the need for group flexibility, we cannot overlook the fact that permanence is a desirable characteristic for some groups. The guidance-oriented group, typically referred to in the secondary schools as the "homeroom," is formed with a concern for human relationships. In grouping and regrouping young people to assure them the best opportunities, the middle school staff must also be aware of their need for stability and security. Certain human relationships must be allowed to continue over extended periods. Time is necessary to form the human bonds that become lasting friendships and mature to a mutual trust where individuals can share their deeper hopes, concerns, and other intimate feelings. If such groups degenerate to serve simply administrative functions, the most important needs will, of course, go unrealized. On the other hand, if students in such a setting can feel that they have a place where educational and personal problems can be shared with an interested and helpful adult and where mutual friendships can be established, the arrangement can reach its highest apex in serving human needs. The school should provide a place where each learner is seen as an entire person and where a responsible professional can keep a finger on the developmental pulse of each child.

For some students, it is necessary to provide highly specialized settings for learning. These individuals have particular needs that cannot be met in regular classrooms, and provisions must be made for them to work in self-contained areas where the setting, the learning materials, and the instructional staff are especially geared to their requirements. Children who have been diagnosed as educationally retarded, socially or emotionally disturbed, brain-injured, and physically impaired need such learning situations. These classes represent a learning group organized around highly specialized considerations.

TYPES OF GROUPS

Seminar Groups. Small groups should consist of fifteen or fewer individuals and should serve to enhance human interaction. The four major purposes of such groups are as follows:

1. Provide opportunities for teachers to measure an individual student's growth and development and to try a variety of teaching techniques which will be suited to a student's needs.
2. Offer the therapy of the group process, whereby students are induced to examine previously held concepts and ideas and to alter sometimes mistaken approaches to issues and people. Students will learn, in other words, how to become better group members.
3. Permit all of the students to discover the significance of the subject matter involved and to discuss its potential uses, rather than to just receive it passively and return it in tests.
4. Provide students with opportunities to know their teachers on a personal, individual basis.[6]

The cue for the teacher's role in the seminar setting is taken from the fact that the small group's particular advantage is in promoting opportunities for human interaction. The teacher must remember that she is simply one of the group, even though she is in a different position from the others. She must avoid taking undue advantage of her privileges as the designated leader. Her role is to promote participation by all, draw out the reticent, and encourage the sharing of ideas, experiences, and points of view. She must act to preserve an atmosphere in which each group member feels comfortable and free to share his own individuality with the others. Only in such an environment is it possible for students to experience the satisfaction of human sharing and honestly examine ideas, concepts, issues, and values in order to open opportunities to develop new insights and change opinions.

In the small group the teacher is just another person, a unique human being with strengths, weaknesses, biases, endearing qualities, hopes, hang-ups, and all the other characteristics of a real person. When the teacher interacts honestly within the group, she opens up a new dimension in student–teacher understanding. If the teacher expects students to become open, sharing, and accepting of others, she must lead the way in openness and acceptance. In the seminar setting, the teacher has an opportunity to come down from the front of the class, enter the group, and know and be known by the students. The teacher should often be a quiet observer within the small group. After helping to establish the necessary environment within which the group can function and helping to stimulate the proper group processes for sharing and exchanging,

6. J. Lloyd Trump and Dorsey Baynham, *Focus on Change: Guide to Better Schools*, © 1961 by Rand McNally and Company, Chicago, pp. 24–25. Adapted and reprinted by permission of Rand McNally College Publishing Company.

the teacher becomes a watcher. She observes the students in action: How do they handle themselves? What does this tell me about the needs of each? Who bullies? Who ignores facts and clings to old biases? Who leads? How does each handle the learning material at hand? Who is the quick intellect with the keen insight? Who is the plodder? Who seems to be making progress? Who is not growing? Who does the group accept or reject and for what apparent reasons? These and many similar questions are flooding through the mind of the quiet teacher who is watching the human dynamics within her seminar group. Based on her astute watching, she plans how to help each of those who need help in a special way.

Large Groups. Some classes should be much larger than those typically found in schools; it can be advantageous for a class to run from 100 to 150 students or more. The specific size should depend on the kind of activities proposed for the group. Experiences that involve a presentation by a teacher or visiting lecturer might be held for 100 or 150 pupils, whereas film presentations might be limited in number only by the capacity of the room. Experimental studies show that both teachers and students adjust the most quickly to large-group instructional situations. Some of the purposes and advantages of large-group instruction are the following:

1. To carry out certain instructional functions compatible with larger groups such as introducing study units, explaining terms or concepts, demonstrating, hearing visiting personalities or special lectures, viewing films, and administering certain tests.
2. To present certain material to all students in a more uniform manner.
3. To expose more students to the more skillful and experienced teachers in all subject fields.
4. To make expensive instructional equipment more economically feasible.[7]

The role of the teacher in the large group varies considerably with the purposes of the class session. Often large-group instruction is handled by a team of teachers and teaching assistants, and other instructional activities are shared among the team members. The setting for all instructional situations is important, but it is particularly so with large groups. Because of the size of the group, an operational faux pas that would be easily adjusted to in a smaller group can cause a major snag, erode instructional time, and ad-

---

7. *Ibid.*, pp. 30–31.

versely affect the learning environment. Therefore, all details regarding the sessions must be carefully considered and proper arrangements provided. Traffic flow, adequate seating, proper lighting, provision for adequate sound amplification, and viewing arrangements are some of the basic considerations. If materials are to be distributed or collected, the method of doing so must be decided beforehand. If questions from the floor are to be entertained, is there a way in which these can be adequately heard? If special equipment is to be involved, how will it be stationed and can it be operated efficiently as required by the lesson? If attendance must be taken, how will this be efficiently accomplished? These may seem to be insignificant considerations compared to the content of the lesson, but they are an important part of the planning for successful large-group sessions. Many a well-conceived lesson has collapsed because elements of the situation were neglected.

In planning the content for a large-group instructional situation, the teacher must also prepare well. The type of group, the particular kinds of individuals who comprise the class, the instructional goals of the session, and integration with other learning experiences must all be considered. Material presented must be relevant and of interest to all members of the group—and there will be a range of differences in any group of this size. The method of presentation must be compatible with the material with which the lesson deals. Attention span of the audience is important; it will depend on age, maturity, and other considerations relative to the individuals in the group. Variety must be built into the presentation. The teacher must have thought through and practiced her every move regarding each aspect of the lesson plan. The lesson must move, hold the attention of the audience, and reach its conclusions in the time allotted to it. Planning such a lesson is not an easy task, but if the preparations are well made, the educational profits can be considerable.

Independent Study. Independent study by individuals is the third type of activity recommended by the Trump studies. Such activities in the past usually have been done on the student's time at home, but these should be expanded and recognized as important by being allotted in-school time. Independent study is not the same as those tasks that have typically been assigned as homework; a closer scrutiny of independent study is in order here.

The term *independent study* has been interpreted in many ways, and there has been no agreement within the profession as to a precise definition. Under a cooperative research project supported by the United States Office of Education, Alexander and Hines surveyed the independent study practices of thirty-six secondary schools in twenty-four states during the 1965–1966 school year. The following definition of independent study was developed as one of the purposes of the study.

> *Independent study* is considered by us to be learning activity largely motivated by the learner's own aims to learn and largely rewarded in terms of intrinsic values. Such activity as carried on under the auspices of secondary schools is somewhat independent of the class or other group organization dominant in past and present secondary school instructional practices, and it utilizes the services of teachers and other professional personnel primarily as resources for the learner.[8]

In the 1969–1970 school year, the Cocalico Middle School in Denver, Pennsylvania, reported seventy-eight students engaged in independent study projects covering topics such as the following:

Viet Nam	*White-Tail Deer*
Napoleon and Caesar	*Wild Turkey*
Patrick Henry	*Reptiles*
Field Hockey	*Sheep*
Forms of Poetry and	*Dogs*
Original Works	*Basic Design and*
Child Care	*Construction of Clothing*
English Grammar	*Nutrition*
Writing	*Nursing*
Nazi Germany	*Interior Decorating*
Civil Rights	*Punic Wars*
Depression Era	*20th-Century American*
Reconstruction Era	*Drama*
Civil War	*Interior Decorating*
Forestry	*Battle of Gettysburg*
Embryology	*Photography and Study of*
Earthquakes	*Wildlife*
Tropical Fish	*Erwin Rommel*
Architecture	*19th-Century American*
Construction	*Presidents*
Wood Lathe	*Track and Field*
People of Germany	*Gymnastics*
World War II	*Ice Skating*
Horses	*History of Physical*
Taxidermy	*Education*
Pharmacy	*Famous Women in Sports*
Rocks and Stones	*Music*

---

8. W. M. Alexander and V. A. Hines, *Independent Study in Secondary Schools*, Cooperative Research Project No. 2969 (Gainesville, Fla.: University of Florida, 1966).

It can be seen from the above list that independent study can cover a large variety of interests and include projects that are oriented to library research or involve the investigation of various kinds of activities or processes.

Not all students will be ready at the same time to pursue special learning projects independently. The general aim of education is to develop individuals to function independently and intelligently. However, this is a long-term goal and should begin in small ways at the earliest ages in the elementary school. Opportunities for small independent tasks can lay the groundwork for larger opportunities to come. Alexander and Hines have listed the specific behaviors that independent study aims to develop.

1. The independent learner undertakes on his own initiative learning tasks that are important to him.
2. He uses sources of information efficiently.
3. He tests out reflectively possible answers, solutions, and ideas to see whether they are adequate.
4. He seeks to apply generalizations from former to new situations.
5. He is not easily discouraged by the difficulty of the learning task nor by forces that would have him accept inadequate answers, solutions, and ideas.
6. He enjoys learning and seeks opportunities to learn.[9]

A middle school staff should encourage the participation of students in unique learning undertakings that promote their ability to function independently.

Before a student is ready to move out on his own, some specific planning must be done. This planning can be accomplished by the student and his faculty sponsor through the formulating of an independent study plan, as shown in Figure 6-1. The plan includes very concise, specific statements outlining the project objectives, procedures, final product, evaluative procedures, and a tentative time schedule. Such a plan establishes from the beginning a common perception of student and sponsor regarding the nature, limits, activities, and outcomes of the project.

Implementing the plan is, of course, primarily the job of the student, since this is what independent study is all about. The teacher is not, however, divorced from the implementation stage; in fact, she has an important role to play in it. Although motivation can come only from the student himself, the teacher who is keenly interested in its maintenance can do things to influence it.

---

9. W. M. Alexander and V. A. Hines, *Independent Study in Secondary Schools* (New York: Holt, Rinehart and Winston, Inc., 1967), p. 4.

STUDENT ___John Wilson___ GRADE LEVEL ___8th___

FACULTY SPONSOR __Mr. William Boyce__ DEPARTMENT __Social Studies__

PROJECT TITLE: __The Role of United Fund Agencies in the Community.__

OBJECTIVES:
1. To identify specific United Fund Agencies in the community.
2. To outline the services of each of the above agencies.
3. To identify the specific community problems to which each agency addresses itself.
4. To present available evidence as to the success of agencies in helping to solve community problems.
5. To produce a report detailing the above information.

PROCEDURES:
1. Conduct necessary library and other research activities to investigate the history, organization, and component agencies of the United Fund.
2. Devise appropriate questionnaires to be mailed to United Fund Agencies.
3. Conduct personal interviews with directors of sample United Fund Agencies.
4. Organize and detail information obtained, draw appropriate conclusions, and detail in a final report.

DESCRIPTION OF FINAL PRODUCT:
A written report detailing the history, organization, component agencies, services, and evidence of effectiveness of United Fund Agencies and appropriate conclusions based on the data produced by the study.

EVALUATION:
Conferences with the sponsor and the content of the final report will be used to provide specific evidence of the degree to which stated objectives of the project have been realized.

PROJECTED SCHEDULE:
An anticipated period of fifteen weeks will be scheduled as follows:
4 weeks — Begin library research and devise and distribute questionnaires.
6 weeks — Continue library research and arrange for and conduct interviews with selected agency directors.
3 weeks — Organize all information from library research, questionnaire returns, and interviews and develop conclusions.
2 weeks — Produce final report and evaluate results.

APPROVED _____
Sponsor's Signature

Figure 6-1.   Independent Study Plan

The teacher should express a sincere interest periodically without seeming to be primarily concerned with "checking up." Being available to counsel in time of difficulty, to act as a resource when progress seems to be stymied, to listen, to direct the student to new sources—all of these and many other supporting acts by the teacher are vital to the student's implementation of his plans. The teacher provides the moral and substantive support that undergirds the student in his individual quest for learning. In guiding such study the teacher must do some delicate balancing between structure and freedom, between guiding and telling, and between monitoring progress and becoming overly involved.

Finally, there will come that moment when the student has run his course and is ready to culminate the activity. At this time, the teacher helps clinch the educational objectives. Have we accomplished what we set out to do? In what ways have we fulfilled our original intentions and in what ways have we been unable to do so? What are some of the outcomes that were not foreseen when we began? What difference has the project made in your thinking? In your life? What can we do with it now? Are there next steps? By reviewing such questions with the student, the teacher helps to unify the entire experience, bring closure, and lay the basis for future learning activity.

Choosing a Plan. For too long most schools failed to look at the formation of learning groups in terms of the activities with which the groups would be involved. A leader in pointing attention to this very logical consideration was J. Lloyd Trump, Associate Secretary of the National Association of Secondary School Principals. His studies received wide attention in the decade of the sixties and have become the basis for a variety of organizational patterns that enhance learning activities by placing them in the most appropriate settings.

Concerned with a shortage of trained professionals to staff the schools, the maintenance of quality education, and the further improvement of schools across the country, a Commission on the Experimental Utilization of Staff in the Secondary Schools was appointed by the National Association of Secondary-School Principals. The studies, supported by the Fund for the Advancement of Education and the Ford Foundation, were directed by J. Lloyd Trump, and thus the resulting proposals came to be identified with his name. The study took place in nearly 100 junior and senior high schools across the country for five years, and the results were reported in *Focus on Change: Guide to Better Schools*.[10]

---

10. Trump and Baynham, *op. cit.*

Trump and his commission analyzed what happened in school instructionally. They divided the activities into categories: those best accommodated in a small-group setting, those amenable to large-group situations, and those that should take place on an individual basis. In school programs they indicated that about 20 percent of the time should be spent in small-group seminars, 40 percent of the time in large-group instruction, and 40 percent of the time should be allowed for individual pursuit of learning tasks. Whether or not these particular time distributions are accepted, this is a different and defensible way of structuring learning activities. Activities can be more efficiently handled by differentiation, and the achievement of goals behind the activity can be enhanced by variation.

Whether you are starting on a large or small scale to reorganize a school according to the Trump proposals, you must begin by examining the program of studies. Which learning experiences are best accomplished in each of the three settings? How much of the instructional time will it be necessary to devote to each instructional setting? When these determinations have been made, the particular strengths and interests of the teachers involved can be analyzed. An effort should be made to utilize these staff considerations to best advantage. The characteristics of the student body to be served can be studied and class and instructional groups can be formed in order to enhance the learning opportunities for each individual. Having analyzed the activities involved in the program of studies, having looked at staffing considerations, and having taken the characteristics and needs of the students into account, you can develop schedules that will provide the time and space allotments necessary. Of course, this is easier said than done; it will involve honest devotion to the task and considerable effort. Any sincere group of staff members can generate the specific activities that will accomplish each of the tasks above. Probably at least a year of planning should precede any operational program, but with such a base from which to operate, the educational system can be successfully changed.

NONGRADED INSTRUCTION

Formal education in the United States did not begin in schools that were organized by grade levels; however, by 1860 such organization existed in nearly all city schools. The graded school with a ratio of about one teacher to thirty pupils housed in "egg-crate" fashion has persisted to the present decade with little change. Although relatively unchanged, the grade-level organization has not gone unchallenged. In the decade of the 1950s there was a swelling tide of criticism, a growing interest in plans for nongraded instruction especially in the elementary schools, and an increasing number of schools turning to ungraded organizational formats.

INADEQUACIES OF GRADE-LEVEL ORGANIZATION   One of the greatest problems with schools organized along grade-level lines is that they do not conform to what we know about individuals and how they grow and develop. Contrary to the theory of this organizational plan, research has established beyond question that individuals of the same age vary widely in physical, mental, and emotional growth and that they develop at different rates and according to different patterns. Every boy and girl of the same age cannot be expected to be ready to have the same learning experiences or to pursue them at the same rate of development. Therefore, the traditional graded school builds in failure and frustration. Children who are not ready for learning accomplishments built into the curriculum for their age level are doomed to fail. They must accept the stigma that goes with being retained, and then plod through the same set of experiences over again—some of which they have mastered and all of which are "old hat" despite the fact that they have not achieved them. Others who might be ready to leap ahead in their learning programs must spend the year the same way as all the other students and wait until "promotion" to be allowed to move on. The whole set of problems that revolves annually around promotion or retention, such as the agonizing of teachers over whether Johnnie has mastered enough of the fifth-grade curriculum to go on to sixth grade, is created by an organizational structure that we now know does not fit the human reality it was designed to serve.

For many children, the graded school organization has promoted "unsuccess," frustration, and feelings of guilt. Schools should be doing exactly the opposite. Schools should be dedicated to the development of each individual's talents to the fullest possible extent. It has been well documented that children vary considerably with respect to past experience, developmental levels, interests, and family backgrounds, and a rigidly structured program of studies organized with graded materials, experiences, and expected outcomes is simply not compatible with the need to customize instruction to the needs of each child.

ORGANIZING A CONTINUOUS PROGRESS SCHOOL   To overcome the inadequacies of the traditional organizational patterns, it is necessary to look at instruction, learning experiences, and growth and development in terms of individuals and to generate new organizational devices that will enable schools to help each child achieve to his fullest potential. There is no one combination of procedures that produces "the" way to accomplish this goal. There are undoubtedly infinite variations that can succeed, depending on local conditions, children to be served, and other community circumstances. There will be in each organizational pattern, however, some common provisions such as the following:

1. The focus of instruction will be on individual learners and will accommodate current knowledge concerning learning theory and human growth and development.
2. Organizations will be flexible, providing variations whenever these are appropriate to accommodate the developmental needs of children.
3. Patterns of staff assignment will provide for better utilization of professional skills both by promoting staff collaboration in working with children and by employing teachers in tasks where their individual strengths and interests can be exploited.
4. Certain curricular programs will be organized in order to allow students to work individually at their own pace; others will be organized around group activity with appropriate variations to accommodate individual circumstances.

Since program is the basic ingredient of school systems, let us consider some possible arrangements that will conform to the needs of individual learners.

Individual Progress. Reading and mathematics both involve skill development, which is sequential and cumulative and which can be organized so that learners proceed through the learning experiences at their own pace. As an example of how such a program might operate, let us look at the model for reading development presented in Figure 6-2.

The eighteen levels indicated on the vertical axis are all skills incorporated into the school's formal reading programs. The eighteen levels are arbitrary for the purposes of the model, but they would represent a normal developmental rate of about two levels per ten-month term up through age fourteen or fifteen. Skill development beyond these levels will be independent of formal instruction, except for specialized elective courses, such as speed reading, which would be available in the secondary school program. Various developmental patterns have been depicted horizontally across the top of the diagram. These show how hypothetical indi-

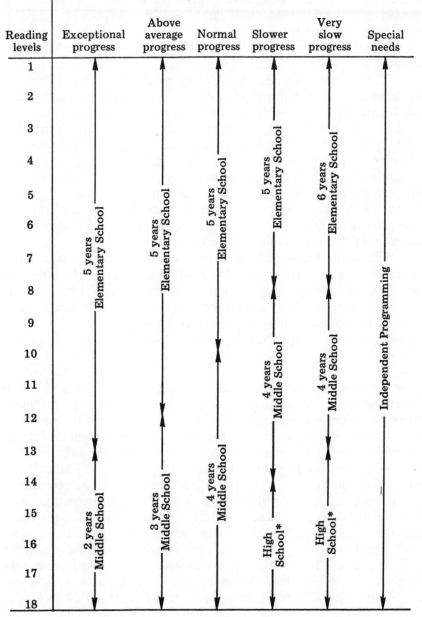

*Program is elective beyond the middle school.

Figure 6-2. A Model of an Individual Progress Plan for Reading Development

viduals conforming to the developmental patterns might progress through the levels of reading skill development. It must be emphasized that these do not represent groups, but rather depict representative patterns that individuals might generate in moving through the learning experiences at their own pace. Each child going through the program would create his own developmental pattern.

To institute such a model, a program of studies would have to be developed for this purpose. This is a challenging undertaking for a staff, but it can be done. Package programs of study are now under development; some are currently available for purchase. The Individually Prescribed Instruction programs discussed in Chapter 7 are representative of such programs and are the result of pioneering efforts to individualize instruction. It is possible to adapt current reading programs to such an organizational arrangement, but one should not underestimate the magnitude of the job. Adequate time, financial resources, consultant service, and the commitment of the staff to the project are necessary.

The model for an individual progress program in mathematics would be similar to the one for the reading program. The language arts program would parallel and be intimately associated with the student's developmental level in reading. Available materials permit the individualization of spelling and handwriting skills so that these can be appropriately integrated into the whole curricular pattern.

Group Activities. Social studies and science are subjects in which instruction can be organized around group activities. Although there are definite skills to be developed in both these instructional areas, there is also a concern for involving all students in broad social and scientific concepts. Thus boys and girls of different abilities with a wide range of developmental levels can, if they have some common interests, pursue a learning task with each contributing in relation to his ability. The goal of such instruction is to achieve through the combined efforts of the group more than any individual could realize if he worked alone. Such situations, however, must still meet individual needs and provide differentiated opportunities. To see how learning groups composed of diverse individuals can be utilized to contribute to the growth of each student and to provide for differentiated instruction, let us look at a short example.

Suppose the middle school staff were concerned with helping thirteen-year-old and fourteen-year-old students to understand some of the basic functions that societies provide for man. Some of the important concepts in such an instructional unit might be the following:

1. Societies are groups of individuals who unite for mutually beneficial reasons.
2. Societies provide protection for group members.
3. Societies provide companionship and define relationships.
4. Societies provide for the care and indoctrination of the young.
5. Societies provide for the resolution of conflict within the group.

The faculty might concentrate on certain skill-development outcomes that are compatible with developing these understandings, such as the following:

1. Use library reference skills.
2. Analyze and develop generalizations about a society's government, legal system, and educational system.
3. Select appropriate information relevant to questions under investigation.
4. Compare and contrast elements in two different societies.
5. Work as productive members of a peer group.

The concepts and skills above could be incorporated in several different learning units, such as studies of the American Indians, the Eskimos, early colonial settlements in America, or African nomads. No matter which general topics are pursued, students can be involved with the same concepts and skills. If several topics are available for students to choose from at this point in their school program, learning groups can be formed around common interests. Also, students who have completed a unit of study but need more experience with the same skills and concepts have a number of other topics readily available to them for further work. Students who have developed sufficiently after completing one unit can proceed to another set of topics which takes them on to other concepts and skills.

Modern teachers recognize that all students do not develop exactly alike even when pursuing the same learning units together. Each student makes his unique contribution to the project. William is good with his hands, Mary has a keen intellect, Jeff can get the group moving together, Sue is an organizer, and Margaret and Charles write well. Each therefore emerges with a slightly different set of experiences, valuable in its own right to his or her development. The individual facts, skills, and concepts and the level of their development are not as much the concern as is the process through which the students have worked. They have interacted together and become deeply involved with a segment of man's life. As a result they have emerged with new conceptual insights, improved skills, and, hopefully, a thirst for more such opportunities.

Learning programs, organized as discussed above, make it possible to promote successful achievement for each student. There is no retention—no repeating of grades or even of learning experiences. Reports and evaluations of learning progress can be related to specific learning achievements at specific levels of development. Children who need repeated exposure to particular concepts can simply become involved with another curriculum unit dealing with the same concepts. The opportunities for outright failure are almost completely eliminated, and the natural momentum of most learning experiences is directed toward some degree of personal development and, thus, toward success.

❧ 7 ❧

TECHNOLOGY
IN THE
MIDDLE SCHOOL

Many new advances in educational technology hold exciting promise for the middle school. Nearly all of these innovations relate in some way to an instructional systems approach to learning. As a result, they are especially applicable to middle grades. These innovations are not only useful as component parts of an integrated learning system, but they also have great capability for enhancing individualized instruction, the heart of the middle school instructional process.

Among the innovations discussed in this chapter are learning packets, instructional systems approaches, new trends in audio and visual instruction and learning, and the emerging role of the media center.

Although all of these innovations relate in some way to advances in technology, the successful inclusion of the innovations into the instructional process is still, as always, dependent on farsighted and inventive teachers and administrators.

LEARNING PACKETS

One of the most promising breakthroughs in the movement toward individualized instruction for middle schools is the development of the learning packet, or learning cell. Simply defined, a learning packet is a structured learning program developed around predetermined instructional objectives. It allows a student to proceed

115

independently yet with direction through a sequential learning experience.

Hopefully, as a result of this experience, the ten- to fourteen-year-old student will learn the process of researching and how to apply the process in other situations. The program content allows the student to acquire the intended learnings in a predetermined sequence so that the higher-order learning skills can be developed from lower-order learnings.

The development of individualized learning packets, or cells, is still in the infancy stage, both in availability and in use. During the 1960s, the repertoire of instructional materials progressed from a disorganized collection of heterogeneous, single-dimension learning activities to a well-ordered, multi-dimensional approach to learning. What were once isolated teaching units have become complete learning systems, structured and sequenced from low-order learning to higher-order cognitive and affective learning experiences. The 1970s and 1980s will certainly see the development of complete series of sequenced learning packets in most of the major disciplines, especially in the middle grades, where the obvious enthusiasm of the student creates an atmosphere receptive to individualized projects.

Middle schools contemplating the use of learning packets should consider certain criteria in the selection of already existing systems or in the development of new learning packet materials. These would include the following:

1. The packets selected for use should be part of a sequential program articulated with the preceding elementary program and the secondary program that follows.
2. The program packets should employ a strategy for mastery and learning easily understood by both the teacher and student.
3. The materials should employ diagnostic procedures early in the program with periodic evaluations of achievement during the learning process.
4. The packets should attempt to develop sequential learning toward a predetermined series of instructional or behavioral outcomes, carefully selected for the ten- to fourteen-year-old.
5. The individual abilities of students should be carefully considered in the development or selection of materials in order to provide for the wide range of student capabilities.
6. The material should be relevant to student interests from pre-teen to emerging adolescent.
7. The process of learning is equally as important as content retention, if not more important. The packets should relate to the acquisition of library skills, research skills, and organiza-

tional skills, which the student will require in secondary school.

8. The packets should attempt to provide mastery in a relatively short period of time. The age of the middle school student requires frequent successful conclusions rather than one extended learning experience ending in limbo. Properly developed learning packets almost guarantee the achieving or learning of the predetermined instructional objective.

9. Learning packets should employ all of the VAKT (visual, auditory, kinesthetic, and tactile) approaches recognized as important to the psychology of learning for ten- to fourteen-year-old students.

10. Learning packets should be open-ended, since some students might be stimulated to explore other related subjects using the processes learned in the structured materials. Avenues for further study should be stressed.

11. Whole kits of varied learning materials and allied equipment should be available to supplement the learning packets. These materials should relate directly to the packets and be available as a resource when the packet directs the learner to specific new sources of information.

12. Alternative paths for learning should be structured into the packets when evaluation reveals that intended learnings are not occurring.

13. Since the learning of the life process itself is not completely an individualized approach, but a shared experience with others, the packets should provide for group, as well as individualized, learning. A complete program based completely on individualized learning packets would lose impact and student interest.

DIFFERENTIATED LEARNING PATHS

The varied learning interests and capacities of middle school students can best be met through the use of many different kinds of educational media and through constant evaluation. The learning packet or system must provide for the use of different media for learning and, when evaluation indicates that the student fails to achieve or comprehend, for alternative paths or tracks for learning.

Constant evaluation of student progress must be structured into the learning packet or instructional systems approach. By pre-testing the student prior to the learning experience, the teacher ensures his proper placement in the program material. In fact, increased pre-testing with increasingly more difficult graded tests allows the individualized learning process to become effective, since the teacher can then prescribe paths for learning, either direct or alternative.

Post-testing the student after the learning process has taken place allows the teacher to determine if the learning objective has been achieved. A low test score points up nonlearning and allows the teacher to prescribe alternative learning paths. These can include different media, different materials, reteaching, or any other proven remedy for nonlearning.

The philosophy that there can and ought to be differentiated learning paths changes the roles of the student and the teacher. The program rather than the teacher's manual or guidebook contains the structure of the discipline. The teacher becomes a facilitator, or a prescriber, of learning paths. The student, hopefully, becomes more independent, since the process of learning becomes an individual responsibility, with expert help and advice readily available.

Contrast these programs with the middle grades programs of the 1950s and 1960s when groups were taught en masse, regardless of prior learning or nonlearning, and when the teacher, even if she were so inclined, was incapable of diagnosing and prescribing for the needs of two dozen or more children on an individual basis in six or more subjects. Is it any wonder that education, by necessity, looked for structured programs that could pace, place, evaluate, diagnose, prescribe, and provide for differentiated learning paths when nonlearning occurred? Thus the instructional systems approach was born.

INSTRUCTIONAL SYSTEMS

A logical extension of the concept of learning packets is the development and use of an entire system for learning. Learning packets can be successfully used for short-term projects within well-defined parameters, but what is more exciting is the idea of structuring a complete new approach to learning an entire discipline through a long-term instructional systems approach. Basically, an instructional system can be defined as a complete program for individualized learning, with accompanying resources and materials, sequentially developed to cover a number of years of study in a discipline.

Whereas learning packets seem to adapt to a unit study of learnings for which predetermined objectives have been drawn, the learning system extends over a number of years, embodying more extended objectives. These extended objectives are carefully sequenced to ensure retention through constant maintenance and reinforcement of skills acquired in the program.

Certain subjects seem to lend themselves to the learning packet or short-term approach. These include social studies, health, language arts, and possibly science. Mathematics, reading, and possibly science could be approached through the instructional system or long-range approach. These subjects require extended study and are sequential in their learning process.

Advances in the technology of educational hardware are beginning to find their way into currently available and well-developed instructional systems. We are now seeing the introduction of complete learning systems in reading, mathematics, and science for middle grades.

All of the criteria recommended for consideration in the section on learning packets are also applicable to instructional systems. Learning systems already in use present middle schools with the possibility of approaching individualized instruction through a carefully researched, long-range approach to instruction, using a number of components over an extended period of time. Following is a discussion of several such programs.

PATTERNS IN ARITHMETIC One learning system available to middle schools is the mathematics program Patterns in Arithmetic (PIA), developed by the Wisconsin Research and Development Center for Cognitive Learning, University of Wisconsin. The completely sequential program extends from grade one through grade six. Through the medium of television, it is designed to bring expert teachers of mathematics into the classroom. The PIA program consists of 336 fifteen-minute television lessons, with exercise books for students and allied teacher's materials.

The use of in-school TV tape players has enabled the local school to use the tapes as needed on a nonbroadcast basis, allowing for instructional pacing and a more individualized approach for the student. The government-funded project provides for continued systems development. More than 389,000 children and 13,000 teachers in twenty-three states were involved in the use of PIA in 1971.

INDIVIDUALIZED MATHEMATICS SYSTEM A systems approach to mathematics instruction for both primary and intermediate grades was considered in the basic rationale of another innovative program developed by the government-funded Regional Educational Laboratory for the Carolinas and Virginia (RELCV).

The Individualized Mathematics System (IMS) contains all of the elements of a system: behavioral objectives, planned sequence, tightly controlled structure, diagnosis and evaluation, individual pacing, remediation through teacher prescription, alternative learning paths, and multi-sensory learning. It is a complete VAKT (visual, auditory, kinesthetic, and tactile) approach to learning.

The program, built around more than 500 instructional objectives, divides the elementary school mathematics curriculum into ten topics: numeration, subtraction, multiplication, division, fractions, mixed operations, money, time, systems of measurement, and geometry.

Each of the ten topics is divided into ten levels of difficulty. At each of these ten levels, there are a number of skills that must be learned. For each skill, there is a folder of from four to twelve teaching pages.[1]

INDIVIDUALLY GUIDED EDUCATION SYSTEM   The Individually Guided Education System (IGE) is being developed at the Research and Development Center for Cognitive Learning, University of Wisconsin. It is being designed as a total educational system. The system provides a model for programming for individual learners based on rates and styles of learning with attention to other considerations such as guidance, curriculum development, educational measurement, evaluation, and home and school communications. The first program is aimed at reorganizing school personnel to help schools improve their curriculum and/or individualize instruction. The Wisconsin Design for Reading Skill Development is being prepared as a management system to expedite individually guided instruction in reading skill development for kindergarten through sixth grade. A more detailed description of the IGE system is presented by Herbert J. Klausmeier in the November 1971 issue of *Phi Delta Kappan*.[2]

PROGRAM FOR LEARNING IN ACCORDANCE WITH NEED   Program for Learning in Accordance with Need (PLAN) is a computer-managed system for individualizing instruction through all grade levels. Both academic and guidance programs are available as part of the system. Academic programs are built around teaching–learning units (TLU), which include a set of objectives, activities, and commercially available resources to achieve each objective.

1. Regional Educational Laboratory for the Carolinas and Virginia, *Educational Development*, Vol. 2, No. 2 (Durham, N.C.: RELCV, 1970), p. 2.

2. H. J. Klausmeier, "The Multi-Unit Elementary School and Individually Guided Instruction," *Phi Delta Kappan*, November, 1971, pp. 181–184.

Alternate TLUs are provided to allow for differences in learning styles. The guidance program deals with the development of attitudinal skills.

THE INDIVIDUALLY PRESCRIBED INSTRUCTION SYSTEM

The IPI system is one of the pioneer projects started as a cooperative venture of the University of Pittsburgh and the staff of the Oakleaf Elementary School. The work was taken over and extended by Research for Better Schools, Inc., a Philadelphia-based, federally funded regional laboratory. A brief overview of IPI is given below as an illustration of how such systems are designed and operate.

Individually Prescribed Instruction is an instructional system that provides for planning and carrying out with each student a program based on his or her particular learning needs and characteristics as a learner. The learning materials in each individualized program developed conform to the following characteristics:

1. The rate of speed at which each child progresses depends upon his own capacities. He places himself on the continuum by taking both placement tests and pre-tests.
2. The curriculum material is arranged in a sequential order called a *continuum*. The assignments are given by a prescription to fit his individual needs. (A prescription is an individual lesson plan for each student each day.)
3. The student's mastery of the curriculum is judged by curriculum-embedded tests and post-tests. He is required to perform at a level of 85 percent.
4. The child works independently in most cases, thus building up his sense of responsibility and his confidence in his own knowledge. He begins to know that learning is a process that is dependent on his own participation and initiative.[3]

IPI programs of study are built upon very specific and detailed learning objectives such as the following:

1. Identify synonyms for specified words when these words are presented in a sentence.
2. Distinguish between a word that names a group and a word that identifies a member of that group.
3. Select from choices the meaning of a specific word in a sentence when the meaning of that word is included as part of the sentence.

---

3. "Individually Prescribed Instruction," Research for Better Better Schools, Inc., Phila., undated.

Each objective is stated so that it communicates to teacher and student exactly what it is that the individual who has mastered the skill or content can do. The objectives are grouped together in meaningful units of content and arranged sequentially so that skill development or content mastery proceeds on a continuum from lower to higher abilities. In Table 7-1, for example, skills in the various competencies are sequenced from simple to more complex through eleven developmental levels, A through K.

All the lesson materials are related exactly to the objectives and are presented in such a way that the student can proceed independently with a minimum of teacher direction. Four types of instruments are utilized to diagnose student needs and monitor their progress. These are the following:

1. *Placement instruments* are tests used to assess mastery of units of work along the learning continuum and to indicate the entering level of the student in the continuum.
2. *Pre-test instruments* are used to discover which specific objectives within a unit and level a student knows or does not know.
3. *Post-test instruments* are alternative forms of the pre-tests given at the end of each unit of work to determine the student's mastery of the unit.
4. *Curriculum-embedded tests* are short tests of a student's progress toward a particular objective within a level and unit of work. Each test has two parts; the first measures progress toward a particular objective, and the second serves as a pre-test of the

Table 7-1

COMPETENCIES	DEVELOPMENTAL LEVELS
	A B C D E F G H I J K
Visual discrimination	⟶
Auditory discrimination	⟶
Literal comprehension	⟶⟶⟶⟶⟶⟶⟶⟶⟶⟶⟶
Interpretive comprehension	⟶⟶⟶⟶⟶⟶⟶⟶⟶⟶
Evaluative comprehension	⟶⟶⟶⟶⟶⟶⟶⟶⟶⟶
Vocabulary development	⟶⟶⟶⟶⟶⟶⟶⟶
Structural analysis	⟶⟶⟶⟶⟶⟶⟶
Library skills	⟶⟶⟶⟶⟶⟶⟶
Reference skills	⟶⟶⟶⟶⟶⟶⟶⟶
Organizational skills	⟶⟶⟶⟶⟶
Related reading	⟶

ability to achieve the next objective within the unit and level of work.

Written lesson plans, called *prescriptions*, are prepared individually for each student. They provide the means for guiding the student through the learning sequences. Figure 7-1 diagrams the process through which students proceed in the IPI program. Figure 7-2 illustrates a reading prescription sheet.

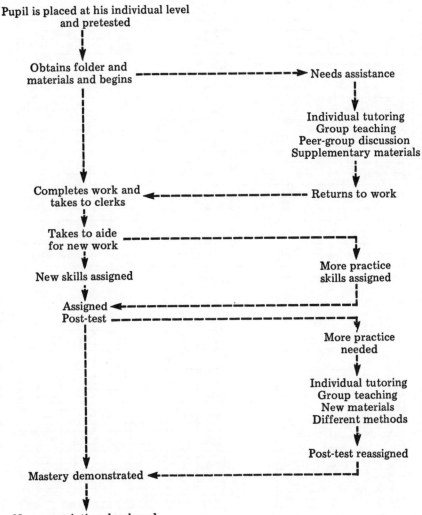

Figure 7-1. Flow of the IPI System (Source: Reprinted from "A Progress Report: Individually Prescribed Instruction," Research for Better Schools, Inc., Philadelphia, 1969.)

READING PRESCRIPTION SHEET

PAGE _____ OF _____

STUDENT NAME	STUDENT NUMBER	SCHOOL NUMBER	GRADE	ROOM

UNIT

UNIT DATES	
UNIT BEGAN	
UNIT ENDED	
DAYS WORKED	

TASKS								CURRICULUM TEST				DAYS WORK-ED
								PART 1		PART 2		
DATE PRES.	PRES. INIT.	SKILL NO.	PAGE NO.	TOTAL POINTS	NUMBER CORRECT	INST. TECH. CODES	INSTRUCTIONAL NOTES	NO. OF POINTS	%	NO. OF POINTS	%	

INSTRUCTIONAL TECHNIQUES

CODE	SETTING
01	Teacher Tutor
02	Peer Tutor
03	Small Group
04	Large Group
05	Seminar

	MATERIALS
06	Curriculum Texts
07	Teacher Made Skillsheets
08	Film Strips
09	Records/Tapes
10	Research
12	Manipulative Devices

9-69   P-1

PRE AND POST TEST SCORES									
SKILL NUMBER	MAX POINTS PER SKILL	PRE SCORE	%	POST SCORE	%	POST SCORE	%	POST SCORE	%
DATES									

Figure 7-2B.   Reading Prescription Sheet, Page 2

READING PRESCRIPTION SHEET

____________________ STUDENT NAME

____________________ UNIT

PAGE _____ OF _____

TASKS								CURRICULUM TEST				DAYS WORK-ED
								PART 1		PART 2		
DATE PRES.	PRES. INIT.	SKILL NO.	PAGE NO.	TOTAL POINTS	NUMBER CORRECT	INST. TECH. CODES	INSTRUCTIONAL NOTES	NO. OF POINTS	%	NO. OF POINTS	%	

Figure 7-2A. Reading Prescription Sheet, Page 1

PROGRAMMED MATERIALS

Programmed materials are the learning components of programmed instruction. They are designed so that a learner attends to a very limited amount of material at one time and makes some kind of response to each segment of the sequence after which he receives immediate feedback concerning the adequacy of his response. The cycle is repeated throughout the program through which the student proceeds at his own pace. Textbooks, workbooks, and self-instructional programs all permit students to move at their own individual rate, but here the similarity ends. Programmed materials are developed with much more attention to the behaviors intended as outcomes of instruction. The psychological analysis of behavior and the experimental approach used in sequencing the learning segments are also much more sophisticated and rigorous.

The underlying principles of programmed instruction, then, are the following. Instruction is goal-oriented and organized into effective sequences. Materials present one simple increment of learning at a time. Students are actively involved in the learning process, receive immediate knowledge of results, and proceed at their own pace.

There are four major steps involved in developing a program, each of which requires skills and understandings for its accomplishment. First the goals must be specified as particular tasks that students must master. The material leading to the accomplishment of these tasks must then be broken down into small units and ordered into individual frames. Each frame is a unit which the learner must focus on and respond to, and the initial program must be tried out, revised, and, finally, validated. A detailed flowchart is presented in the National Society for the Study of Education Yearbook, which outlines and orders the steps in developing a program.[4] Considerable training and experience are necessary to complete this process and produce worthwhile programs.

Programmed materials are presented in a variety of formats. Many are published in written form with various devices used to present the learning sequences and provide for the immediate reinforcement. Others are developed to be used with particular mechanical aids.

There are a variety of types of mechanical aids that qualify under the general category of teaching machines. Some are simple devices that provide for covering correct answers until the student

---

4. Phil Lange, ed., *Programmed Instruction*, National Society for the Study of Education, 66th Yearbook, Pt. 2 (Chicago: University of Chicago Press, 1967), p. 58.

responds to a frame of material, then advancing the device exposing the correct answer, and giving directions for the next segment. Other machines utilize recordings, tapes, slides, and filmstrips. Some teaching devices combine various components of audiovisual machinery into one system. The highest form of such devices is, of course, the computer. Computer-assisted instruction is an accomplished fact in many school situations.

COMPUTERS FOR MIDDLE SCHOOLS

The use of the computer in education has shown a slow but continuous growth in the past decade. As both the price and size of computers have decreased, their use in American schools has increased proportionally.

Computer use in schools has generally been concentrated in the four areas of (1) computer-assisted instruction; (2) computer management of instructional systems and programs; (3) instruction in the programming and use of computers; and (4) a tool for administration.

Few middle schools have successfully used computers "in-house" in any of the four areas. The prohibitive cost of installation, the scarcity of trained personnel, and the lack of receptivity of school administrators have been major forces impeding the rapid spread of this tool. However, more and more senior high schools have begun to lease terminal time and to purchase service bureau assistance for scheduling, class listing, reporting and grading, attendance, and other administrative chores.

Computer-assisted instruction (CAI) is a two-way interaction system (computer and learner) that results in behavior modification. It is a highly sophisticated application of the principles of programmed instruction to machine technology, utilizing the digital computer as its central component. It is based on behavioral objectives and provides a well-tested system for achieving specific learning goals. It individualizes instruction by varying the rate of learning as well as the pathways of learning. The systems now available have the capability to keep accurate records of students' progress and to make available summarized data for research purposes.

How does CAI happen? A programmer takes the material for a given course of study, identifies the behavioral objectives involved in the learning, and develops a learning program compatible with a given computer. The program is entered into the computer and is then available for use from any properly connected remote terminal. A terminal usually consists of a typewriter-like keyboard which the student uses to interact with the computer program. Messages to and from the computer appear on a printout sheet which is incorporated into the terminal unit. Some terminals have also included visual devices for the presentation of nonlanguage material. In some installations these can be viewed and then responded to with electronic pens. In the circuit between the terminal and the computer an electronic switching device called a *multiplexer* makes it possible for the computer to handle communications with many terminals.

Computer-assisted instruction has not spread as rapidly as was first anticipated. The problems inherent in the initiation of computer-assisted programs have mainly been classified under the following categories:

1. Cost problems.
2. Lack of worthwhile software (programs).
3. Tie-up of terminals by one student, with a resultant lack of flexibility.
4. Opposition to a passive, stimulus-response instructional approach.
5. Lack of conclusive research to demonstrate that computers were cost effective in terms of learning growth for students.

Computer-managed instruction deserves a closer look than it has received to date. As individualized programs of instruction become more available, and the educational systems approach to learning becomes more common, the problem of management of the programs becomes more pronounced. Scoring, record keeping, branching, and alternative tracking for each student can easily be programmed and managed by computer systems, which allow teachers and administrators instant access to student record data.

Instruction in the use and programming of computers seems to be better suited to high school and college-age students than to the middle school child. Mastery of computer language and program design is easier for older students. For the present and forseeable future, instruction in the use of computers for middle school students will probably receive little emphasis.

Administration at all levels has made increasingly larger use of the computer to assist in administrative chores. As costs continue to decrease, more use of the computer can be anticipated in middle schools, enabling administrators to instantly retrieve data for current and future planning needs.

LANGUAGE LABORATORIES

The current use in the middle school instructional program of audio equipment for the teaching of language and other subjects will expand even more as structured learning systems are developed and marketed. The early use of audio laboratories as a tool to enhance the teaching of foreign languages has been expanded into the areas of reading, social sciences, mathematics, and spelling. The growth in the use of audio learning laboratories has occurred as cassettes and other kinds of portable equipment have become cheaper and more available.

Early language laboratories were generally fixed installations using expensive carrels, individual tape recorders, consoles, and miles of wire. As the technology of audio laboratories progressed, wireless systems using audio loops became prominent. These allow for greater flexibility at lower cost.

Systems have generally been of three major types. The least expensive (and least adaptable) is the audio-passive system, allowing for simple listening to a program. Slightly more expensive (and more complex) is the audio-active system, allowing for listening and repetition of the listener's voice, but without the capability to store the listener-speaker's voice.

The most complex (and most adaptable) is the audio-active system with return voice (storage) capability. This system allows the listener to hear, to react to the program, and to store his reactions on tape for later review.

For middle school use, it seems obvious that inexpensive, portable systems utilizing the loop transmission devices would suffice. These can be either audio-passive or audio-active. When voice storage is needed, inexpensive cassette tape recorders can be used.

Individualized instructional programs can be greatly enhanced by audio components. As more instructional systems are marketed, audio programs will play an increasingly more important role, since these systems stress a multi-dimensional approach to learning.

SCIENCE LABORATORIES

The advent of "packaged" science programs and National Science Foundation–sponsored science programs has radically changed the teaching of science in the intermediate grades. Long-standing programs such as the AAAS (American Association for the Advancement of Science), ESS (Elementary Science Study), SCIS (Science

Curriculum Improvement Study), Elementary School Science Project (University of Illinois), and QAESS (Quantitative Approach in Elementary School Science) have been published commercially by various textbook companies. These elementary programs, added to already existing intermediate grade programs such as ISCS (Intermediate Science Curriculum Study), IPS (Introductory Physical Science), and ESCP (Earth Science Curriculum Project), have changed the dimensions of middle school science instruction.

Certain recurrent educational themes run through each program. These include the following:

1. Stress on the process of science approach.
2. Laboratory experimentation.
3. Development of student learning through inquiry.
4. The need for and use of science-trained teachers.
5. Use of science equipment and apparatus.
6. Desirability of laboratories for teaching.
7. Use of multi-media for instruction.
8. Integration, where possible, with other disciplines.

The science program requirements generally dictate the need for as much laboratory space and equipment as can be obtained, since intermediate grade science programs have built in most of the educational themes listed above. As the middle school idea grows, the use of science laboratories will grow with it.

TELEVISION AND FILMS

Films and television have undergone a tremendous change during the last few years of the 1960s. The directions for the 1970s indicate an exciting future. Branching out from the rather lackluster approach of educational television, the electronics industry has brought ETV into the classroom, on demand and at reasonable cost, through new videotape systems. Among the systems available are the Columbia Broadcasting System's EVR system (Electronic Video Recording), which allows for color video through the use of a cartridge viewed through a player and video receiver. This relatively inexpensive system enables a school to utilize a twenty-five minute color program (or fifty-minute black-and-white program) at a cost considerably under the cost of a comparable 16mm film. Lower costs, improved shelf life, self-rewinding features, and the lack of direct handling seem to indicate a real potential for education. Coupled with broadcasting possibilities to many locations in the same building, these technological advances have moved visual education a giant step forward.

To compete with the already available EVR cartridge, such companies as RCA, Sony, Ampex, and Norelco are promoting videocassette as an even better technique for projecting educational programs. The videocassette systems are slightly larger than the audiotape cassettes, and have great potential for low-cost classroom use. Whether through cartridge or cassette, it is obvious that the electronics industry means to change audiovisual instruction.

In addition to the new cartridge or cassette programs, a large number of schools have purchased videotape systems and have begun to make increasingly greater use of the equipment in instruction. Experimentally, the equipment has been used in special education, athletics, drama, physical education, science, and other fields by ingenious teachers and media specialists. In addition, many schools have built up collections of TV tapes made from regular TV broadcasts. Thus they have captured shows for future use as program needs require.

Even the well-regarded 16mm film industry has shown potential for change by developing the Super-8mm sound movie and the Super-8 single-concept film loop. These two developments, however, still lack the potential of an EVR or TV cassette in both cost and flexibility of use, as they involve rather expensive production costs.

The field of video playback is fluid at the moment, but all companies indicate that production models of television cassette players will be marketed soon. Major problems confronting schools considering these playback systems are the lack of industry-wide standardization, cost differences between companies both for players and tapes, program availability, and the lack of a structured application in already developed instructional systems. The exciting potential applicability of these programs for instructional systems may be the single greatest reason why the development process will be speeded up by the electronics industry and accepted by schools. The need for inexpensive video viewing is evident to all those advocating the instructional systems approach to learning.

The middle grades possess the potential for expanded use of films and television. Among the best known and recognized stimuli for learning among the ten- to fourteen-year-olds are those projecting through the visual and auditory senses, yet these stimulus techniques seem to be those least exploited in education.

Middle schools, however, charged with the responsibility of introducing new skills and reinforcing old ones, are beginning to recognize the need for more structured instructional systems allowing for a VAKT approach to learning, capable of being individualized for pacing of instruction, and inherently diagnostic and prescriptive. Multi-media equipment is effective both as motivation and as a learning stimulus. What better approach is there for middle grades than a video system capable of being handled by a pre-adolescent and geared to introducing, reinforcing, or maintaining his skills?

INSTRUCTIONAL MATERIAL MEDIA CENTERS

A necessary and vital part of the middle school is the instructional material media center. In order to support individualized learning, the middle school program requires a strong and well-supported instructional material center. Both the physical environment and the variety and quality of materials and media available must be determined with the ten- to fourteen-year-old in mind.

One of the major drawbacks of the new material media centers has been the lack of vision of the personnel who man the centers. They tend to be librarians from the "old school," trained in the tradition of books rather than of media. Most librarians, fearful of machines, cassettes, and video equipment, have forced administrators to place the care and feeding of these vital tools into the hands of another person, who is generally designated the audiovisual coordinator. This results in a chaotic, uncoordinated program of instructional materials, books, equipment, and films. Another major problem is that the untrained teacher does not or can not look beyond the medium of a textbook as a means for acquiring knowledge.

The choice of an untrained media center specialist incapable of coordinating and advising on the use of all types of media will result in a less than complete and less than satisfactory program. Since a variety of media and materials are crucial to individualized learning, the media specialist must have depth and breadth of vision.

The following are criteria that are considered important in the media program.

PERSONNEL
1. Is the media specialist knowledgeable about all phases of the program from books and films to television, cassettes, and microfiche, and can he or she relate these to the middle school curriculum?

2. Can the specialist relate well enough to his equipment to lead in the use of the materials rather than reacting passively, as most school librarians do?
3. Has the librarian image been erased, or do the administration and faculty view the media center as a library?

PROGRAM
1. Does the program require specific use of varied media and materials at designated points in the instructional system?
2. Can the students manipulate the audio equipment, slide projector, film loops, television tapes or cartridges, audio cassettes, and reference collections in order to enhance individualized learning?
3. Does the planning process involve the media specialist in continued planning with the instructional teams, or is the typical pattern of sporadic or periodic involvement the only contact between the program and the media center?

FACILITIES AND EQUIPMENT
1. Is the center carpeted for acoustical control?
2. Does the environment attract, or does it have the stereotyped library image?
3. Can one study individually? Work in a group? Confer one to one? Read for fun? Browse? Listen? View a visual? Relax? The physical design should permit all of these without disturbing the other necessary functions.
4. Is equipment available for individual student use in the following areas?
   a. Microfilm and microfiche viewers.
   b. Television tape, cassette, and broadcast reception capability.
   c. 16mm, super-8mm, reel, and loop film.
   d. Audio tapes and cassettes for instruction.
   e. Record and tape cassettes for music listening.
   f. Filmstrip viewing with audio capability.

STUDY CARRELS What forward-looking school administrator would approve plans for a media center without study carrels? Observers visiting centers with these facilities wonder why they receive little or no use. For carrels to be used effectively, the instructional program must require individual study. This can best be achieved by constant teacher planning or through a structured instructional system design. As more learning systems are marketed, media equipment and study carrels will be used more, since the student will be required to use these aids in an integrated fashion in sequentially planned instruction.

Study carrels are being designed both dry and wet. Dry carrels require isolated desk space for individual study, pencils, paper, and books. Wet carrels, in any variety, need electrical connections and use of a variety of equipment including tape or cassette recorders, TV or film viewers, headphones for listening, and computer terminals and screens.

DIAL ACCESS AND RETRIEVAL EQUIPMENT Many new middle school plants are being designed to allow teacher or student dial access and retrieval of audio and/or visual programs on television screens in classrooms or media centers. The designs of many new types of study carrels permit students to dial a program for listening or viewing. All of these originate from the media center or some central station and are available upon request by telephone or cable. As EVR or video cassettes become more plentiful, the use of this dial access capability will grow, especially as more instructional systems require integrated program use of many forms of media.

Creative solutions to the problems of how to store material and how to provide for better use of the stored data necessitate the use of technology. Many schools were granted funds from federal sources to explore new ways of storing and retrieving data. In order to achieve maximum benefits from the retrieval system, adequate planning was necessary. The Oak Park and River Forest High School, Oak Park, Illinois, defined its criteria for data retrieval as follows:

> In seeking constructive solutions to all or part of these two problems, the faculty study committee defined a new type of retrieval system which would provide instant, individual and remote access to audio and visual instructional materials. Essentially, five functional specifications were insisted upon. Together they required the ability to devise a new technology for educational retrieval systems by calling for a level of service not available in standard systems. The five specifications were defined as: 1) Random access to stored materials must be provided. That is, each request for materials must be honored when made and instantly. Materials in the system must never be "not available now" or "now in process." 2) Access must be provided for both audio and visual materials. 3) The individual user must have full control over the selection and use of the instructional materials. 4) Remote access to the materials in the system must be supplied on the widest possible scales. Individual carrels, conference rooms, classrooms,

other schools and private residences must be potential receiver points. 5) The efficiencies of a single, central storage and control facility must be provided.[5]

Middle schools of the future can look forward to functional new ways to store and use information and materials. As the uses of these systems become more plentiful, the price will probably be reduced to the point where it becomes economically feasible for most school districts to consider. The software necessary to complement the hardware is becoming consistently more available and is now better planned for integrated learning systems. Coupling retrieval capability and software with EVR, video cassettes, and the next generation of hardware could make the era of educational technology an exciting one for middle schools.

CONTRIBUTIONS OF REGIONAL LABORATORIES

Title IV, Elementary and Secondary Education Act, authorized and provided funds for fifteen regional educational laboratories to operate throughout the United States. These laboratories were instrumental in developing and disseminating educational ideas and programs to the ultimate consumer, the local school system.

Among those regional laboratories developing usable programs for middle grades were the following:

1. Research for Better Schools, Philadelphia, Pennsylvania—developer of Individually Prescribed Instruction (IPI) in reading, math, spelling, and science.
2. Regional Educational Laboratory of the Carolinas and Virginia —developer of Instructional Math System (IMS) for elementary grades.
3. Northwest Regional Laboratory, Portland, Oregon—developer of teacher training programs, videotaped math programs, and Patterns in Arithmetic (PIA).
4. Mid-Continent Regional Educational Laboratory, Kansas City, Missouri—developer of programs for dropout prevention in inner-city schools.
5. Appalachia Educational Laboratory, St. Ann, Missouri—developer of programs in reading, language development, and media.
6. Central Midwestern Regional Laboratory, St. Ann, Missouri— developer of programs in aesthetic education and the arts, lab

---

5. "Report II, Random Access Information Center," Oak Park and River Forest High School, Illinois, September, 1968, p. 2.

theater, and instructional systems for students with learning disabilities.
7. Far Western Laboratory for Educational Research and Development, San Francisco, California—developer of a teacher training program using micro-teaching and mini-courses.

The laboratories were charged with the responsibility of innovating through research on a large scale and of diffusing the programs once models were developed. Cutbacks in funds and duplication of effort have caused the U.S. Office of Education to close some programs and to curtail others. Curriculum planners, however, recognize that for the first time coordinated research has effectively cut the lag time from development to implementation and has speeded up the process of improving education. The regional laboratory idea certainly deserves a large part of the credit for recent action research in education.

≫ 8 ≪

THE
ACTIVITY PROGRAM

Many activities that were once outside the regular school program have become part of the school curriculum. Schools should pursue this course with caution, however, for it is probably desirable that certain activities remain outside the structured curriculum; otherwise, they might not be as attractive to the students. At as early an age as twelve or thirteen, a student needs to begin to practice self-direction, and the balance between student initiative and direction by the teacher becomes very important.

BACKGROUND

Student activity programs can be traced back as far as the academy of Benjamin Franklin's period. They were probably developed as a means of providing recreational activities for students, since schools were mainly residential. Sports and forensics were the original activities in the early programs. It was not until after 1900 that student activities were really looked upon favorably by educators. Their viewpoints advanced from ignorance to toleration and, finally, to acceptance.

The term extracurricular belongs to the period when activities were the stepchildren of the school program. It implies that they were beyond the scope of the curriculum, even though some might have developed from subject-area interests. They were looked upon as a source of entertainment or as a means for providing structured recreational opportunities for children. At times, the term extra-class was used. This had the same implication—outside the curriculum, not part of the regular program as provided in classes.

Cocurricular, a term later applied and still used today, seems to give more status to the program, but also implies that the activity program is separate, but of an importance equal to that of the regular curriculum. Cocurricular is no longer a completely accurate term, since some program activities such as band and chorus have become an integral part of the regular curriculum in many schools.

Student activities is a much more comprehensive term. It implies that the activities are part of the regular program, and it breaks down the distinction between curricular and extracurricular. Student activities can become an important means of achieving educational objectives rather than being a recreational pastime. The term also implies that there is no regular pattern or uniform program for all schools or students.

EMPHASIS Middle school personnel who administer and implement student activity programs must be firm believers in "student-centered learning" if programs are to be successful. New theories of learning and development must be taken into account, along with the implications of earlier adolescence. In this way, the activities can become a means of supplementing the formal educational program.

A student activity program can be successful only if its emphasis is on student function, formal or informal. A particular activity can be formally organized with specific students serving as officers and meetings conducted according to Robert's Rules of Order. This type of situation provides opportunities for development of leadership ability within a formal structure. Responsibility and ability to work with others will naturally develop. A more informal situation might be appropriate for an activity whose objectives emphasize social development. As part of a cooperative group without a formal slate of officers, students learn to work together toward common objectives. A very successful after-school party might result from such an informal committee working under the guidance of a skillful faculty sponsor.

Whether the group of students involved in an activity is part of a formal, organized structure or part of an informal group, the emphasis must be on student participation and operation. These are *student activities* and the program cannot be successful unless they are truly that. The instant a teacher assumes complete control the activity loses its value.

VALUES Participation in a student activity program can have positive effects on the development of student interests. The program provides a means for extending the academic curriculum and providing a broad, exploratory experience. For some students it provides motivation that might be the impetus needed to keep them interested in school. For others, it offers opportunities to develop creative abilities and gain satisfaction from doing things that they enjoy and find interesting.

A good student activity program is also a means of satisfying psychological needs, such as the need for recognition and approval. Cooperation, responsibility, and respect for others can develop along with social competence, and there is an opportunity for students to socialize in a way that is not possible in the formal classroom. An activity program provides an opportunity for a constructive release of youthful energy that might otherwise be turned into less productive channels. A good, vital program arouses and capitalizes on natural youthful spontaneity and enthusiasm in ways that will affect its participants in other facets of their school life.

Finally, the student activity program can be a valuable supplement to the usual classroom program. It can assist students in exploring various interests, talents, and abilities in a way not possible in a regular classroom. It can also provide an opportunity for the student to apply fundamental skills and knowledge acquired in the classroom program and to make a gradual transition from pre-adolescent activities to the type of activities, education, and specialization appropriate for older adolescents.

In a book that appeared a number of years ago, Miller, Moyer, and Patrick presented the following outline, one of the most comprehensive statements of the values of student activities.

CONTRIBUTIONS TO STUDENTS

1. To provide opportunities for the pursuit of established interests and the development of new interests.
2. To educate for citizenship through experiences and insights that stress leadership, fellowship, cooperation, and independent action.
3. To develop school spirit and morale.
4. To provide opportunities for satisfying the gregarious urge of children and youth.
5. To encourage moral and spiritual development.
6. To strengthen the mental and physical health of students.
7. To provide for a well-rounded social development of students.
8. To widen school contacts.
9. To provide opportunities for students to exercise their creative capacities more fully.

CONTRIBUTIONS TO CURRICULUM IMPROVEMENT

1. To supplement or enrich classroom experiences.
2. To explore new learning experiences which may ultimately be incorporated into the curriculum.
3. To provide additional opportunity for individual and group guidance.
4. To motivate classroom instruction.

CONTRIBUTIONS TO MORE EFFECTIVE SCHOOL ADMINISTRATION

1. To foster more effective teamwork between students, faculty, and administrative and supervisory personnel.
2. To integrate more closely the several divisions of the school system.
3. To provide less restricted opportunities designed to assist youth in the worthwhile utilization of their spare time.
4. To enable teachers to understand better the forces that motivate pupils to react as they do to many of the problematic situations with which they are confronted.

CONTRIBUTIONS TO THE COMMUNITY

1. To promote better school and community relations.
2. To encourage greater community interest in and support of the school.[1]

TYPES OF ACTIVITY PROGRAMS

Student activities are of various types. Some are related to the curriculum in that they extend or enrich the content found in the formal instructional program. Some activities are related to physical development; they are an extension of the gym program. Others might be termed interest activities; they offer physical and emotional release. Two additional types are service and social activities, which are important means of improving interpersonal relationships, enhancing an individual's self-perception, and increasing self-confidence.

CLUBS A very common form of activity is the club. Most often it is a local group which is not part of a national organization. A club usually meets once a week for thirty minutes, or, if it meets more than once a week, for less than thirty minutes. Several kinds

---

1. Franklin Miller, James Moyer, and Robert Patrick, *Planning Student Activities* (Englewood Cliffs, N.J.: Prentice-Hall, © 1956), pp. 13–19. By permission of Prentice-Hall, Inc.

of clubs are recommended to ensure a comprehensive program. The following provide an adequate coverage: interest, subject-related, and service.

Activities that focus on special interests might utilize common hobbies as a base. A small school could have a hobby club where its members pursue their hobbies on an individual basis and acquaint others with them, but a large school should have a variety which would include the following:

Marionette Making	*Hiking*
Wood Carving	*Chess and Checkers*
Photography	*Arts and Crafts*
Sketching	

Hobby clubs are frequently more popular than subject-related clubs, because the student gains satisfaction from working on and/or completing a project or task that he himself has selected.

Subject-related clubs help motivate the development of skills. There should be a wide range for student selection. Possibilities include language clubs, a science club (which is more appropriate for the middle school than a very specialized club in biology or chemistry), a home economics club, and, perhaps, a local history club. These activities supplement and enhance basic skills and knowledge taught in the classroom. They also provide an opportunity for the academically talented to concentrate more intensively on a particular academic interest.

Service activities are oriented to school and/or community needs. They offer an opportunity for practical experience and participation in projects defined by a group. One kind of service activity is the student council, which will be discussed as part of the larger question of student governance. Escort-service groups which provide student hosts and hostesses for school visitors are a possibility. Library and office assistants are another. Common groups include stage managers, audiovisual equipment assistants, and traffic control personnel. Students frequently consider it an honor to be part of such groups.

Community-oriented service groups might focus on a project such as converting a local lot into an attractive play area for neighborhood children. Assisting at local nursing homes, working at child care centers, and providing tutoring services at local community centers are other possibilities.

ATHLETICS Most educators and medical experts agree that participation in highly competitive interscholastic athletic programs is undesirable for middle school boys and girls. In 1952, a joint committee of representatives from the National Education Association, the Department of Elementary School Principals, the American Association of Health, Physical Education, and Recreation, the National Council of State Consultants in Elementary Education, and the Society of State Directors of Health, Physical Education, and Recreation issued a statement disapproving of sports programs involving intense competition for children prior to the ninth grade. Later the Educational Policies Commission of the National Education Association and the American Association of School Administrators issued a strong statement recommending that varsity-type interscholastic athletics not be permitted for junior high boys and girls. This was based on the opinions of 220 physicians who were consulted about the suitability of interscholastic competition for boys between the ages of twelve and fifteen. During this age period, bones are still tender and muscle growth uneven. Although boys may grow rapidly, growth is uneven, and one of its by-products is low endurance. Thus intense competition can be damaging to the individual.

A strong intramural program makes it possible for any student, regardless of his degree of ability or talent, to participate in activities if he wishes. It also provides for the unequal rates of development in boys and girls and for the uneven opportunities they might have experienced during their earlier school years to develop athletic skills. A sound intramural program begins within the framework of the regular physical education program and is then extended to other periods, such as before and after school and during the lunch periods. This kind of program nurtures a healthier spirit of competition, sportsmanship, and teamwork than the high emotionalism of interscholastic activity.

Another advantage of a strong intramural program is that it provides equal opportunities for boys and girls, in contrast to the usual senior high school situation where the activities for boys overshadow those for girls. Boys and girls can participate either separately or together in sports such as tennis, badminton, volleyball, bowling, and table tennis. Other sports, including touch football, track, softball, wrestling, basketball, and soccer, are more appropriate for separate participation. Even croquet and horseshoes can have a place in the middle school program.

Rather than having interscholastic programs, many schools find the field-day approach to be a suitable way of developing both community interest in athletic programs and the motivational force so often created when boys and girls perform in public. Three or four schools join together in athletic events that provide an opportunity for each individual to objectively evaluate his own performance and that of others. Good sportsmanship and fun are emphasized rather than competition.

Such programs will arouse recreational interests and provide an educational experience for their participants if they are carefully organized and supervised. They provide an opportunity to learn rules and sports appreciation. Teams can be developed according to weight, age, or grade, depending on the type of activity and the situation. A grade organization might be preferable for basketball, whereas weight should be the guiding factor in wrestling.

DRAMATICS   Young people have a natural flair for the dramatic. Given ample opportunity to develop, it can become the base for a marvelous learning opportunity. As in the athletic program, participation by many is preferable to professional-type performances by a select, talented few. Skits and short plays presented by one sixth-grade class for the other sixth-grade students are one way of achieving this. A half-hour play involving as many members of a class as possible might be presented to parents early in the evening with refreshments served afterwards by the participants.

Creative drama should be completely student-oriented; middle schools should not follow the lead of senior high schools in using commercially prepared plays, since many ideas can and should come from the regular instructional program. The culmination of a unit in social studies, science, or any other subject area can be a satisfying production in which the students not only write the script but also prepare their own costumes and scenery. The assistance of the art and music teachers will help the students to recognize the integration of various components of the instructional program. Writing even short skits for presentation can be exciting. They may be inspired by a poem, a song, or a work of art.

Plays provide many opportunities for students to work together toward common objectives. The quality of the end product is not as important as the experiences of those involved in producing it. An added awareness of self, other people, and the ideas confronting students can all be developed through original dramatic productions.

PUBLICATIONS   As in other activity areas, the major objective in the production of various kinds of publications should be widespread participation. The slick, high-cost, professional-type newspaper or magazine is most inappropriate for the middle school. A mimeographed newspaper that appears frequently can keep students aware of school events, give recognition to students, groups, and classes for their particular achievements, and make the community aware of what is happening in the middle school. This kind of publication makes it unnecessary to depend on local businessmen for the advertisements that are so often needed to subsidize the high cost of some publications.

The same principle should be applied to any kind of literary production. With a little thought students can produce attractive publications of excellent quality. Colored stencils were used by one class to produce a booklet containing writing efforts. There was at least one contribution from each child; pieces ranged from the simple haiku to a short story. Each child made his own stencil by printing, typing, or handwriting stories and illustrating them with simple, suitable artwork.

In another school, one English teacher introduced a project in which she and a panel of students selected what they considered to be the best short essays, stories, and poems produced by the seventh-grade students and had them reproduced in a mimeographed magazine. The art teacher assisted students in preparing appropriate artwork and attractive covers. The result was a production that aroused much interest throughout the school. This student activity was very closely related to the regular school program.

School publications can exert a strong influence on the student body. They can be produced on a school-wide basis, by departments and clubs, or by classes, either grade-level classes or individual classes. No matter what form the publications take, they provide a real opportunity and incentive for an expression of student ideas and accomplishments.

MUSICAL ACTIVITIES   Disagreement often arises among music educators and administrators regarding the major objectives of musical activities. Should only the talented participate, or should such activities be open to all interested participants regardless of ability? Should musical activities focus on fostering school–community relationships through their entertainment value, or on the enjoyment and personal development of the participants? In keeping with the middle school philosophy, middle school activities must focus on the development of the individual student and the pleasure he can gain from participation in school musical activities.

Development of a prize-winning marching band should not be a major goal. In addition to the regular band organization, a small feeder band might be organized for beginners and less advanced students. Instruction must be available at least for beginners and intermediate students. Most school districts then anticipate that parents will provide advanced instruction if and when a child becomes ready.

Exploratory opportunities with musical instruments are just as important in the middle school as other kinds of exploratory experiences. Some of the less common instruments, such as oboes and bass clarinets, should be introduced even if it is necessary to borrow them or to share them with a local high school. Experiences with stringed instruments are also essential.

In some situations, full-fledged bands and orchestras may not be possible because the level of achievement is inadequate. Small ensembles are then appropriate and possibly even preferable, because they increase opportunity for individualized instruction. In addition, the small-group situation gives the participant a feeling of security.

A variety of vocal activities is also desirable. Small and large groups, boys' and girls' groups, plus mixed groups from duos to large choruses make it possible for each and every child who so desires to participate. Participation in choral singing provides much enjoyment and is within the ability of everyone. In one school, so many girls wanted to join the Girls' Chorus that it was impossible to accommodate them in the choral room. The teacher initiated a policy that no girl in her final year in that school would be turned away. Thus everyone had an opportunity to participate. Even "monotones" were accepted and then placed in the alto section between the "strongest" singers. The elementary school child's natural love for singing should be fostered in the middle school—he should be encouraged to participate.

OUTDOOR EDUCATION   As national and international interest continues to focus on environmental problems, increased attention is being given to opportunities for outdoor education. These range from ongoing activities on school grounds to weekends or two- or three-day experiences away from school.

In one suburban New Jersey district, Board of Education subsidies enable all fifth-grade students to participate in a two-day visit to a nearby camp. Outdoor activities, related arts and crafts, and science activities form the nucleus of the program. Parents attend as chaperones. Students pay a minimal charge for meals and overnight lodging. Those who cannot afford the expense are completely carried by Board of Education funds. In fact, on a recent trip, only one student remained behind; that was because of a severe allergy to poison ivy.

Outdoor education also offers opportunities for social development, as boys and girls share duties at mealtime, clean-up periods, and so on. As the area of environmental education increases in importance, the outdoor program will be given greater emphasis. Some urban districts have recognized this fact and are purchasing sites outside the school district to provide natural areas for fairly extensive outdoor education programs.

ORGANIZING AN ACTIVITIES PROGRAM

No two schools should necessarily have identical student activity programs. The activity program should be tailored to meet the needs of the particular student body it serves. Student activities must become an integral part of the school program; the values of each activity must be identified.

CRITERIA FOR SELECTION A well-developed activity program provides each student with an opportunity to experiment or explore in a nonthreatening atmosphere. He is able to experience new activities, have his interest aroused, and develop new abilities. Sometimes new subject areas can be made available for exploration through the activity program. Certain types of language and science clubs fall into this category. In one school, an English teacher with foreign language training conducted a language club after school. Because the club interested students very much, the language became part of the regular curriculum one year later.

An effective program should provide desirable activities that might not be possible in the regular classroom. They may offer an opportunity to discover or identify special abilities and to smooth the gradual transition from preadolescent education to the specialization required of older adolescents.

Balance among the various activities must be maintained. Athletic or musical programs must not be permitted to overshadow the other areas. The contributions of each activity to educational objectives must be studied and, on this basis, the priorities of staffing, financing, facilities, and time determined. The activity program must be part of a balanced offering that supplies students with educational experiences that have not yet become part of the regular curriculum.

SCHEDULING Many schools use an extended day to provide time for activities, although they are regarded as part of the curriculum. In one particular school, the intramural program has been scheduled into this extended day, whereas other activities, which are an integral part of the students' schedules, are scheduled by the team teachers, who also serve as advisors. Opportunities in dance and dramatics are particularly emphasized. Community volunteers are used wherever and whenever possible. In that same school, there is a school governmental body consisting of representatives from both the teaching and nonteaching staff members and students. There is no faculty sponsor. Meetings are called by the principal, although she is not always present. The principal is kept informed and, ultimately, considers herself responsible for decisions made. She often analyzes tapes of the meetings and uses these as a basis for guiding the group.

Another school also uses a combination of extended day and regular school day to provide time for activities. Rather than studying during their scheduled study periods, some students elect to participate in teacher-sponsored activities. This option is available on a limited basis. Other students choose to participate in intramural activities at the end of the regular school day. Still others take advantage of activities sponsored by community volunteers from the home and school association. The program includes guitar, bowling, knitting, crocheting, needlepoint, oil painting, public speaking, and drama. An evening review at the close of the year provides an opportunity for participants to perform, receive their bowling trophies, and display painting and needlework projects. The community-sponsored program is particularly helpful in filling the gap between fall and spring sports activities.

EVALUATION OF THE PROGRAM   Continuous evaluation of the activity program is just as important as continuous evaluation of any other aspect of the total educational experience. The program must be assessed in terms of the needs and interests of individual students and of the community. Evaluation should be the responsibility of a representative committee that includes in its membership community representatives, faculty, and students. Specific activities that are needed must be identified and existing activities evaluated. Some methods for producing such data might include the following:

1. Student interest inventories.
2. Determination of the amount and pattern of participation in individual activities.
3. Evaluation of contributions by sponsors.
4. Study of the values to which activities contribute.
5. Surveys of use and availability of school and community facilities.

6. Cost studies of the activity program.
7. Study of the relationship between the activity program and the regular classroom program.
8. Study of individual activities.
    a. Identification of objectives.
    b. Chief accomplishments as related to the objectives.
    c. Major difficulties preventing achievement of objectives.
    d. Principal projects of the group.
    e. Recommendations for improving a particular activity.

A truly adequate activity program must reflect the needs and interests of the students in a particular school. Evaluators must determine whether or not there is provision for the less talented to participate in the skill activities such as music, dramatics, and athletics. The extent of student participation must be examined by comparing the number of boys and girls who participate with the total enrollment of the school, with the goal being participation by each student in at least one activity. The other extreme, overemphasis and overparticipation, must be examined. Is there guidance available to ensure against overparticipation by some individuals? The extent of influence of the expectations of the senior high school on the activity program must be assessed. The middle school must not become a training ground for high school activities, as has occasionally happened in the past, particularly in athletics.

The evaluating committee should also examine the relationship between the activity program and the regular instructional program. There should be apparent relationships, and both should be consistent with the school's philosophy and objectives. A related question is the cost of participation to the student. If the activity program is an important area with specific educational objectives, there should be no cost to the student, just as he is not required to pay a fee for participating in an English class. While the financing is being examined, a study should be made of how money is handled. Is the accounting system an accepted one? Are students involved in the handling of money? If not, they should be. Studies of the above matters will provide a basis for sound decision making.

STUDENT GOVERNANCE

Participation in a student governance organization can provide opportunities for students to develop good habits, responsibility, and self-identification. Student governance does not mean that the students rule themselves or the school, but that they have the opportunity to participate. As their responsibilities are gradually increased, they will develop increased competence, receive a psychological lift, and become more self-disciplined. A student governance structure is the cornerstone for the entire activity program. The capabilities of the students must not be underestimated.

HOMEROOM ACTIVITIES   A school needs to be humane. One means of accomplishing this is to provide a home base for each student. A homeroom organization can provide a place where each student feels secure, because the teacher is concerned about him and recognizes him as an individual. The most extensive participation involving all students takes place at the homeroom level.

Care must be taken that the homeroom does not become an administrative convenience for making announcements and taking attendance, or an extension of the study hall. Time and attention must be given to extensive planning of a program that is an outgrowth of the needs of the students. The program should range from an orientation type of introduction to the middle school for new students to an introduction to the senior high school for those who are ready to be transferred.

Unfortunately, orientation programs have too often been a half-day experience comprising perhaps a large-group meeting and a whirlwind tour of the building. Much more appropriate is immediate assignment to a homeroom teacher who then undertakes to provide a well-planned program that might extend for several weeks. Topics for the orientation program and experiences, such as becoming acquainted with the building, should be sequential. For example, the first homeroom meeting might include an introduction to the functions of the homeroom, assignment and discussion of the class schedule, and a guided tour limited to the areas and rooms on the class schedule. A tour of the total building is more appropriate for a later meeting when students have a partial knowledge of the building layout and are less apt to become confused.

Additional topics for subsequent homeroom periods might include policies and procedures for the homeroom and the school, curricular opportunities (including required and elective courses), opportunities available in the school activity program, how the middle school differs from the elementary school, objectives of the middle school, development of objectives for the class and by each individual in the class for himself, and effective study habits.

When a class enters its final year in the middle school, visits to the senior high school by individuals and small groups of students who then report back are appropriate. A visit by an entire class might be desirable. Senior high school representatives should be invited to the middle school. Some excellent programs result when the high school wrestling team provides a demonstration or high school newspaper editors discuss their publications with groups of interested middle school students.

STUDENT COUNCIL   The homeroom serves as a subunit of the larger student government organization, which is represented by the student council. With appropriate freedom and guidance, a student council can manage certain school activities and clubs. The student council itself provides excellent opportunities for self-management.

The student council is an appropriate vehicle for the promotion of school activities. It can not only contribute to an all-school program by sponsoring specific activities such as a talent show or an after-school square dance, but it can provide an opportunity for discussion of the values in student activities and provide leadership and guidelines for participation in them. Routine matters such as making announcements and coordinating the school calendar of activities are additional ways in which it can assist in maintaining the entire activity program.

If it is to be effective, the student council itself must be representative not only of students but also of the administration, teachers, and guidance staff. Students need to have adequate supervision without having their initiative stifled. Limits must be established that define students' responsibilities and authority, and then they must be permitted to operate within these limits.

Council members must not be expected to serve as policemen or custodians, nor should they serve as judge and jury in cases of student misbehavior. They may assist in these areas, but their main function is to meet the needs of the student body at large. An effective student council provides training in democratic processes and governmental procedures, teaches group cooperation, raises the morale of the student body, and fosters self-discipline.

Some common projects for a student council might include the following:

1. Assisting community organizations.
2. Maintaining a lost-and-found office.
3. Maintaining school bulletin boards.
4. Publishing a school handbook and subsequent revisions.
5. Acting as ushers and receptionists.
6. Assisting in evaluating the school activity program.
7. Assisting in organizing new clubs.

8. Assisting in orientation programs.
9. Keeping the calendar of school activities.
10. Assisting in lunchroom maintenance and with lunch-hour programs.

In *Secondary Education in the United States,* Douglass lists the following principles, which are appropriate for application to middle school councils:

1. The principal and the majority of the teachers must be thoroughly in sympathy with the fundamental philosophy of the idea.
2. The principal and those to be associated with the council as sponsors or advisers must be well read in the theory and practice of student participation in management and administration as organized in a secondary school.
3. There must be a desire on the part of the great majority of the students for student participation.
4. Both students and faculty must have a clear idea of the plan, its scope, and its limitations.
5. The development and extension of student participation, particularly in organized form, must be practiced; the students participating must be prepared in advance by discussions and, perhaps, by reading materials before each successive step in the development and expansion of participation, and before the initial organization for participation.
6. The faculty advisers must be carefully selected on the basis of their sympathy, understanding, training, and the reading they have done in the field of student government and management; as far as possible, they should have personalities that are attractive to young people and will cause them to be readily liked, accepted, and respected.
7. A carefully worked out constitution should be adopted as the result of a great deal of deliberation by various groups specially appointed for the purpose. Its various drafts should be discussed by small groups of the students and later by the entire student body at the time of its adoption.
8. It is necessary that the students have confidence in the council, its operations, and its officers, and in the attitudes of the faculty in the matter of noninterference.
9. From the outset there should be cordial cooperation and constructive criticism on the part of members of the faculty.
10. As far as is practical, considerable numbers of students must be given responsibilities of some importance, though not onerous ones, in connection with the activities of the council.

11. The principal should retain a veto power, which he should exercise in a very limited way, permitting the students to move ahead even along lines that may be somewhat doubtful but not definitely disasterous.
12. There should be definite business-like organization for the collection, expenditure, and supervision of the finances. Usually the assistant principal or a member of the faculty of the business department is appointed as the supervisor of student funds with whom the student council and other student organizations work.
13. There should be an annual audit; indeed, many schools have a semiannual audit.
14. The plan of organization must provide for adequate representation of all the students, regardless of grade, sex, etc.
15. The student government should be developed gradually, in proportion to the developing maturity and sense of responsibility of the students.[2]

PRACTICAL POLICIES

The student activity program must serve the students. Each student should have an opportunity to succeed at something, whether it be giving a good performance or participating in a meeting. He needs an opportunity to participate without worrying about a grade or about reaching a certain level of achievement. In order for every student to gain maximum benefit from participation in activities, a clear set of policies governing activity operation should be established by a committee whose membership includes representatives from administration, faculty, and students. Frequent review of the policies by the same kind of representative committee is essential.

INTRAMURAL VS. INTERMURAL   The advantages of intramural over intermural activities were discussed in an earlier part of this chapter. A firm policy establishing an intramural program must be developed. The same policy should exclude intermural or interscholastic athletics, for the existence of such policies will make it more difficult for community members to press for an intermural program, which unfortunately does happen. The pressures of Little League competition with the attendant parental emphasis on

---

2. Harl R. Douglass, *Secondary Education in the United States,* Second Edition, Copyright © 1964, The Ronald Press Company, New York.

winning must not be permitted to become part of the middle school sports program.

EXPENSE   There should be little or no cost to the participants for student activities.   Membership dues, high admission fees to athletic events, and excessive costs for rental of musical instruments prevent participation.   A school must constantly examine its program to make certain that excessive costs are not hindering student participation.   Fees, if any, must be nominal, since the activity program must be looked upon as an integral part of the ongoing school program with educational value.

Where money is involved, accepted accounting procedures must be followed.   A central treasurer for the entire program is recommended.   Although all activities money should be in a common bank account, a definite budgetary allowance must be made for each activity.   Where disbursements are made by check, at least two signatures should be required for authorization.   The two might be the principal and the faculty sponsor.

Each activity that in any way involves expenditures must have an operational budget.   A budget review committee is recommended not only for the essential function it might serve, but also because it provides an excellent learning opportunity for its student members.

ELIGIBILITY   All must have an equal opportunity to participate if activities are to have educational value.   Race, religious belief, economic status, and scholastic standing must not become criteria for membership.   An obvious exception is the honor society (and one might question whether such a group should be part of a middle school activity program).

The time of day at which activities are scheduled must encourage, not discourage, participation.   Ideally, time should be provided within the school day.   A regular period every day or two periods per week could provide time for clubs, various activities, and assemblies.   If too many activities are offered outside normal school hours, some students will be ineligible because they are unable to remain for various reasons.

PROTECTION OF STUDENTS   The only value in an activity program is the benefit it provides to the participants.   The welfare of the individual is of the utmost importance.   Students must not be permitted to become so extensively involved that their health becomes endangered or that their academic progress is detrimentally affected.

The amount and type of participation by individual students should be determined in a counseling situation. Each student should participate in at least one activity; some are eager to become involved in several and are capable of doing so in combination with their academic programs.

The physical well-being of each student is important, as is his emotional stability. An emphasis on competitiveness and finished performances has no place in the middle school. The shy, quiet girl must be encouraged to participate as an active member of an activity rather than a silent observer. Aggressive students who tend to take over and "run the show" must be counseled carefully so that other students have an equal opportunity. No group of students should ever be permitted to form a clique that takes over the program. Officers of various organizations should rotate; no one should succeed himself.

Each student's participation should be limited by the time required for each activity, the difficulty of his academic program, his interests and abilities, and demands on his time and energy by non-school activities. A maximum of five hours of participation in middle school activities per week is recommended.

Occasionally programs outside school hours for parents and community members are desirable. These should begin early in the evening, and they should be no more than one to one and a half hours in length. Students must be able to return home at a reasonable hour to be rested for the next day in school. At all times, the educational value of the activity and the welfare of the students it serves must be more important than the performance value for the community.

SOCIAL ACTIVITIES   Social activities in a school program provide opportunities for boys and girls to work together. These should be group-type activities that do not stress boy–girl relationships. Their major objectives should be development of personality, self-confidence, and skill in social behavior.

Many boys and girls do not know how to act in social situations and need to learn the social amenities without social pressure. Square dances, large circle dances, and games such as table tennis and shuffleboard are possible kinds of activities for social gatherings in the middle school. Grade-level socials with some kind of instruction by faculty members before the social event itself are recommended.

Some students are eager to have dances. A limit of two during the year is recommended for the eighth grade, one of which might be scheduled in the evening. One afternoon dance should be sufficient for seventh graders; younger students should participate in a social activity that includes games and group dances. Regardless of the kind of event, students should assume responsibility and leadership in planning, decorating, and implementing their plans.

STAFF INVOLVEMENT   The student activity program is a vital part of the educational program. The degree of its educational effectiveness is dependent upon the philosophy, enthusiasm, and competence of the faculty. All faculty members should be involved with the program in some way and fully understand its objectives.

Organizational Role.   The role of the faculty member in a school activity is not very different from the role of a teacher in the classroom. He must assist in providing learning experiences that fit the program to the interests and needs of the students. He must be willing to give time and effort to planning and working with groups. A special effort must be made to stimulate student groups to organize their own programs and to develop student self-direction without exercising arbitrary controls.

Members of the school staff have a vital role to play in encouraging students to join activities, helping students to formulate policies concerning their activities, establishing meeting dates, and determining the qualifications for membership. Even more important is their role in assisting students in establishing goals for their activities, in developing ways of achieving these goals, and, at that point, in planning programs based on the established goals. Throughout the teacher must encourage group control, as he gradually reduces his own control.

An effective activity program requires time and effort from staff members, whose organizational role might include calling members together for their first meeting, assisting in the election of officers or starting a discussion of the kind of organization that would be most appropriate for the situation, assisting student leaders in conducting meetings, helping in the formulation of objectives, and providing needed information.

Guidance Role.   The role of faculty members is also one of guidance. They must provide the necessary direction where needed, yet they must determine the times at which students must be allowed to proceed on their own, even if they make mistakes. Effective staff members will encourage the development of leadership. They will be concerned with the personal and social development of each student and continually guide students in their growth toward realization of established educational objectives.

Staff members associated with middle school activities must understand the age group with which they are involved. They must thoroughly understand how they grow, their likes and dislikes, their problems, and the reasons for their various kinds of behavior patterns. They must be a constant source of counsel, influencing attitudes and behavior without coercion. A command of the techniques of the group-work approach to learning is essential.

Balance with Teaching Duties. Staff members must desire to be effective in whatever roles they play in the total activity program. Their participation must not become a burden added to an already heavy teaching load. The activities in which they are involved must be of interest to them if their enthusiasm is to be a factor in the successful operation of the program.

It is also important that involvement with an activity not overshadow the teaching assignment. The coach who relegates everything but coaching to a lesser degree of importance is all too familiar. The music teacher who views his annual concert as the only important event in the school year is also undesirable. An appropriate balance between involvement with activities and teaching must be maintained. Ideally the activity program should be viewed as a teaching situation, and staff involvement in activities should be viewed as part of the individual staff member's teaching load.

Vested Interests. It must be remembered at all times that the activity program is for the students and should focus on their needs and interests. Unfortunately, this does not always happen. Sponsors of musical and athletic activities particularly have been accused of furthering their own careers by means of overemphasized activities in their area. Staff members from athletic departments often view their assignments as stepping stones to high school coaching jobs; they encourage middle school participation in interscholastic competition as one means of achieving this goal.

No staff member should ever be permitted to take over a student activity to the extent that it is viewed as his alone. Care must be taken that each activity be viewed in its proper perspective as part of the total activity program and, most important of all, as part of the total educational program.

Utilization of Resource Personnel. In the early history of school activities, it was not uncommon for a school to employ an individual who was not a regular staff member as sponsor of an activity.

In fact, sponsorship was considered to be a nonprofessional task unbefitting a teacher. As the educational value of activities became increasingly apparent, their sponsorship shifted to the regular teaching staff. Today there appears to be another shift developing.

In many situations, teachers are not interested in the additional burden of involvement with an activity. In fact, many do not have the particular skills required to be effective. As a result, some schools are utilizing individuals from the community who are qualified by interest and training. The local resident who makes jewelry from polished stones and the dramatic coach for the local community theater organization can make valuable contributions to a school's activity program. They might prove to be the ideal individuals to encourage students to participate in very satisfying activities that can become lifetime hobbies.

THE STUDENT VOICE Parents, teachers, and administrators must all develop sensitivity to student feelings and perceptions. They must learn to see the world as their students do. No longer are teachers and administrators in a position to establish policies and determine all aspects of the curriculum and classroom activity. Students are clamoring to be heard, and adults must listen.

The day of the faculty-sponsored student council with its token decision-making process has passed. No longer will students accept a situation where their recommendations are forwarded to the principal by the faculty sponsor, ignored by the principal, and then forgotten.

Students want to discuss issues much more crucial than the date of the next social event or how to decrease the noise in the cafeteria. From the long-hair issue which created a furor about student rights, students have moved to demanding black studies and the right to publish and distribute their own newspapers and other publications. One eleven-year-old became involved in a court case in which he sued for the right to continue circulating a petition for the removal of his principal.

Communication and the flow of information once moved in one direction—from teacher to student. Now communication must flow in many directions. Adults can learn from and with students. Some teachers feel threatened by these developments, but they must work toward a situation where teachers and the students are involved together in appropriate decision making.

Community Involvement. The effectiveness of students is influenced by the community. A community that is apathetic about its schools will only reinforce student attitudes about the lack of concern on the part of adults. A community must show its concern for students by helping to create a climate that will lead to satisfaction and harmony, and by working with students to improve society.

Parents should be encouraged to become involved in school activities as much as possible, either on a volunteer basis or as paid teacher aides. They will then be part of the school situation, view it firsthand, and, perhaps, better understand student concerns and reactions.

It might be appropriate in some instances to develop a school council rather than a student council. As mentioned above, faculty and administrators should work together. Why not add parents and board-of-education members to such a body? Awareness, concern, and involvement should be shared by all in a situation that will foster mutual decision making.

Policy Making. Policy making must be a mutual activity involving staff and students. What better way is there for students in a middle school to learn how to develop effective and appropriate policies that they and their peers will accept? Student dissent has been increasing among younger students. It has even extended down into the elementary school. Preventive measures for avoiding disruption and violence are more important than determining a course of action after overt dissension has disrupted the operation of an entire school.

Guidelines for dealing with open dissent should be developed in advance. Activities to be taken into consideration might include disruption of classes, chanting, distribution of printed materials, marches, and sit-ins. Provision should also be made for handling false fire alarms.

Legal aspects of disruptive situations must be clarified and students made aware of the legal implications of their involvement in any kind of disruption. They must also know beforehand how disruptive situations will be handled and, where applicable, be aware of school-board policy. One of the most comprehensive policy statements on student involvement in the educational process is that adopted by the Board of Education of Montgomery County, Maryland, in August, 1969. Its ten items range from a statement describing student participation in the learning process to the establishment of a procedure for consideration of student problems and the processing of student complaints.[3]

One of the first areas of dissent was student dress. This is a matter to be determined by parents, administrators, and students

---

3. "Student Involvement in the Educational Process," Board of Education Policy Statement, Montgomery County, Maryland, 1969.

together.   Many schools are adopting a policy similar to the following, which was taken from the Montgomery County policies.

> Students' dress and grooming is the responsibility of students and their parents, unless some standard of dress and grooming is a reasonable requirement of a course of activity or necessary for reasons of health and safety.
>
> Schools may develop advisory guidelines for dress and grooming through the cooperation of students, parents and teachers.   School personnel may counsel with those who affect extreme styles of dress and grooming.
>
> Unless a student's dress or grooming causes or is likely to cause a disruption of the educational process, he shall not be disciplined because of the way he dresses or grooms himself.[4]

Growing up in today's society is difficult and demanding.   Responsible participation by students in an activity program and in the development of policies by which they are affected can be of immeasurable value in aiding them in this process.

---

4. *Ibid.*

≥ 9 ≤

STAFF
ORGANIZATION
AND UTILIZATION

Staff organization and utilization in a middle school may follow numerous patterns. There may be, for example, the line and staff arrangements with which most people are familiar—arrangements that typically start with the principal at the top, the department head in the middle, and the teacher at the bottom. Although line and staff arrangements have merit if the roles and relationships of personnel are defined functionally, there are other ways of organizing and using staff that deserve special consideration in a school geared to youngsters ten to fourteen years of age.

TEAM TEACHING

Many changes in the techniques of grouping and regrouping students have occurred during the past ten years. Some have been masquerading as "team teaching." Ask any group of educators to define team teaching and you begin to hear a variety of definitions that relate to large-group instruction, small-group instruction, shared instruction, and/or shared planning.

Simply stated, team teaching is the cooperative or collaborative effort of two or more teachers who share in the planning and in the conduct of instruction. The term team teaching is a misnomer. A better titular description would be team organization or team planning.

A major problem with team teaching is the tendency for the teachers comprising the team to "turn" teach rather than team

161

teach. This practice has done much to diminish the positive effect that cooperative–collaborative teaching and planning has on the improvement of instruction.

An open-plan, multi-graded, flexible middle school program will be more successful if it stresses cooperative planning and teaching. A middle school organizational plan stressing the team approach to planning has a more cohesive curriculum and a more integrated approach to instruction from both the teacher's and the student's viewpoints.

Some educators in middle schools advocate cooperative–collaborative arrangements where teachers in a single discipline plan and teach a block of instruction for two or three classes at the same time. Another variation is the assignment of an interdisciplinary or cross-discipline team to plan and teach interrelated subjects. These teachers generally represent all major subject areas and are concerned with planning for and teaching the same common group of students. Imaginative middle school staff designs encourage interdisciplinary planning and teaching by allowing the team authority to rearrange blocks of time to suit instructional needs.

Inherent in any successful design for cooperative–collaborative teaching are the following criteria:

1. The group is able to set long-range and short-range goals and to develop the techniques for meeting these goals.
2. A climate exists that encourages the team to become involved in curriculum decision making.
3. Authority for rearrangement of instructional groups of students is given to the team.
4. Adequate time is scheduled for team planning.
5. Leadership potential is placed in each team.
6. Personalities, potentialities, and abilities of teachers are considered in organizing the team.
7. Various disciplines are represented on the team planning the instructional process.
8. Communication channels with the administrative team are built into the structure.

If these criteria are successfully integrated into the staff design for middle schools, the goals of a student-centered middle school can be met. Time, space, and personnel can be rearranged by cooperative–collaborative planning, allowing for the full flexibility that best serves the needs of instruction. Of these possible patterns, two will be emphasized in this chapter because it is felt that these patterns are best adapted to a dynamic middle school and the implementation of its curriculum.

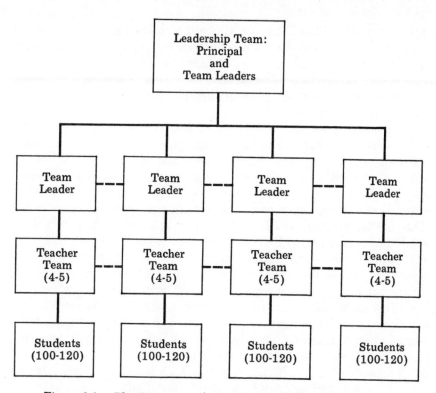

Figure 9-1.   The Team Approach to Middle School Organization

THE LEADERSHIP–TEACHER TEAM   A leadership–teacher team with an organizational arrangement similar to that shown in Figure 9-1 has a definite place in a middle school and offers excellent opportunities for strengthening the instructional program.   Before discussing its place in the organizational structure and the advantages it provides, we should look at the composition of a team and the number of staff members involved.

Each teacher team is headed by a leader who chairs team meetings, arranges agendas for meetings, establishes contact with resource people, and performs such other activities as are deemed essential to the successful operation of the team.   The leader is usually a teacher in one of the major disciplines.

As depicted in the diagram, all team leaders constitute a leadership team or a steering committee which meets regularly with the principal.   In these meetings questions of policy are discussed, needs defined, procedures worked out, resources determined, and related questions considered.   In this respect the leadership team or steering committee serves as a clearing house.   Ideas and suggestions offered by the principal and team leaders are discussed and evaluated. Those that are thought to have merit are taken by the team leaders back to team members for review and judgment. In turn, the ideas and opinions of team members are presented to the steering committee by team leaders. This organizational setup permits an easy, two-way flow of information which helps to weld each team into a strong unit.

Teams are composed of four to five teachers, with each one being responsible for 100 to 120 pupils. On this basis, it is a simple matter to determine how many teams are required for a middle school of any given enrollment. For example, a typical 800-student school would need a maximum of forty team teachers or a minimum of thirty-two team teachers in major disciplines such as English, social studies, mathematics, and science. These teachers would be supplemented by a series of specialists, as shown in Figure 9-2. These specialists would include a guidance person and individuals in the fields of art, music, health and physical education, vocational arts, media resources, and medical services.

Two kinds of advantages are associated with the leadership–teacher team. One concerns instructional development, and the other involves learning problems of individual students. On the instructional side, the whole team is in a position to look carefully at all aspects of the curriculum with which it is concerned. It can examine scope and sequence, determine curricular design, agree on teaching strategies, outline means for effecting correlation and integration, participate in the selection of instructional supplies and

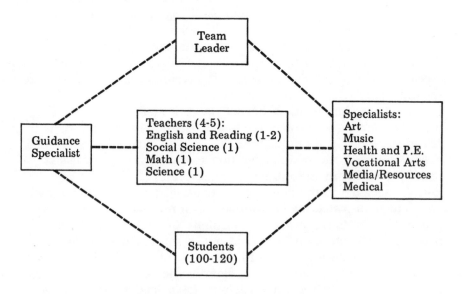

Figure 9-2. The Teacher Team

equipment, and formulate policies on these and related matters. The team arrangement is a natural vehicle for ongoing curriculum study and improvement.

The other advantage associated with the leadership–teacher team is that commonly observed problems and behavior manifestations can be identified and shared by teachers and other adults. Decisions can then be made regarding remedial or corrective actions. The efforts of the entire team can be brought to bear to observe and evaluate progress or the extent to which action taken has been successful. Without doubt, the efforts of four or five teachers can have a more salutory effect than the efforts of a single teacher in dealing with either a learning or a behavior problem.

Professional assistance from a psychologist, social worker, learning disability specialist, or counselor should be available to the team upon request. These specialists broaden the talents brought to bear on a problem and can often produce a more tenable working hypothesis or solution. When necessary, parents should be invited to meet with the team and exchange ideas as to causative elements and possible ways of dealing with a troublesome question. This type of cooperative approach has a sharp impact on parents and leaves them with the feeling that the school is genuinely interested in the welfare of their children.

Another positive aspect of team-directed guidance is the possibility of having one team member serve as the primary counselor to each individual student. Each team member, then, is responsible for counseling twenty-five to thirty students. This counseling approach necessitates the development of a rapport between the teacher and student, if students are going to bring their personal problems to such teachers. Children of middle school age must feel comfortable with and trust the adults to whom they look for understanding and guidance.

Role of the Principal. If the concept of the leadership–teacher team is to function properly, then it must be set against a background of dynamic, democratic, and constructive leadership on the part of the building principal. Although he undertakes administrative responsibilities in such areas as management, school–community relations, child guidance, and plant supervision, his primary task is that of instructional leadership. Instructional leadership encompasses a number of activities directed toward the steady and continuous improvement of the educational program within the school. It is through these activities that the principal facilitates the tasks of leadership–teacher teams in their work of helping students to learn.

Although the principal is responsible in the final analysis for the educational program, he shares his authority and responsibility with team members. In so doing, he operates under the assumption that staff personnel should have a voice in making recommendations and arriving at decisions that concern their work. He believes that the quality of the recommendations and decisions is much higher when decisions are developed jointly. This does not preclude his making decisions based on established policies or the need for arriving at quick judgments when circumstances dictate that action be taken. Team members should understand what he must do to handle administrative matters so that they do not feel that he is working in an authoritarian way.

The middle school principal's role is that of a change agent and a facilitator of services performed by members of the staff. As a change agent, he exercises his talents to create a tone or a climate in the school that fosters open, cooperative relationships among those with whom he is associated. He knows that unless people are free to speak their minds on professional matters, feel good about themselves and others, and have a sense of personal worth and dignity, change is not likely to occur. The making of change requires an environment that encourages people to exchange views, examine ideas, study innovations, and experiment with new ways of thinking and acting.

As a facilitator of services performed by staff personnel, the principal arranges for materials and resources when they are needed. He is concerned with doing everything possible to enable the staff to achieve the major purposes of the school. This calls for ready assistance in the search for solutions to problems that staff members think are important and the expediting of actions that contribute to the smooth operation of the teaching–learning process.

The middle school principal should be a communications expert. He needs to know what people in the organization think and feel, whether or not they are experiencing a sense of progress in their work, and if they have desires and frustrations with which he should be concerned. Both as a listener and a communicator, he establishes channels for the two-way flow of information and ideas. He encourages feedback to proposals and suggestions offered by himself and by colleagues. He tries to make certain that staff members possess the understandings and have the perceptions required for sound decision making. He is fully aware that his method of operation in listening and communicating is a vital factor in the success of the leadership–teacher team.

Responsibilities of Team Members. All members of the teacher team must possess certain attitudes and understandings along with a willingness to accept responsibility, if the group decision-making process is to be successful. There must be a genuine desire on their part to cooperate fully in attacking problems, studying the implications of events occurring in school and community, framing and receiving propositions to be tested, making recommendations, and formulating policy statements based on rational review and assessment of pertinent information.

At the same time, team members must feel a strong sense of individual and group accountability for the decisions made and the actions that follow. They must take it upon themselves to help define the purpose or purposes for which they are meeting and to acquire an adequate knowledge of the subject under discussion. Once decisions have been reached, they have a moral obligation to implement assigned duties to the best of their ability even though they may disagree with the decision. Loyalty in this instance is to the group and not to themselves, the leader, or the principal.

The effectiveness of the team approach to decision making rests largely upon the application of group process to the treatment of professional matters. Members must acquire skills in the identification and understanding of problems and in the use of democratic methods of working as a group for their solution. They must know the limits within which the group can function, including the nature of the decisions to be made and where the line is to be drawn between their authority and that reserved for the principal. They must learn to empty themselves of pride in their own points of view and eliminate the conviction that they know the whole truth. Group process calls for a spirit of give and take, an atmosphere that is appropriate for exploring problems, and a testing for consensus without creating pressures for uniformity. If these conditions prevail, then both productivity and member satisfaction will be achieved in a minimum amount of time.

Parent and Student Involvement. Parents and students have a role to play in decision making by members of the leadership–teacher team. When a particular issue or problem concerns them, they should be invited to take part in the study and deliberations. Generally, parents and students are willing to participate if it appears that the final determination of an issue or a problem may affect them in some significant way. For example, they would have a natural interest in such matters as a change in homework policy, the introduction of nongraded instruction, or a new system of reporting student progress. There are times, however, when they do not feel strongly about a proposal and are rather indifferent about their involvement in it.

In selecting parents and students to take part in team discussions, every effort should be made to secure those who have the most to contribute. The real challenge is to involve them in ways that will satisfy them and, at the same time, enrich the decision-making process.

DIFFERENTIATED STAFFING   Another pattern of staffing that is somewhat similar to the concept behind the leadership–teacher team is differentiated staffing. Differentiated staffing is an organizational arrangement in which various levels of teaching responsibility are designated. Teachers within a team are assigned in a way that matches their talents to the needs of students. There are many definitions of differentiated staffing, but almost all of them divide the professional staff into levels and include teaching aides.

Figure 9-3 shows how the level idea works. At the top is a team leader. This individual heads the team and provides the expertise needed to stimulate and give direction to team efforts. Next, in descending order, are staff teachers, or teachers who perform a variety of services that are in keeping with their specialties, such as curriculum study, curriculum guides, activity packages, testing programs, programmed materials, and audio tapes. Assistant or apprentice teachers constitute the next level of personnel. As their title implies, they assist the staff teachers in various ways and frequently assume responsibility for lecturing, small-group instruction, remedial tutoring, translating goals and curriculum units into lesson plans, and devising tests. The various kinds of aides or para-

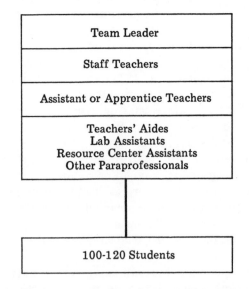

Figure 9-3.   Differentiated Staffing Team Approach

professionals depicted in the model work with all team members in taking care of routine matters and noninstructional activities so that professionals have more time available for their specialties. Figure 9-4 shows the relationship of the instructional team to students and instructional support centers.

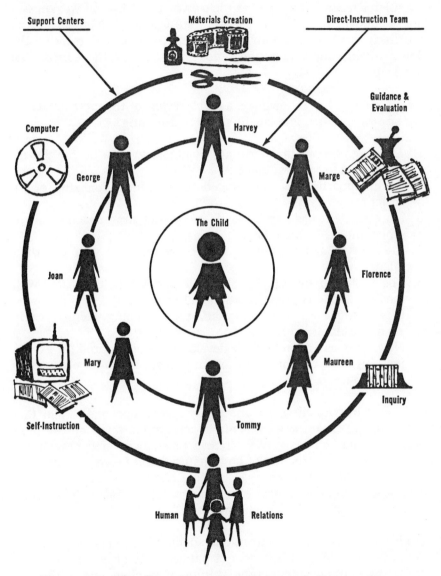

Figure 9-4. The Direct-Instruction Team and Support Centers (Source: Bruce R. Joyce, *The Teacher & His Staff: Man, Media & Machines* [Washington, D.C.: National Education Association, 1967.])

There are four principal ideas that make up the rationale for differentiated staffing. First, it creates an incentive system which places a career label on teaching. Teachers have a ladder they can climb; they make progress in accordance with their ability to grow and improve. Second, financial rewards are in keeping with responsibilities at different levels in the organizational structure of the team. Third, differentiated staffing provides a climate that stimulates teachers to discover their own strengths and weaknesses and to move into new areas of interest and competency. And fourth, it creates a team approach to instruction, underscoring the development, implementation, and evaluation of the educational program.

Advantages. The following is a quick review of the more outstanding advantages attributed to differentiated staffing:

1. A larger number of adults are available to provide for the instructional needs of students.
2. Better opportunities are created for the individualizing of instruction.
3. More efficient use can be made of teacher time, teacher talent, school facilities, and other resources.
4. Greater job satisfaction is derived by teachers who put their talents to use.
5. The staffing pattern is flexible and can easily be correlated with the introduction of new instructional systems.
6. It is a unique way of compensating and keeping talented teachers in the classroom.
7. New avenues are created for developing concepts and for experimenting in ways that help to bring about essential changes in education.

Tied in with these advantages is recognition of the fact that the development of new kinds of curriculum materials and systems will shift the emphasis away from a teacher-centered program to one in which the structure of both material and process is built into student learning experiences. As these changes occur, the teacher will become more and more of a diagnostician, a facilitator, and an evaluator of individual student progress.

Problems. Like other innovations adopted by middle schools, differentiated staffing in a variety of patterns has given rise to a few problems. Among them is the attitude of teachers and of the professional organizations to which they belong. They oppose the idea of paying salaries according to the levels on which teachers are functioning. Such a plan, they fear, will destroy the concept of the single-salary schedule and result in the allocation of good salaries to only a few people at the top of the team. They view the differentiated-salary plan as a disguised merit rating and would prefer to have all teachers receive higher salaries so they can afford to stay in teaching.

Another problem emerges when schools look upon differentiated staffing as a cost saver. Existing models in such states as California, Florida, and Kansas do not indicate any real savings. In fact, the opposite is more apt to be the case, because more professionals and paraprofessionals are used than in conventional staffing patterns. To meet increased costs, schools using differentiated staffing may find it necessary to raise the number of students assigned to a team. Even so, it is likely that the ratio of staff to students will still permit greater individualization of instruction.

Effective use of differentiated staffing presupposes the availability of learning materials and systems to provide for the articulation of content and process on both an individualized and group basis. Without these materials and systems, the end product of instruction will probably fall short of established goals.

One other problem sometimes develops in schools using differentiated staffing. With new roles for team members and new patterns of interpersonal relationships, the chances of personality conflicts are greater than normal. Their severity can be controlled if the principal sets a wholesome tone in the school and the team leader is sensitive in identifying trouble spots and taking constructive action to control them.

USING SPECIALISTS AND AIDES

The advent of differentiated staffing allows the school to look closely at the feasibility of using a larger number of adults in the learning process.

SPECIAL RESOURCE PERSONNEL   The teacher alone cannot effectively individualize instruction for all students. Such an expectation would be professionally naive. There are a significant number of children whose development deviates in some way from the normal so that they are considered exceptional. When learning is not progressing normally for a particular child, it is essential that the teacher be able to call upon the services of specialized personnel to help pinpoint the exact nature of the problem.

The group of specialists whose particular skills are necessary to identify the physical and/or psychological impairments causing underachievement and to devise an appropriate strategy for removing or circumventing these problems is the diagnostic team. Because there will be various specialties represented and because it is necessary that their work be coordinated and integrated to be effective, these professionals must operate as a team. The actual composition of the diagnostic team will vary from case to case, depending on its particular nature. The school principal or counselor, the teacher, and the school psychologist would be a basic nucleus for all such teams. Other possible team members would be drawn from such specialties as pediatrics, neurology, psychiatry, and social service. It is also likely that where circumstances warrant, various educational personnel from areas such as reading, speech, vision, hearing, adaptive physical education, and special education might become a part of the team.

A constant effort must be made in every school to prevent serious long-term consequences that can and do occur in the lives of children because of unrecognized physical and psychological problems. The teacher is perhaps one of the most important people in the child's life when it comes to the early recognition of such problems. Although perceptive parents and medical personnel sometimes discover impairments, it is often in the school situation under the eye of a professional teacher who knows normal developmental patterns that the first evidence of a problem is detected. It is the teacher's keen sensitivities that are important in noting early difficulties, alerting others, and initiating the process of diagnosis and remediation.

It is also the teacher who will carry out many of the prescriptions for helping children that grow out of the diagnostic team's efforts. When she follows the advice and direction of these specialists, the classroom teacher makes a unique contribution to improving the impaired child's ability to function normally. By utilizing the special competencies of professionals on a diagnostic team, the teacher brings to her command new information about specific children and thus increases her ability to provide, for each of her students, a meaningful and effective individual program for learning.

INSTRUCTIONAL AIDES   Teacher aides or instructional assistants should be employed by school districts whenever they can economically relieve professional teachers of nonprofessional tasks. The term "economically" must be considered, because the employment of aides, as recommended by teacher unions or associations, does not relate directly to increasing the professional efficiency of the teacher. Many teacher groups advocate employment of aides in their negotiations without thinking through the effective use of these paraprofessionals in instruction.

The employment of instructional aides should relate directly to the following criteria:

1. The amount of material used in individualized instructional programs requiring scoring or record keeping.
2. The number of the large-group/small-group instructional situations.
3. The size of the team.
4. The number of students needing individual help that could be supplied by a nonprofessional.
5. The possibilities for differentiated staff assignments in the school district staffing pattern.

TUTORS   The advent of Title I, Elementary and Secondary Education Act, gave birth to a proliferation of tutorial projects in schools throughout the country.   The lack of individual achievement in reading, mathematics, and other disciplines could be remedied, it was felt, if the nonachievers could receive one-to-one (tutor to student) assistance.   Schools have used various kinds of tutoring arrangements, including paid adult tutors, adult volunteers from the community, and, in many cases, student tutors, both paid and volunteer.

Many schools have found that student tutors are effective in the one-to-one tutoring arrangement.   In fact, the use of older student tutors, who are themselves experiencing difficulty in a subject, to tutor younger students helps both students to learn and to achieve.

Middle school staff designs should include personnel to assist in tutoring.   Benefits accrue not only to students, but to the school itself, as more of the community becomes involved in helping the school to achieve its instructional goals.

CLERICAL AIDES AND PRODUCTION PERSONNEL   Middle school teacher teams need clerical and production assistants in order to perform their tasks efficiently.   Assistants do not necessarily have to be provided to each team; they can be centrally located to perform similar services for all teams in the school.

The larger the number of available instructional systems, the more clerical help is required for scoring, record keeping, production of allied materials, mimeographing, xeroxing, and the myriad of other necessary services.   These should be performed by nonprofessionals when possible, leaving teachers more time for instruction and students.

QUALIFICATIONS OF STAFF

ADAPTABILITY TO STUDENTS OF MIDDLE SCHOOL AGE
Coping with the ten- to fourteen-year-old is not always as easy as many adults imagine. The junior high child has always been considered the most difficult to handle by teachers who have taught a wide range of ages. Teachers find the naiveté and enthusiasm of the ten- to fourteen-year-old to be most delightful when harnessed purposefully, and most rigorous when left undirected.

Teachers of the middle grades, then, must be warm, capable, child-oriented, subject-knowledgeable leaders of youth. It is far easier to teach high school students than it is to teach the ten- to fourteen-year-old, who is looking for an identity.

Unfortunately, some teachers of the ten- to fourteen-year-old tend ultimately to tire of the challenge and to request a transfer to the high school. One of the major factors causing staff mobility at the middle school level is the lack in most teacher-training institutions of programs to prepare future teachers for middle grades. The common practice of state departments of permitting either elementary or secondary training as an acceptable preparation program for the middle school generally leaves us with a neither-fish-nor-fowl arrangement for staff training. This problem will continue until something is done to change it. Accordingly, we believe that standards like the following should be adopted by state education departments for the approval of preparation programs for middle school teachers. Certificates for teaching in the middle school should be issued only to those individuals who have attained the competencies implied.

Standard I   Knowledge of the developmental stages of late childhood and early adolescence in the physical, intellectual, psychological, and social–emotional areas.

Standard II   Knowledge of the learning processes appropriate to the above stages.

Standard III   Understanding of the nature and objectives of the kindergarten through twelfth-grade curriculum with emphasis on the place of the middle school in its sequential development.

Standard IV   Fundamental knowledge of curriculum construction and its bases.

Standard V   The ability to work with children at many different reading levels.

Standard VI   Depth in two content areas (combined time should equal about one quarter of the total time spent in the program of preparation).

Standard VII Completion of a methods course based on methods common to good teaching rather than on specific content areas.

Standard VIII Observation of and participation in middle school situations as part of professional courses.

Standard IX   Student-teaching experience in a middle school unit.

BALANCE ON THE TEAM   Schools function best when the leadership team can draw on the talents and enthusiasm of a faculty with both experience and recent training.   A well-balanced staff with levels of both experience and inexperience adds to the potential for inspired instruction.

The placement of "has-been" or "never-was" teachers on faculties has been one of the major reasons why the junior high school has never reached its full potential.   Teachers assigned to junior high schools were often unwanted high school teachers or new teachers training or waiting for high school placement.   The problem was sometimes further complicated by the assignment of elementary teachers who never fitted into the pattern.   All of these factors together helped to diminish the effectiveness of junior high schools.

It is obvious that if the personnel for the middle school are selected as haphazardly as were those in the junior high school, the success of the new model can be no greater than that of the one it replaces.   The ultimate weapon in the army is the infantry soldier; in education, the teacher makes or breaks the program and the school.

By careful selection, the planning process in which the instructional team engages is strengthened, particularly when teachers who comprise the team are able to relate to both materials and systems in more than one discipline.   A mix of talent should step up the quality of the planning almost in proportion to the number of disciplines represented on the team.   This conjecture has been borne out in the work done by outstanding teacher teams.

How can the talents of both the professionals and nonprofessionals be utilized to provide the most meaningful educational program? There are many answers to this question, all dealing in some way with or at least related to how well the school district can afford to support the program.

OPTIMUM USE OF TEACHER TIME AND TALENTS   Where resources are available, the leadership–teacher team or differentiated staff team can be assigned to work exclusively with one group of students.   Where resources are limited, it might be best to explore the possibility of assigning the team two groups of students, possibly smaller in number.   It might also be remembered that some part of the student day must be reserved for individual or small-group work.

Schedules must allow for group planning, both for instruction and for problems related to students.   These meetings should be scheduled and all personnel required to attend.   The effectiveness of the team relates directly to the outcomes of these team meetings. Therefore, the leadership–teacher team must keep abreast of developments within each team.

The teacher's program in Table 9-1 shows one possible program or schedule that could effectively serve the needs of the student-centered middle school.   The schedule allows for large-group and small-group instruction, individual study and counseling, as well as for teacher team planning for both instruction and pupil personnel study.   The time distribution may vary from week to week.

The effective use of teacher time can be evaluated best by the

Table 9-1   TEACHER'S PROGRAM

ACTIVITY	FRACTION OF SCHOOL DAY
Instruction	$\frac{1}{2} - \frac{5}{8}$
Team planning for instruction	$\frac{1}{8}$
Team planning for pupil personnel study and problems	$\frac{1}{8}$
Individual counseling— independent study preceptor	$\frac{1}{8} - \frac{1}{4}$

faculty, since they are most closely connected with the problem. Effective programming allows the teacher time to prepare for instruction, to consult professionally with other teachers, and to meet individually with students needing personal guidance. If teachers feel that their program offers opportunities for a professional challenge and a sense of accomplishment, then the program should succeed.

OPTIMUM USE OF STUDENT TIME   As students progress from one level to the next, the amount of time spent in self-contained or block-of-time instruction in skills and general studies should begin to decrease.   Older students should be able to spend more time in meaningfully structured independent study with less direction from the teacher team.   A typical program of student time utilization in middle schools is shown in Table 9-2.

Modular scheduling could be utilized by the teacher team in planning the student's schedule and in tailoring the time required for instruction as necessary.   Modular scheduling can be defined as a method of flexible scheduling that allows for the utilization of short modules of time, normally twenty to thirty minutes, rather than the more conventional and rigid periods of forty-five to sixty minutes found in most secondary schools.

The teacher team, during its daily planning sessions, can rearrange the modules as needed for effective instruction, since all those involved teach the same group of students.   This flexibility offered to the team of teachers to rearrange instructional time should make instruction even more viable.   When necessary, the team can combine the talents of a number of adults for instruction or divide the group of students for learning.

Table 9-2   STUDENT'S PROGRAM

ACTIVITY	FRACTION OF SCHOOL DAY (BY GRADE)			
	5	6	7	8
Block-of-time instruction in skills and general studies	$\frac{1}{2} - \frac{2}{3}$	$\frac{1}{2} - \frac{2}{3}$	$\frac{1}{3} - \frac{1}{2}$	$\frac{1}{3} - \frac{1}{2}$
Specialized instruction and independent study	$\frac{1}{3} - \frac{1}{2}$	$\frac{1}{3} - \frac{1}{2}$	$\frac{1}{2} - \frac{2}{3}$	$\frac{1}{2} - \frac{2}{3}$

The possibilities for more effective instruction are limitless when flexibility and decision-making power are provided to the teacher team. When instruction time is needed, it can be provided. When instruction requires different modes of grouping, they can be arranged. When added staff is required, differentiated staff aides are available. With all of these advantages, combined with effective and available leadership, the middle school of the future could indeed become a real student-centered environment for learning.

AN ORGANIZATIONAL DESIGN FOR MIDDLE SCHOOLS

What does the staff design of the middle school look like in actual practice? How can channels for staff communication be designed to enhance a quality instructional program in a student-centered school? What criteria does a middle school planner use to design an effective staff organization scheme?

Appropriate planning of the organization of the staff is necessary if a middle school program is to be truly effective. As a point of departure for evaluating an organizational chart, one should look at the following criteria:

1. Is the principal released from administrative tasks so that he can consider the instructional program his primary responsibility?
2. Are job descriptions available to spell out in detail each person's area of responsibility?
3. Are team leaders and other staff personnel able to become involved in decision making? How close or accessible to the principal are these people?
4. Does the organizational chart help or hinder communication flow?
5. Is the organizational chart geared primarily to facilitating instruction and secondarily to administration areas?
6. How can communication occur between teams? Between disciplines? Across disciplines?
7. What is the role of the student in the whole organizational pattern?
8. Is the community involved in organizing the school? If so, how?
9. Is the organizational scheme flexible enough to allow change to occur?

10. Are planning and evaluation built into the organizational chart? Into the job descriptions?

   A discerning middle school planner can quickly determine how well the school staff design can function by applying the criteria listed above to both the chart of organization and the job descriptions. Although many practitioners scoff at extensive organizational planning, a knowledgeable observer inherently senses the possibility of a more effective instructional program where everyone knows his area of responsibility and understands his relationship to the total program.

   With these criteria in mind, we will look at two operational models. The models selected use different kinds of organizational planning, yet they are similar in the respect that they were both designed to meet the criteria discussed in this chapter.

RUSSELL H. CONWELL MIDDLE MAGNET SCHOOL   The Philadelphia school system reorganized the existing grade structure in many areas of the city to include the middle school concept. Among the outstanding programs is the one designed at the Conwell Middle School, which embodies individualized instruction, team planning, cooperative efforts, community involvement by aides and volunteers, cultural enrichment programs, and an intensive evaluation program to measure the effectiveness of teaching and learning. The staff organization chart in Figure 9-5 shows the organizational pattern of the Conwell School.

LAGUNA BEACH UNIFIED SCHOOL DISTRICT   The Thurston Intermediate School in Laguna Beach, California, organized its middle grades program around the team approach to instruction. Unique in the organizational approach is the description of the principal's role as instructional leader, and the assistant principal's role as administrative and counseling functionary.

   The staff design incorporates aides and paraprofessionals, who assist the certificated personnel in instructional tasks. The design is shown in Figure 9-6.

   Interesting job descriptions for the student services counselor and the assistant principal at the Thurston Intermediate School are detailed in Figure 9-7. These job descriptions help to detail the many mundane chores from which an instruction-oriented principal can be relieved in a well-planned organizational scheme.

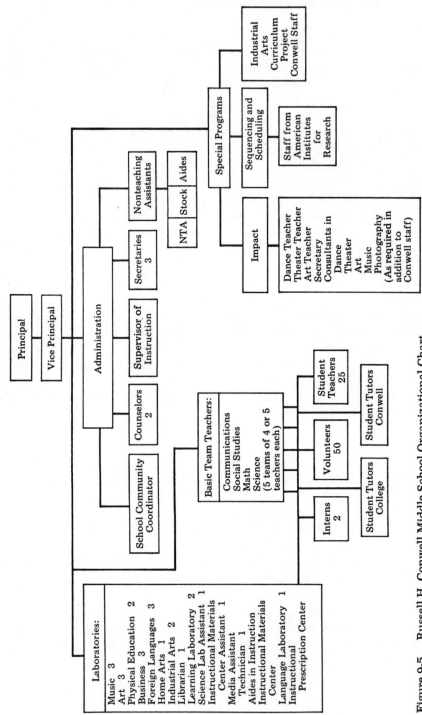

Figure 9-5. Russell H. Conwell Middle School Organizational Chart

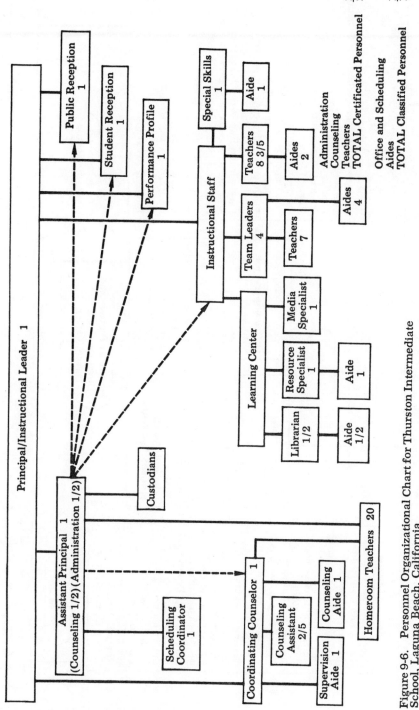

Figure 9-6. Personnel Organizational Chart for Thurston Intermediate
School, Laguna Beach, California

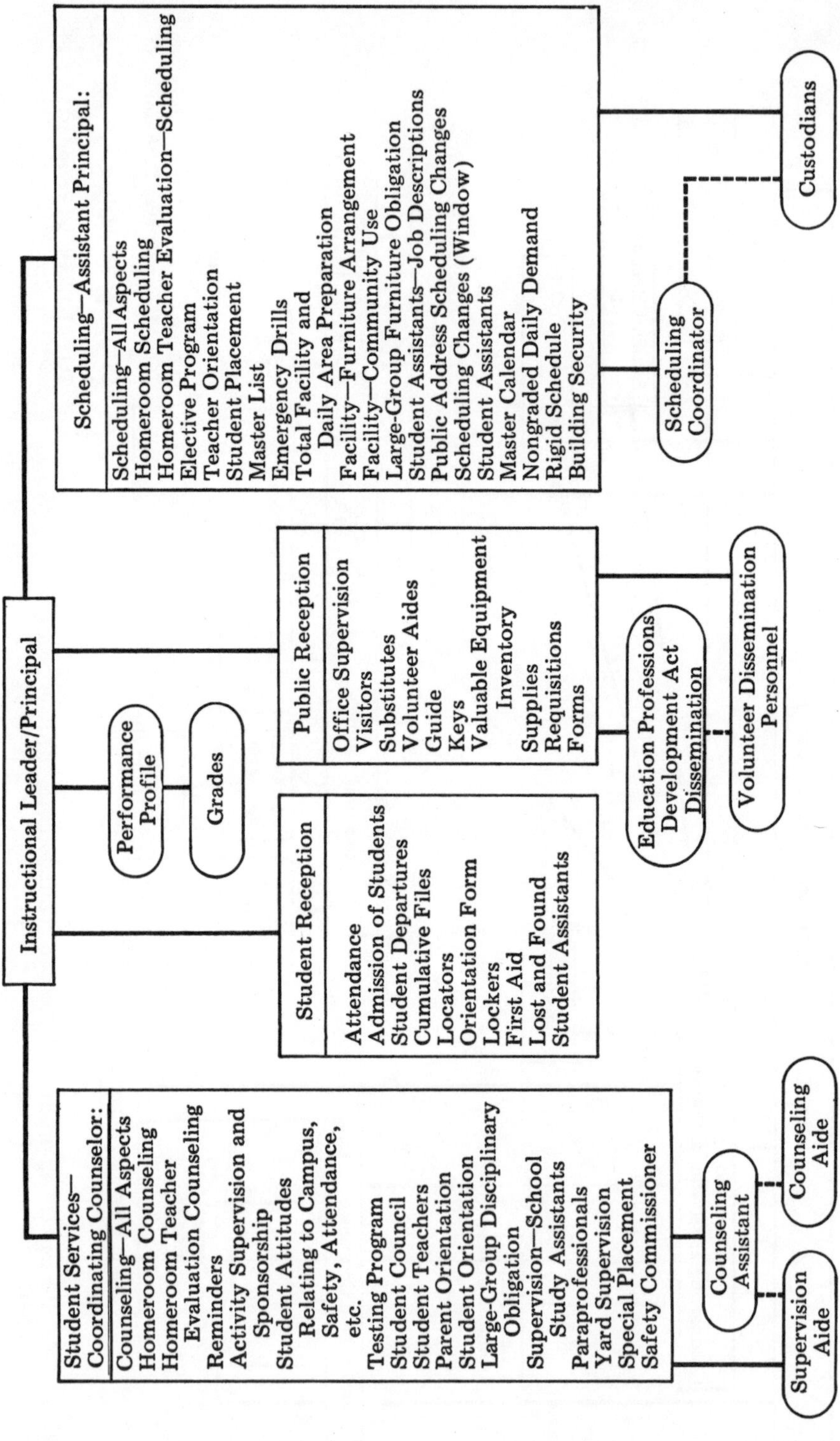

Instructional Leader/Principal

Scheduling—Assistant Principal:
- Scheduling—All Aspects
- Homeroom Scheduling
- Homeroom Teacher Evaluation—Scheduling
- Elective Program
- Teacher Orientation
- Student Placement
- Master List
- Emergency Drills
- Total Facility and Daily Area Preparation
- Facility—Furniture Arrangement
- Facility—Community Use
- Large-Group Furniture Obligation
- Student Assistants—Job Descriptions
- Public Address Scheduling Changes
- Scheduling Changes (Window)
- Student Assistants
- Master Calendar
- Nongraded Daily Demand
- Rigid Schedule
- Building Security

- Scheduling Coordinator
- Custodians

Performance Profile

Grades

Public Reception
- Office Supervision
- Visitors
- Substitutes
- Volunteer Aides
- Guide
- Keys
- Valuable Equipment Inventory
- Supplies
- Requisitions
- Forms

- Education Professions Development Act Dissemination
- Volunteer Dissemination Personnel

Student Reception
- Attendance
- Admission of Students
- Student Departures
- Cumulative Files
- Locators
- Orientation Form
- Lockers
- First Aid
- Lost and Found
- Student Assistants

Student Services—Coordinating Counselor:
- Counseling—All Aspects
- Homeroom Counseling
- Homeroom Teacher Evaluation Counseling
- Reminders
- Activity Supervision and Sponsorship
- Student Attitudes Relating to Campus, Safety, Attendance, etc.
- Testing Program
- Student Council
- Student Teachers
- Parent Orientation
- Student Orientation
- Large-Group Disciplinary Obligation
- Supervision—School
- Study Assistants
- Paraprofessionals
- Yard Supervision
- Special Placement
- Safety Commissioner

- Counseling Assistant
  - Counseling Aide
- Supervision Aide

Figure 9-7. Administrative Areas of Responsibility at Thurston Intermediate School, Laguna Beach, California

COMMUNICATION

An important element in the effective operation of the leadership–teaching team or in a differentiated staffing arrangement is communication. Although there are a variety of meanings connected with this term, as used here it will refer to the free flow of information and ideas among staff personnel and the resultant degree of understanding.

An efficient communications system is vital to a middle school for several reasons. The primary one is to facilitate consistent action on the part of all individuals within the institution toward the achievement of educational goals. Another is that of bringing about the unity of thought and feeling or the sense of cohesiveness that is so essential to the maintenance of harmonious interpersonal relationships among members of the group. Clear-cut and efficient channels of communication are necessary for the transmittal and receipt of the orders, directions, and requests that serve as command messages. Failure to communicate efficiently within the school system and within an individual building usually gives rise to poor work performance, unhealthy attitudes, misunderstandings between administration and staff, and lack of serious concern for the attainment of educational goals.

A good communications system is one that employs various channels—up, down, and horizontal—that are both formal and informal. Messages are sent through formal channels from one part of the institution to another. They may pertain to routine matters, important information, new procedures, personnel decisions, and the like. Associated with the formal network are individuals who decide when a message should be transmitted, what its content should be, who should receive it, and the form in which it should be dispatched and recorded.

Informal communication is carried on largely through face-to-face relations among teachers, principals, supervisors, and other employees. It is more characteristic of the way ideas and information are exchanged in an individual school. Often this method of communication revolves around the analysis and interpretation of messages received through formal channels. Much of the time, it concerns speculation about people, policies, and consequences of anticipated action as well as the discussion of rumors. The latter is especially common in school systems where little has been done to set up formal means of establishing a two-way flow of information. It is the job of the superintendent and his staff, including the middle school principal, to integrate the formal and informal channels of communication. By doing so, they improve the chances of increasing unity of understanding, cooperation, and the satisfaction of individual needs.

Four principal types of communication are used for the transmission of messages. They are writing, reading, speaking, and listening. However, more than this is needed to impart information, attitudes, and interests. The unspoken message that is conveyed by facial expressions, physical gestures, tone of voice, small favors, and implied suggestions means much in the communication of a message and the effect the message has on the behavior of an individual or a group.

In order to create an atmosphere in which the middle school principal can communicate freely with teachers, teachers with the principal, and teachers among themselves, the principal must have a fairly good understanding of how the communication process operates. This calls for the setting up of means or channels through which information and ideas can be disseminated to staff personnel and through which feedback can be received. He needs to know how his messages are being interpreted and what his co-workers are thinking. For this process to operate efficiently and effectively, the principal must have the ability to listen, read, speak, and write. He must be open to advantageous persuasion by staff personnel and be competent himself in the art of persuasion.

≥ 10 ≤

EVALUATING
PERFORMANCE

This chapter concerns the nature and place of evaluation in the modern middle school. Attention is directed first to the meaning of the term and the need for evaluation. This discussion is followed by one dealing with the analysis of student performance and the instruments that are available for doing the job. The chapter next takes up the question of marking student performance and reporting the same to parents. It closes with a somewhat detailed treatment of curriculum evaluation, or the task of finding out how well the whole program or specific parts of it are suited to student needs.

THE RATIONALE

Much of man's progress over the past years can be fitted to a rather simple developmental model. In this model he begins with a goal, applies efforts to reach the goal, observes the results, refines his techniques on the basis of the observations, makes renewed efforts to reach the goal, observes the results of what has been done, and so continues the cycle. A diagram of this process appears in Figure 10-1.

In light of this diagram, evaluation may be regarded as a process of finding out how well stated objectives have been met. There are two elements involved in this process: assessment and appraisal. Assessment has to do with the direct measurement of something in order to determine the rate, the level, or the amount. Appraisal, on the other hand, concerns the making of a judgment as

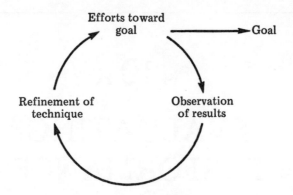

Figure 10-1.   Goal-Seeking Process

to quality, status, or effectiveness, and thus incorporates the results of assessment.

There are a number of reasons why the evaluative process should be an integral part of the middle school program.   Briefly, the reasons are as follows:

1. To find out how much achievement students have made in a given field.
2. To find out what sort of achievement students have made in a given field.
3. To supply students with information that enables them to understand their own progress toward established goals.
4. To create a learning situation that is appropriate for each student, since each one has his or her own unique learning style.
5. To stimulate the student in a positive way so that he may progress at his own ability level.
6. To help students to identify their own learning problems and to find solutions to them.
7. To bring about in students a state of readiness for teacher aid based upon an understanding of their own needs and weaknesses.
8. To report to parents how well their children are doing in achieving their own goals and those of the school.
9. To determine how well the instructional program is meeting the personal and social needs of students.

Implied in these reasons is the emphasis placed in middle school education upon individualizing and humanizing the instructional process.

DIAGNOSING STUDENT PERFORMANCE

The diagnosis of student performance in the classroom may be undertaken by the student in a self-evaluation of his own work, by the group to which he belongs, or by the teacher in charge of the learning situation. Generally all of these avenues are brought into play when adequate provision is made for evaluation as part of an ongoing instructional process.

STUDENT SELF-EVALUATION A unique purpose of a student-centered middle school is that of encouraging and assisting the individual to evaluate his own progress. This is one of the strongest values associated with middle school education. It is believed that each student should develop a healthy self-image as well as the ability to undertake self-direction. A feasible way of achieving these ends is through a process of self-evaluation. This means that the individual student, with teacher assistance, establishes his own learning goals and then ascertains how well he is achieving them. In the course of doing this, he makes a systematic analysis of his own strengths and weaknesses and of his assets and learning deficiencies, and plans his program of action. He may emphasize the need to capitalize on those aspects of learning that he handles well or to adopt measures for overcoming deficiencies within the limits of his own capacity, or both.

In helping to establish goals toward which the student directs his efforts, the teacher must take care to see that the goals are reasonable ones, that they are compatible with what is known about the learning process, that they are consistent with each other and with the goals of the class and the school, and that they are appropriate for the student. In this respect, it should be recognized that every student should not be expected to acquire similar concepts, attitudes, or bodies of information at different rates, but rather to acquire those ideas, attitudes, and bodies of information that are in keeping with his goals and what he is capable of learning.

It has been shown many times that the kind of feedback a student receives from systematic self-evaluation is significant in directing his future learning. It conditions his decision about what he will do next. For example, if he discovers that an inability to express himself clearly in writing is due to a limited vocabulary, then he might decide to start listing words that are unfamiliar and to look up their meaning until he has compiled and mastered a substantial number of them.

To live comfortably with themselves in the self-evaluative

process, students need teacher assistance as well as a sense of personal well-being. It is the teacher's role to encourage the student and members of the group to select and apply instruments and skills that will produce the information being sought. As a diagnostician, the teacher is seriously concerned with the behavioral characteristics of each student in his or her class and with directing individual effort into areas where a need for improvement is indicated. Usually, the teacher helps the student identify a weakness and then stimulates him to suggest how he plans to deal with it, holding his own suggestions back unless they are needed. At the same time the teacher makes it a point to help the student overcome any fear of failure he may have and to aid him in moving toward his goals. Such a teacher is more interested in promoting individual achievement of self-selected goals than in comparing one student's progress with that of another student in the class. The self-evaluative process is facilitated when teachers help students to develop a sense of self-respect and to experience a feeling of progress.

Reference has been made in the discussion of student self-evaluation to the necessity for gathering reliable evidence concerning progress or lack of progress toward goal achievement. Not much has been said specifically about the means for undertaking this task. Although the general methodologies of evaluation will be dealt with in a subsequent section of the chapter, a few procedures will be described that suggest ways for students to secure evidence they need in order to make judgments about their own work and to help them decide the next steps they will take.

A device that has proven useful in directing student self-evaluation is a checklist. The checklist consists of a sequential arrangement of the activities that are included in a given assignment or a given unit of study. When the assignment or unit has been completed, the student checks off the activities he has engaged in. If devised properly and adapted to a particular group or situation, the checklist helps to awaken in the student a concern about the progress he has made in specific areas of growth and development, such as participation in class discussions, assumption of named responsibilities, cooperation with other members of the group, preparation of particular reports, and the like. Other devices include questionnaires that force the student to react to his own classroom performance; the use of descriptive statements that characterize qualities of personality, social attitudes, and emotional controls; tape recordings that may be valuable in helping a student to evaluate his speech performance; the maintenance of folders containing written work that enable the student to compare present with past efforts;

and special self-evaluative report cards on which the grades are recorded in sequence for work corrected and marked by the teacher.

GROUP EVALUATION   In addition to individually defined goals, teachers and students establish group goals.   Common agreement on the ends toward which they should direct their work may be reached in a single class, a team arrangement, a core program, or some other instructional plan.   Generally, when group goals are agreed upon they are then compared with those of the school and any inconsistencies are eliminated.   Not only are the goals that are arrived at through teacher–student planning taken seriously by members of the group, but also the process of developing them is a valuable learning experience.

Once goals are mutually acceptable and consistent with those of the school, it is possible to make provision for group evaluation of learning outcomes.   In other words, plans are developed to under-take the gathering of evidence in order to find out how the group as a group, not as individuals, performed with reference to its objectives.   The concern is that of finding answers to such questions as the following: How close are we coming to the goals we set up?   In what areas did we make our best gains?   Where did we fall down?   How can our performance be improved?   Group evaluation of group performance acts as a stimulant to motivate group effort to improve the effectiveness of its work.

Evaluation procedures are usually selected by the group as a result of teacher–student discussions of how best to secure the information needed for assessment and appraisal purposes.   Sometimes the group decides to convert its statement of objectives into rating scales or checklists that can be used by both teacher and students in determining progress.   Peer evaluation may be employed by asking for written judgments about committee reports and related matters.   These appraisals may then be taken up and reviewed critically through oral discussion.   There is likewise a place for the use of selected tests, questionnaires, informal discussions, and structured observations, to mention but a few of the possibilities.

TEACHER EVALUATION   The third approach to the evaluation of student performance is centered around the teacher.   The teacher may be in charge of a self-contained classroom, instruction in a single subject in a departmental organization, or he may work with one or more teachers in a block-of-time, core, or team teaching arrangement. No matter what the instructional setup may be, the teacher has his own perceptions of learning and he employs whatever diagnostic devices he knows how to use to reach judgments about student performance and to decide what steps should be taken to further the learning progress.

But before the teacher can undertake a diagnosis of student performance, either by himself or with other teachers, he must have a well-defined series of goals. These goals should be peculiar to student needs in a particular area of the curriculum as well as consonant with the self-determined goals of students and the group, and the goals of the school. It does not matter whether the teacher's goals are worked out before or after those of the individuals and the group. Preferably, they should be stated in terms of terminal behavior or of changes desired in students as a result of teaching–learning activities. For example, one way of stating behavioral objectives is as follows: The student will be able to distinguish between the actual and the implied meaning in magazine advertisements. Or an objective might be handled in the following way: At the end of the course, the learner will be able to perform such tasks as engaging in a foreign language conversation with a native speaker of the language, etc. There are other patterns for expressing behavior that are specific, measurable, or observable, but these two are sufficient for illustrative purposes.

In middle school education, the goals today are not limited to the dispensing of subject matter and the teaching of subject matter skills. They are concerned also with such matters as the development of attitudes, ideals, interests, and critical thinking; with writing and speaking competencies, work habits, and acceptance by peers; with the personal–emotional, personal–social, and personal–physical aspects of daily living; and with problem-solving abilities, the making of intelligent choices, and the reaching of sound conclusions.

Evaluation by the teacher should be done on an individual-student basis. In this way, the teacher is in a position to note changes that have occurred from one period of time to another. Sometimes it is advisable for him to administer pre-tests and so establish a base line against which progress can be seen. For example, a student could be asked to use the facilities and resources of the library for preparing a paper or a report and a careful record would be kept of his activities. This record could then serve as a base for comparing his performance on a similar assignment sometime later in the year.

Heavy dependence was formerly placed upon pencil-and-paper tests to assess student performance. Today teachers still rely on this type of measurement, but it has been supplemented with a broad assortment of instruments, devices, and procedures that deal with other aspects of learning. For example, a teacher is able to judge to a respectable degree of accuracy how well a student can plan, engage in critical thinking, or follow the steps in problem-solving by arranging pertinent situations and then observing and recording behavior. Or, if the teacher wants to find out how well a student attacks a social problem, he selects and administers instruments that yield measures of a student's ability to gather information and use it in dealing with the problem. And if the teacher is interested in knowing whether or not a student is acquiring a particular skill or a particular understanding, he uses appropriate instruments to sample thoroughly enough the fundamental ideas of the concept or the relevant aspects of the skill.

The former dependence upon pencil-and-paper tests rested upon the idea that all students could be handled at the same time with a consequent saving of teacher time and labor. Although this idea has merit, it is entirely possible to accomplish the same thing by testing and interviewing only a sample of a class. By taking six students from a class of thirty, the teacher can obtain a useful picture of the learning that is taking place in the group and the attitudes that are being developed.

Team teachers and those in block-of-time and core classes are in a position to share and pool information about individual students. Even though their observations and judgments are subjective in nature, still they have a real place in evaluation when they represent a team conclusion. There is a strong likelihood that in many instances the collective judgment of team members is more valid in assessing student progress than a battery of pencil-and-paper tests.

The collective contribution can be increased when teachers apply suitable instruments and devices to their appraisal of student performance. If appraisal is carried on over a considerable period of time, the findings enable team members to identify more accurately the students with problems that call for the services of counselors, nurses, home and school visitors, and other specialists.

All classroom teachers face the question of what techniques to use for evaluative purposes. Although the selection will vary in terms of objectives, situation, and facilities, nevertheless there are many techniques that appear to have rather wide application. Some of these are as follows:

1. The construction and maintenance of an individual student record system which contains information on such items as standardized test results, performance patterns, and samples of classwork.

2. The creation of special conditions in classes which enable the teacher to observe and appraise progress in specific areas of learning, responses to suggestions, the application of correctional measures, etc.
3. A comparison of teacher and student judgments on a rating scale dealing with specific aspects of learning.
4. A discussion of papers by the student and the teacher when the pupil is satisfied with his work; otherwise, grading of the papers by the teacher.
5. The development of pencil-and-paper tests that reflect the objectives of teaching and the work carried on in class.

Techniques of this kind and others make it possible to appraise student learning throughout the year in a variety of learning situations.

EVALUATIVE INSTRUMENTS

Even though a number of evaluative instruments and techniques have already been discussed, it might be helpful for the middle school teacher to see them arranged in some sort of a systematic order and to gain more information about how they are used. Accordingly, seven different categories of evaluative instruments and techniques will be presented below.

SELF-REPORTING DEVICES   Included in this category are questionnaires, checklists, rating scales, autobiographies, and sociometric tests.   They are self-administered by students and, with the exception of autobiographies, may be applied by teachers in their appraisal of performance.   They assist the teacher in better understanding the student as a person.   They are helpful in problem situations in providing clues as to student reactions to particular issues and convictions held.   They are valuable in assessing progress toward objectives when progress is difficult to appraise by other means.   Some of these devices enable the teacher to see that things are checked off according to a fixed schedule or sequence.

OBSERVATION   Observation is a procedure that is brought into play by all teachers in the evaluation of student performance.   It may be carried on informally, formally, or in a combination of the two ways.   If done informally, it takes place during regular class activities and is, for the most part, unplanned.   The perceptive teacher notes and tries to interpret the behavior of various students. For example, his observations may lead to a careful analysis of student participation in class work and to certain conclusions about some members of the group. He may become aware that a few boys and girls are experiencing real difficulties in handling particular assignments but are trying to conceal their lack of understanding. He may develop a sensitivity to the nature of interpersonal relations among students and search for its effect on learning outcomes.

Informal observation frequently creates the need for engaging in a more formal type of observation in order to acquire more information about a student. A previously identified situation may be watched carefully for patterns of student behavior or new situations may be created as a means of determining how students react to or deal with a different set of conditions. Usually, the teacher keeps a running record of the student's actions, how long it took him to accomplish a particular task, what sort of difficulties he encountered, the degree of intensity with which he worked, from whom he sought help, and so on. After the teacher has accumulated enough data, he then analyzes his findings, draws conclusions, and plans what he thinks should be done to overcome learning obstacles or to raise the quality of the next assignment.

SITUATIONAL TASKS   Complementary to observation as an evaluative technique is the use of situational tasks. Developed by the teacher, they become practical tests of how well a student can apply the information, skills, and concepts that have been studied. The nature of this technique and the ease with which it can be utilized are brought out in the illustrations that follow. If reading and interpreting graphs has been a subject of class work, a simple test of how well students have mastered these skills would consist of exposure to a new set of graphs with instructions to write out the story they depict. Or a set of facts could be given to students with the directive that they be presented in graphic form along with an interpretation of their meaning. Assuming that one or two fundamental scientific principles were dealt with in a unit under study, their application could be tested by presenting students with a situation or a problem that called for the use of these principles in resolving a difficulty or in reaching an acceptable conclusion. In similar fashion, the ability to arrive at valid generalizations based on evidence could be tested by creating a situation involving the analysis of historical data. Reactions may be tested through other situations presented to students by means of films, slides, filmstrips, recordings, a sociodrama, or a story told by the teacher.

WORK SAMPLES   Analyzing samples of a student's work is an excellent means of finding out how much progress is being made toward particular objectives.   The samples may be taken at any time during the year.   Their selection will vary with the area of study and the amount of information needed for assessing perform-ance.   They may include special homework assignments, oral re-ports, panel discussions, essays, research papers, dramatic sketches, letters, and so on.

From these samples, it is possible to determine subject matter assimilation, application of knowledge, organizational ability, logi-cal thinking, depth of understanding, nature of attitudes, and skill in oral and written expression, among other accomplishments.

The findings from sample analysis furnish a natural oppor-tunity for the teacher to confer with the student about the results. Together they can review the quality of the work and decide how to go about a similar task in the future.   The point of the conference is the mutual sharing of something that each regards as being important.

If grading the sample is in the picture, it may hurt the teacher–student relationship unless the purpose is understood by the student and accepted ahead of time.   Not only should the purpose be ex-plained before the sample is prepared, but also the criteria should be reviewed so that the student knows what the teacher will be look-ing for in the work he does.   Preferably, grading should be avoided in the evaluation of work samples.

INTERVIEWS   Interviews can be used as a diagnostic device for evaluating student performance.   Unfortunately, their use is lim-ited in many schools because teachers do not have time during the regular day to schedule interviews.   If they are held, it is necessary to see a student either before or after school.   Increasingly, how-ever, more schools are providing a daily period during which a teacher and student may confer about a topic related to the stu-dent's welfare.   This is especially true in modern middle schools where time is provided for teachers to meet with students and their parents and to bring in specialists when their services are needed.

Interviews become a diagnostic device when they are directed toward the satisfaction of an evaluative purpose.   The purpose may be that of reviewing an analysis of work samples, discussing diffi-culties experienced by a student in everyday class activities, com-paring teacher and student ratings on a scale for assessing student performance, working out remedial procedures for dealing with a learning problem, or trying to pinpoint the causes for conflicts in interpersonal relations in school and family.

The achievement of evaluative purposes depends to a large extent upon the skill of the teacher in handling an interview. He must be able to establish rapport with the student, assist him in the identification of his own problem, offer suggestions without cutting off thinking, and help the student to reach conclusions and to decide upon future courses of action. Detailed information on the refined use of these procedures is available in books on guidance and supervision.

CUMULATIVE RECORDS   The cumulative record is regarded as an essential tool in the evaluation of student performance. It is a record that follows a student through school from the time he enters until he leaves or graduates from high school. Each year new information is added to it so that it becomes a resource file of fact and opinion as well as the most comprehensive record maintained about the student during his school career.

Although variations in the content of the cumulative record are found among districts, most records include data relating to family background, test results, health examinations, previous academic grades, interests, correspondence, special awards, cocurricular activities, conferences, learning problems, and anecdotes about classroom experiences. The inclusion of other items depends mostly upon the needs of personnel who use the record or the purposes to which it is applied.

The information in the cumulative record is particularly helpful in the evaluation of students and the nature of their progress. By bringing past achievement into the foreground, the teacher can determine whether or not a student is living up to his achievement expectancy level. If special learning problems arise, then an analysis of the contents of the record can be made for information that bears upon the problem. Such analysis also aids the teacher in getting a better understanding of the student and any special needs that require immediate and long-range attention. The information in the cumulative record frequently puts the teacher in a better position to plan individualized learning situations and to work with the student more constructively on self-evaluation.

TESTS AND INVENTORIES   When mastery of subject matter and related skills was the main purpose of education, tests were the principal device for evaluating pupil progress. They were used for arriving at marks, issuing progress reports, and determining promotion. Today the situation is different. Tests still have a significant place in the evaluative process, but their use is primarily a diagnostic one. They now cover, along with special inventories, several facets of an individual's growth and development, such as academic achievement, special aptitudes, interests, personality factors, and vocational skills and preferences.

For convenience of treatment, the discussion here of tests and inventories will be divided into two parts. One part will deal with standardized instruments, the other with those that are constructed by the teacher.

Standardized Instruments. A standardized instrument is one that has norms. These norms are the product of careful experimentation with a nation-wide or regional sample of students. They represent the distribution of scores made on the instrument by members of the sample group. Before the instrument is placed on the market, it undergoes systematic study to determine its reliability, validity, and usability. The norms make it possible to compare a student or a group of students with the sample group with reference to scores for age, grade level, percentiles, intelligence quotient, or standard scores.

The middle school teacher should become acquainted with the various types of standardized instruments with which he is apt to come into contact. They have a significant place in the evaluation of student performance, particularly in diagnosing strengths and weaknesses and in helping to understand a student better. Following are the types of tests and inventories administered most frequently in middle schools:

The general intelligence test is also known as a scholastic aptitude test or a mental ability test. It is administered on a group basis. It purports to measure how well an individual can learn now and in the future. In this respect, it identifies students with either high or low learning ability. This information is valuable to the teacher in planning educational experiences for and with a student. However, there is some skepticism regarding the validity of this test when a student has low reading ability, an emotional disturbance is apparent, or his cultural background is at variance with that of the group.

Achievement tests are designed to measure how well students have assimilated various outcomes of instruction. Traditionally, achievement tests were limited to the measurement of knowledge and skills pertaining to specific subject areas in the curriculum. But in recent years they have been broadened in scope and now provide measures of achievement in such things as problem-solving, critical thinking, application of principles, logical reasoning, propaganda analysis, and evaluation of factual data. Although the outcomes of achievement tests can shed light on only a small part of an individual's growth pattern, nevertheless they are valuable diagnostic tools in determining learning difficulties, discovering the nature of gains and losses, planning appropriate learning activities, channeling students into proper groups and challenging situations, and relating performance and abilities to defined behavioral objectives.

An interest inventory is an instrument that is constructed to survey a student's interests in various fields of work. It differs from a test in that there are no right and wrong answers. The answers given by the student merely indicate a preference for something—a part of a personality pattern. Although interest inventories are used largely to suggest possible occupational fields for exploration, they are important in helping the student to gain an insight into his own interests and to see a relationship between what is being studied and vocational fields.

Personality inventories, like interest inventories, have no correct or incorrect responses. The choices made among the items comprising the inventory are assumed to indicate gradations in personality structure. Differences are revealed in such characteristics as extroversion–introversion, masculinity–femininity, tolerance–intolerance levels, and manic-depressive reactions. Considerable doubt has been expressed about the advisability of having teachers administer and use the results of personality inventories. It is felt that special skills are needed to administer them properly and that the results are too difficult to interpret. Moreover, if the results are discussed with the student, there is strong likelihood of destroying the student–teacher rapport and even creating some psychological problems. It is recommended by experts in the testing field that personality inventories be used only by trained educators and clinical psychologists. This does not preclude, however, the inclusion of interpreted results in the cumulative record. These results often supply supporting data that reinforce other information about the student or perhaps shed new light on a personality problem.

Teacher-Made Tests. Student progress is monitored more with teacher-made tests than with those that are standardized and sold commercially. Standardized tests are viewed only as supplements to teacher-devised and teacher-administered test instruments. This is because teachers can construct tests that reveal more directly the kind of progress students are making toward the goals they are trying to reach. They can construct the tests in light of classroom experiences and their knowledge of the students themselves. There are usually two types of tests built by teachers: essay tests and objective tests. Each type will be reviewed briefly.

READINGS FOR TEACHERS

Ahmann, J. Stanley, and Glock, Marvin D., *Evaluating Pupil Growth*, 5th ed. Boston: Allyn and Bacon, Inc., 1975. A comprehensive work on evaluation; useful to the teacher.

Payne, David A., *The Specification and Measurement of Learning Outcomes*. Waltham, Mass.: Blaisdell Publishing Co., 1968 (paperback). Designed for teachers; its focus is the classroom.

Wood, Dorothy, *Test Construction: Development and Interpretation of Achievement Tests*. Columbus, Ohio: Charles E. Merrill Publishing Co., 1974 (paperback). Designed especially for use by classroom teachers.

An essay test is made up of one or more questions that must be answered in written form. The answers cannot be given with a checkmark, a single word, or by filling in blanks on an answer sheet. The essay-type test requires that the student express the answer in his own words after he has thought through and organized what he is going to say.

Essay tests have advantages that make them valuable in evaluating student performance. They can be used to gain insight into a student's ability to organize material, to analyze and synthesize factual data, to transfer concepts from one situation to another, and to arrange ideas in logical sequence. Problem questions included in essay tests can call for comparisons, cause and effect, and decisions for and against an issue. Questions may be asked that involve the discussion of a topic, an explanation of an event, or a description of something. These are but some of the advantages that essay tests provide in appraising student progress.

The disadvantages associated with essay tests are their lack of high validity and reliability, bias on the teacher's part due to illegible handwriting and poor use of English, subjectivity in scoring, limited sampling of knowledge about a subject, and allowing knowledge of a student to affect the grade assigned to an answer.

Objective tests consist of a series of items of various kinds arranged in various ways but for which the answers are either right or wrong. They are classified according to their arrangement as recall, completion, alternate response, multiple choice, matching, and rearrangement. Each type is used by teachers for the purpose it serves best.

The recall test has a series of statements or questions that require definite answers. The answers are either right or wrong. For example, a test item may ask for the name of the secretary of state of the United States or for the names of the president's cabinet members. A similar test of memory, the completion type has a series of statements containing blank spaces which the student fills in with an answer. There is but one correct answer for each blank space. In some instances, this test is arranged so that the answers are placed in a column to the right of the statements.

The alternate response test contains statements or questions and two choices for the answer. The student is asked to select the correct one. Its more common form is a true–false test, which is designed to inventory factual knowledge on a particular subject. Another test containing alternative answers is the multiple-choice test. In this test each item is accompanied by four or five responses and the student is requested to indicate which one is the correct answer. This test is excellent for measuring achievement in skills and factual information. If it is very well constructed, it can also yield measures relating to the application of facts, generalizations, and understandings.

The matching test usually has a column of items on one side of the examination and a related column of answers on the opposite side. The student, as the test type suggests, is instructed to match the items in one column with those in the other. There may be an identical number of items per question in both columns, though practice seems to favor having a larger number in the second column. The matching test is useful in measuring ability to associate facts or ideas. It is especially helpful in determining how well a student can associate certain terms with their counterparts, can match personalities with events and places, and can put dates and happenings together.

The rearrangement test is used for finding out how well a student knows a given sequence of events, whether he is able to place things in a certain order, and if he has an understanding of a particular chronology of events and happenings. Accordingly, he is asked to rearrange a series of items in a desired sequence using the numbers 1, 2, 3, and so on, to indicate the order in which they should appear.

Generally, the advantages claimed for teacher-made objective tests are (1) they sample a wider scope of knowledge than do essay tests; (2) they are consistent in the results produced; (3) they are accurate in measurement; (4) they can be scored rapidly; and (5) teacher bias does not affect the scores. However, the disadvantages of these tests have been recognized for some years. It is pointed out by critics that they invite the guessing of answers, take too much time and thought to construct, require unusually precise use of language, measure retention of facts more than application of knowledge, focus more on details than upon generalizations and understanding, and place a premium more on memory than upon reasoning.

MARKING STUDENT PERFORMANCE

Perhaps one of the things teachers dislike most about their work is marking or grading student performance, especially at report card periods during the school year. Some teachers strongly oppose this practice and would like to see it eliminated entirely. Then there are others who feel that marking is necessary and should be continued. This is a long-standing issue which has received much attention. Without doubt, the weight of opinion among middle school educators favors a change in the traditional system of using a single-symbol mark to indicate the quality of a student's achievement. They maintain that the single-symbol mark such as "A" or "B" is undiagnostic and so simple as to be nearly meaningless. In order to arrive at a recommendation on the issue, it would be useful to get an overview of marking practices and the possibilities for modifying and improving them.

PURPOSES OF MARKS   School marks serve a number of worthwhile purposes. The most important one is that of motivating and directing student growth and development. When a student learns that he is making progress, he is encouraged to continue his effort. If he is not succeeding in his work, then marks should help to indicate where improvement is needed and foster the setting of more realistic goals for the future. At the same time, marks enable parents to become aware of students' progress and to decide whether something should be done to bring about improvement. Marks are used also as a basis for promotion and graduation and for according various types of honors. As a part of his permanent school record, marks make it possible to compare past and present achievement and to discuss with the student the probability of success along certain lines of future education.

GRADING STANDARDS   In examining current grading practices, it is necessary to look at the standards used by teachers in arriving at a mark for a student. Three kinds of standards are employed in schools today: absolute, comparative, and clinical standards. An absolute standard of grading represents a measuring rod devised by the teacher and applied to the accomplishments of the student. For example, if a social studies teachers drilled a class on place geography in Latin America, he would determine prior to testing how many correct answers were needed for an "A," a "B," and so on. This position assumes that the teacher is correct in his determination of the scale and is willing to live with the results of the testing. It assumes further that individual differences among students will not be unduly overlooked.

In contrast, the comparative standard of marking is based on the relative standing of students in a classroom situation or among students in different sections of the same grade and subject. After test scores are arranged in rank order, high marks are assigned to those who received better scores than others and low marks to those who did more poorly than others. This system can be justified when competition among students is fairly even; otherwise those who cannot compete are punished for lack of ability. Similarly, allocating grades according to the relative standing of students in a low-ability class as against students in a high-ability class is nothing more than a punishment and reward system. More important than this is the fact that comparative marking ignores almost completely the student who tries to achieve within the limits of his capacity. In other words, there is neither recognition nor reward for a student who is "doing his best."

The clinical standard of determining marks revolves around the uniqueness of the student. Each student is regarded as a person in his own right. He is encouraged to use the capabilities he has and to develop them as much as possible. In applying this standard, the teacher has a responsibility to understand the student, to render help as needed, and to evaluate the student as a person apart from the group. When this approach to marking is implemented fully and correctly, a curriculum evolves, replete with appropriate learning experiences, that ties in more closely to the nature of the middle school child. Unfortunately, the clinical standard of marking is not used widely in schools today. It has been rejected because there is a lack of essential instruments for clinical use and because teachers are too busy to devote the time it requires.

MARKING SYSTEMS   A variety of symbols are used in marking systems to indicate the quality of a student's achievement on a test or an assignment or a composite mark for grades received over a given period of time. The percentage system of marking is perhaps the oldest in practice at this time. In this system, grades are expressed as precise percentage points on a scale from 0 to 100. Thus a student might receive 85 in language arts, or 85 points out of a possible 100. The system also carries an arbitrary passing score. The passing score could be 60 percent or some other percentage of 100, depending upon the marker's decision or the policy of the school. The percentage system of marking implies a precision that is difficult to determine. For example, can an English teacher evaluate the worth of a student's theme as 92 instead of 89? Can a social studies teacher decide that a student's performance in using library resources is worth 80 rather than 79? The question is likewise raised about how a teacher can indicate on a 100-point scale such complex concerns as habits, attitudes, and abilities.

The five-point scale of grading represents an attempt at improving the percentage system. Used more widely than any other system, it employs the symbols A, B, C, D, and F. In this gradation, the symbol "A" is the highest mark and stands for excellent achievement; the symbol "F" is the lowest mark and stands for failure. The scale also includes the symbol "I" to indicate incomplete work on the part of the student. Because the five-point scale involves fewer categories than the 100-point scale, it is easier to arrive at a mark. However, the complaint is made frequently that the mark is too general to convey much meaning or to indicate with enough precision the nature of the achievement. The problem, of course, with any symbol is the matter of its interpretation. This can be facilitated somewhat by defining what each symbol denotes on the scale or describing the behavior involved.

A system that developed to meet the criticisms of the percentage and five-point scales is known as the pass–fail method of grading. Here the student receives either a "pass" or a "fail" as an evaluation of his work, although sometimes the terms "satisfactory" and "unsatisfactory" are used instead. Proponents of this grading system point out that it eliminates harmful competition among students by no longer putting a premium on high marks. Opponents of the system, however, claim that it does not reflect a student's progress nor show his achievement compared with that of his classmates. Generally, the pass–fail method of grading has been dropped by schools after an experimental period.

The descriptive system is an abrupt departure from traditional ways of marking. Instead of sending a report card home, the teacher either writes a letter to the parents of each student in his class or else sets up a conference with them. Sometimes both the letter and conference are used. The letter contains a description of the student's performance and other pertinent notations regarding such matters as study habits, personality factors, and social attitudes. A similar procedure is followed in conferences with parents where total growth is discussed. Child and parent can review the content of the discussion and profit from it. The real drawback to the descriptive system is the amount of teacher time required for preparing letters and planning and holding conferences. The load seems too heavy for most teachers to carry, despite the fact that the letter and the conference are more constructive and helpful than the one-symbol mark.

MARKING IN MIDDLE SCHOOL Teachers in most middle schools are required to rate student performance periodically and then to report their ratings to students, parents, and school officials. If procedures by which they judge a student's performance could be analyzed, analysis would undoubtedly disclose the presence of many subjective factors. Some teachers are influenced strongly by deportment, physical appearance, and native endowment, whereas others let class activities, cooperativeness, and family background play a part in their decisions. These and other subjective elements can be partially controlled when a school adopts a basic marking policy that spells out the guidelines for teachers to follow. Such guidelines do not restrict teacher freedom to supplement and implement the policy in their own way. They merely help to bring about a consistency in marking among teachers and to reduce elements of subjectivity. The teacher still has the right to follow a grading system he believes is right, but it also represents the essential concepts behind middle school education. The position he takes on marking must be one that he can live with comfortably and defend.

In arriving at a position on marking, what are some of the important considerations that the teacher should take into account? Is a marking system that uses a single symbol for reporting various kinds of growth satisfactory for a modern middle school? Does such a system run counter to the objectives of middle school education? Is it out of line to establish uniform standards of accomplishment for students of middle school years, who are in the period of rapid growth? Is the real purpose of grading students that of comparing performance with some set standard or establishing their relative positions in a competitive situation? Or should the goal of marking be that of trying to find out how well a student has determined his own objectives and moved toward them? Does a consideration of individual differences reduce and even prevent some of the anxieties tied in with a period in life that is replete with concerns and doubts about personal worth and identity? If these last two questions carry affirmative answers, then the middle school should certainly employ some kind of clinical approach in its system of marking.

The introduction of a clinical approach to marking is difficult in some school districts, because tradition is strong and hard to modify. However, in systems where tradition blocks major marking changes, improvements nevertheless can be brought about by combining the best in absolute and comparative systems with parts of the clinical method. Here are some possibilities that are worth examining.

1. Use descriptive comments on work done by students rather than one-symbol marks. Descriptive comments on term reports, special projects, regular themes, and oral presentations not only tell the student more about the quality of his work but also reduce the emotionalism often connected with the single-symbol system of marking. A similar method can be used in reporting to parents on a student's performance at stated intervals during the year.
2. If a single mark is required for each subject on the report to parents, it can be accompanied by a definition of the competencies that an "A" student, a "B" student, etc., should be able to demonstrate. For example, an "A" student should be able to organize his work carefully, show superior study habits, participate constructively in class discussion, and so on.
3. Employ a split-grade system when a symbol mark is required. In this system, a mark is given for each objective or point that is stressed in class work. For example, a report in social studies might be marked for originality and accuracy of content, for organization of the material, and for clarity of written expression. A combination of such points can be included in the periodic reports that go home.
4. Assign grades in accordance with different standards of marking. Assign one for achievement compared with an absolute standard, one for achievement relative to other members of the class, and one for achievement based upon personal ability.
5. Define the competencies a student demonstrates for each single-symbol grade in achievement compared with classmates, achievement in terms of personal ability, and in personal–social development.

It is possible to make other modifications as well in traditional marking practices in order to place more emphasis upon clinical approaches to the evaluation of student performance.

READINGS FOR TEACHERS

Gronlund, Norman E., *Improving Marking and Reporting in Classroom Instruction*. New York: Macmillan Publishing Co., Inc., 1974 (paperback). Prepared by an expert and geared to the needs of the classroom teacher.

National School Public Relations Association, *Grading and Reporting: Current Trends in School Policies and Programs*. Arlington, Va.: The Association, 1972 (paperback). Brief but very useful survey of current trends.

Wrinkle, William L., *Improving Marking and Reporting Practices in Elementary and Secondary Schools*. New York: Holt, Rinehart and Winston, Inc., 1956. A small volume yet one of the most comprehensive treatments available.

REPORTING STUDENT PERFORMANCE

The purposes of reporting on student performance in school work are similar to those behind a marking system. Reporting informs the student about how well he is doing and supplies the parent with the same information. If necessary, both can seek help and take constructive measures for bringing about improvement. Reporting also sets the stage for closer home and school cooperation. Often a report card or other reporting form serves as a motivational force for a student. He studies harder and makes gains that otherwise might be difficult to accomplish. And reporting becomes a means of recording information that is necessary for administration and counseling, especially when the information is incorporated into the student's permanent record.

Whatever form reporting takes, there should be agreement among staff members on the purposes and content of the report. If the school is concerned only with scholastic achievement on an absolute standard of marking, then the report form should express this purpose and arrange the content accordingly. If the intent of the report is that of comparing the relative standing of a student with that of other members of the group, it should be designed to provide for this end. If progress toward stated behavioral goals is the purpose, then the report form should carry descriptions of behavioral goals and indicate where the student stands with respect to them. In essence, the report form should reflect the educational beliefs of the school, which are built into the standards and system of evaluating student performance.

It is important that parents receive a careful explanation of the reporting system. Unless they understand it, trouble is bound to follow. One way of assuring better parental understanding is to involve them in the development of the reporting form. As a rule, they have many excellent ideas, particularly with reference to the method of reporting they think most useful. Students also have fine contributions to make in shaping a reporting system; they should be involved as well.

It is standard practice for schools to issue printed report cards for parents four to six times a year. Usually, the reporting is done by means of symbols on a five-point scale of letter grades—A, B, C, D, F. A small amount of space is provided on the card for both teacher and parent comments. The student's attendance record is

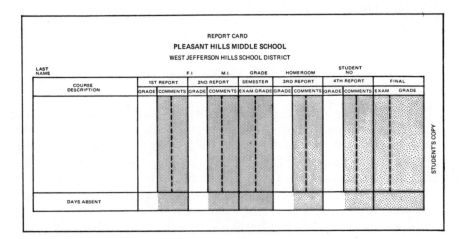

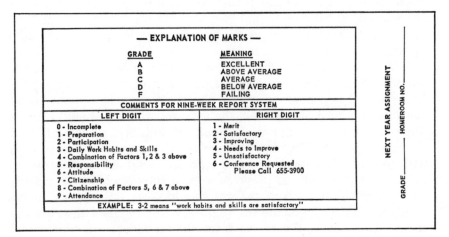

Figure 10-2. Pleasant Hills Report Card

shown for the period covered by the report. An example of such a card is shown in Figure 10-2. Besides the letter marks for scholastic achievement, the cards may reflect other aspects of growth and development. The growth and development may be indicated by means of descriptive or narrative statements prepared by the teacher, by means of other symbols or checkmarks for particular character traits listed on the card, and by means of a code connected with a list of descriptive behavior statements.

In some of the more modern schools the traditional report card, or a modified version of it, may be supplemented at regular intervals by progress reports, or occasionally as the teacher sees fit. These reports apprise the parent of changes in student performance, both deficiencies and improvements. The combination of the regular report card and the progress report makes an effective communication system between school and home.

Some intermediate schools report to parents in written note form. The teacher writes out his judgments about the student's performance, using anecdotes now and then to illustrate the points he is making. The written note may be combined with a checklist or another printed form on which the teacher indicates the nature of the progress being made toward the stated goals of instruction.

Another type of report used in middle schools contains a list of items reflecting educational objectives and learning behaviors. The student places his self-evaluation on each item in a column provided for this purpose. The self-evaluations may be expressed in either number or letter symbols on a three-point or a five-point scale. Then in a parallel column the evaluations of the teacher are recorded.

If real differences stand out between their respective ratings, a conference is arranged between the teacher and the student. They examine the reasons for their differences. Any adjustments made as a result are placed in a third column. The teacher, however, is the final judge. This report is sent to parents. It can be used as a base for a parent–teacher conference.

A new development in reporting is the looseleaf report card. It has a format that reflects the unique aspects of a student's learning program and the growth through which he is going. The report card in Figure 10-3 is a report on social studies progress. The assumption is made in this report that the goals of social studies instruction fall into three categories—content knowledge, skill development, and concept understanding. Separate pages are constructed around these objects for each social studies unit. In other words, the major learning objectives for any given unit are divided into content knowledge, skill development, and concept understand-

Unit: The United States at the Beginning of the Twentieth Century

	REPORT PERIODS		
	Date:	Date:	Date:

Skill Development*			
1. Can read and interpret graphs depicting such information as economic growth of the country, source of immigrants to U.S., percentage of population casting election ballots, etc.	A		
2. Can locate on an outline map cities, states, rivers, and other areas pertinent to events studied.	A		
3. Given election results can identify a majority, plurality, minority.	B		
4. Can interpret and read a map depicting population density.	A		
5. Demonstrates ability to analyze historical data and arrive at valid generalizations based on evidence.	B		

Concept Understanding*			
1. Economic and social conditions can cause large-scale immigration.	C		
2. Large-scale immigration leads to cultural conflict.	B		
3. Men with similar grievances can band together to increase their effectiveness.	B		
4. With leadership comes responsibility.	C		
5. Changing times bring new forms of expression in arts and advances in technology.	C		

Content Knowledge†			
1. Assimilation of factual information concerning the factors that led to the U. S. becoming a world power.	51		
2. Assimilation of factual information regarding social, political, and economic reform movements in the early 1900s.	65		
3. Assimilation of factual information regarding the influence of journalism in the early 1900s.	45		
4. Assimilation of factual information concerning the social processes that result from cultural conflict: amalgamation. assimilation, accommodation, or extermination.	55		

* Competence is expressed in letter form. The letter is based on results of mastery tests.

A—Mastery or understanding at advanced level
B—Mastery or understanding at intermediate level
C—Mastery or understanding at fundamental level

D—Development in progress
E—Shows no development at present
NA—Not applicable at this time

†Competence is expressed as a percentile. It indicates comparative standing of accomplishments in relation to those of other students.

Figure 10-3. Report Card for Social Studies (Source: Items under each classification taken from "Individually Prescribed Instruction," Research for Better Schools, Philadelphia, Pa. [brochure].)

ing. There is a code for reporting progress in these three categories.

In reporting on skill development and concept understanding mastery tests are used as the assessment instruments. Separate mastery tests are administered for determining competence at fundamental, intermediate, and advanced levels. In reporting on the assimilation of content knowledge, the teacher is concerned with how well students can do things with the facts that are available to them rather than how many they have acquired. Reporting in this area of learning thus becomes a comparative matter; it should be done in relationship to what other students have accomplished. This calls for achievement tests in which a student's score is expressed as a percentile rank.

In Figure 10-3 the progress of one student is reported. His percentile rank in the class with respect to content knowledge places him at or around the mid-point of his fellow students' accomplishments. In the other two areas, he has well mastered the skills described and has achieved an understanding of all the concepts at either a fundamental or intermediate level of comprehension.

The reporting procedures outlined here can be applied to all subjects represented in the middle school curriculum. Developing the learning programs and testing devices necessary to make such reporting practices a reality is a difficult undertaking, although the skills and understandings involved are available to the profession.

A different type of report card is reproduced in Figure 10-4. Issued by the Reed Union School District for grades 6, 7, and 8, it is expanded far beyond conventional cards. It is built around specific behavioral outcomes. The card is filled out manually instead of by data processing procedures. Checkmarks are employed, not letter symbols, but nothing is said concerning levels of achievement. The format of the card suggests lines along which reporting practices in middle schools can be developed and strengthened.

Some middle school educators believe that the best way of reporting is the student–parent–teacher conference. Instead of reporting a mark, the student and teacher discuss with the parents the accomplishments or lack of accomplishments being made by the student in school. The emphasis is almost exclusively on student attainment of self-determined goals rather than on the relative standing of the student in his group or how he compares with class norms. Emphasis is placed on positive achievement and success, not failure.

In preparation for the conference the teacher raises several questions with the student: What does the student plan to tell his parents? How will he explain his progress or his lack of progress? What will his goals be for the future? Do they differ from those of

Interim Profile of Student Participation and Performance for Students Grades 6, 7, 8

A = Excellent
B = Above Average
C = Average
D = Below Average
U = Unsatisfactory

Materials above grade level
blank Materials on grade level
Materials below grade level

School

_____ _____ _____
Student   Grade/Section   Section/Teacher Advisor

Report Period
| 1 | 2 | 3 | 4 |

_____ School Year

LITERATURE READING: TEACHER _____
Materials being used _____

| | Drama | | Poetry | | Novel |

| | Short Story | | Mythology | | _____ |

GENERAL ACHIEVEMENT

	Yes	No	Comments:
Shows evidence of comprehending			
Completes reading assignments			
Uses literary terms appropriately			
Pursues individual reading			

SOCIAL CONDUCT

Shows self-control			
Works well with others			
Observes property rights			
Shows respect for others			

LANGUAGE ARTS SKILLS: TEACHER_____

	Excellent	Satisfactory	Needs Improvement
1. Uses class time to full advantage			
2. Works constructively in small groups on cooperative assignments			
3. Completes majority of assignments on time			
4. Consistantly revises writing from original to rough draft			
5. Successfully revises rough draft from writing to final			
6. Consistently makes effort to note and eliminate his writing errors			
7. Consistently keeps up personal spelling chart and individual tests			
8. Other _____			

SPECIFIC COMMENTS:
Improvement noted:

Improvement needed:

MATHEMATICS: TEACHER _____
Skill or concept currently being emphasized: _____

One or more may be checked:
___ Understands processes but makes errors in drill or repetitive assignments.

___ Understands processes and does repetitive assignments carefully and accurately.

___ Prefers not to do repetitive assignments after having mastered a process.

___ Seems to have difficulty in mastering _____
_____

___ Other _____

SOCIAL CONDUCT

	Yes	No	Comments:
Shows self-control			
Works well with others			
Observes property rights			
Shows respect for others			

Parents are to keep this copy of the report form. The school maintains a copy. Parent comments should be sent to the school addressed to the section advisor - written on a separate sheet of paper.

Figure 10-4A.   Reed Union School District Report Card, Page 1

the past?   As an outcome of such preparation, students seem to commit themselves more strongly to their programs of studies and to see more clearly what they are trying to accomplish.

In a school using a team arrangement, each member has

Student				Grade/Section

SCIENCE: TEACHER _____

	Yes	No	Comments
Shows growth in developing solutions to problems independently			
Participates in seminars and discussion groups and projects			
Completes majority of assigned tasks on time			

SOCIAL CONDUCT
Shows self-control
Works well with others
Observes property rights
Shows respect for others

SOCIAL SCIENCE:TEACHER _____   Comments

Shows growth in developing solutions to problems independently
Participates in seminars and discussion groups and projects
Completes majority of assigned tasks on time

SOCIAL CONDUCT
Shows self-control
Works well with others
Observes property rights
Shows respect for others

☐ PHYSICAL EDUCATION

☐ MUSIC

☐ TYPING

☐ ART

☐ SPANISH

☐ _____

COMMUNICATIONS AND MINIMUM DAYS

Parent -Teacher Conference arrangements may be initiated by note or phone to provide time for teacher conferences and in-service activities - every Thursday - starting in October and continuing through May - sdudents are dismissed at 2:10 rather than the regular 3:10 dismissal.

Grades are but one indication of how well both the student and the school are accomplishing their educational tasks.

Primary purposes of grades are:
To present an appraisal of accomplishments
To guide parents and students in planning realistically for the future
To maintain communication between home and school

All evaluation is based on the judgement of the teacher, who has sole responsibility for assignment of grades. Achievement is measured in terms of:
Tests and examinations
Preparation of assignments, including neatness and promtness
Ability to organize and present written or oral material
Contributions to class discussions and group participation
Application of facts and principals to new and unfamiliar situations
Initiation and originality in independent work
Conduct as a helpful influence in the class
Regular and punctual attendance

Evaluation and reporting pupil progress is an important, complex, and not always satisfying experience for pupil, parent, and teacher. Our intent is to be as objective and scientific as possible. By combining grades, parent-teacher conferences and periodical phone calls, we have a means to better understand student performance and adherence to standards of conduct. This combined reporting procedure provides information about the following questions:
How well do the teachers feel the student is performing in terms of what is expected in those classes in which he is enrolled? (This information is all that is included in this student report).
To what extent is my child able to perform his various school responsibilities successfully?
How does my child compare with the other children at the same grade level?
Various school personnel, including the administrative staff, are available to interpret the grading practices, but individual grades are the province of the teachers. Any concern about grades or school accomplishments should be discussed first with your child and then with the teacher. All teachers are available to amplify their evaluation of a student's progress.

Figure 10-4B.   Reed Union School District Report Card, Page 2

twenty to thirty students for whom he is responsible.   Since the number of students is limited and time for conferences with students and parents is scheduled during school hours, the load can be carried without added difficulty.   Even in a school where there are no team arrangements, individual teachers can be assigned a similar number of students for reporting purposes.

In selecting a form or method of reporting on student performance, the following points appear to constitute fundamental criteria:

1. The evaluation should be in terms of behavioral objectives.
2. The evaluation should be in terms of student ability, not norms for the group.
3. The evaluation should be in terms of attitudes, personality characteristics, citizenship behaviors, and study habits.
4. The evaluations should be on separate report forms for different subjects.
5. The evaluations should be prepared less often but in more detail.
6. The evaluations should facilitate the educational development of the student as it relates to his ability.

CURRICULUM EVALUATION

Curriculum evaluation may be regarded as the collecting and applying of information for making instructional decisions. It may also be considered as a means for determining how effectively accepted goals are being reached and for identifying those aspects of the program most needing improvement.

There are several reasons for undertaking curriculum evaluation. First, the middle school is still thought of as an innovation in some communities. Board members, teachers, students, parents, and taxpayers want to know how well this new unit is accomplishing the ends claimed for it. Secondly, decisions must be made, among other things, on what is to be studied, how it is to be studied, who will study it, when it will be studied, and how outcomes will be determined. Only careful evaluation of the curriculum can supply answers to the concerns expressed by interested persons and to the questions raised as bases for educational decision making.

Curriculum evaluation is a descriptive process that focuses on a particular program or some part of it and tells a story about it. To tell the story, it is necessary to gather information, to process it, and then to interpret it. The information gathered always includes the worth and value of the goals of instruction and the progress students are making toward the achievement of these goals. It may also include descriptions of ethnic balance and integration, school organization and services, school personnel and facilities, curricular content and arrangement, student growth in self-concept, compatibility of methods, curriculum materials, psychological climate, guidance, and student activities. The inclusion of some or all of these items as well as others depends on what is to be evaluated. However, no single side of the curriculum can be judged without taking into account related aspects of the whole picture.

Though the task of curriculum evaluation appears to be monumental in size, actually it can be handled in a middle school without imposing undue hardship on the staff. As will be shown in an example of a language arts program, the evaluation is limited to one aspect of the curriculum and the work is spread over a fairly substantial period of time. The task can likewise be reduced in size if information is collected on a sample basis. There is actually no need to measure the accomplishments of all students in a grade, a class, or a school in order to collect enough data to reach sound decisions. Sampling not only saves much labor and time, but it is also reliable from a statistical point of view. Still another approach to economy is the handling of goals or objectives. Instead of searching for information on a long list of objectives, it is far wiser to define four or five of those most widely recognized in each field of study and search for information about student progress toward them. They should be objectives that teachers are able and willing to measure in one way or another.

Successful curriculum assessment is a team affair. It calls for close cooperation among staff personnel and an organizational design through which the load can be shared and direction provided. The arrangement often includes a steering committee at the top and a series of subcommittees in areas related to the purposes of the investigation. For example, the steering committee might be composed of team leaders. Qualified teachers and specialists would serve on such subcommittees as mathematics, social studies, language arts, instructional resources, guidance, and physical facilities. Each of these subcommittees would be responsible for selecting data-gathering instruments and techniques, analyzing the information collected, and drawing appropriate conclusions. The steering committee would define the work of the subcommittees, set up time schedules, provide needed materials and services, organize and edit the final report, and present the report to school authorities. Frequently, the steering committee may be assisted by an outside consultant in planning an evaluative undertaking and in making pertinent decisions.

It is a good practice to consider inviting laymen to take part shortly after the decision to appraise all or part of a program has been made. Their involvement adds a richness of experience and opinions to the project. Not only do they have much to offer in subject matter knowledge, but their participation ensures more reasonable judgments and valid recommendations.

READINGS FOR TEACHERS

Grobman, Hulda, *Evaluation Activities of Curriculum Projects: A Starting Point,* AERA Monograph Series on Curriculum Evaluation, No. 2. Chicago: Rand McNally & Co., 1968 (paperback). A good overview of problems and practices in curriculum evaluation.

Payne, David A., ed., *Curriculum Evaluation: Commentaries on Purpose, Process, Product.* Lexington, Mass.: D. C. Heath and Company, 1974 (paperback). An excellent collection of readings on curriculum evaluation.

Taylor, Peter A., and Doris M. Cowley, eds., *Readings in Curriculum Evaluation.* Dubuque, Iowa: William C. Brown & Co., Publishers, 1972 (paperback). Another very useful collection of readings on curriculum evaluation.

The procedures that one school took to appraise the effectiveness of a new language arts program provide a concrete illustration of curriculum evaluation. Faced with a growing dissatisfaction among teachers regarding the effectiveness of certain aspects of the language arts program, the school district formed a staff committee to study the problem and make recommendations. After a detailed survey of staff concerns regarding the teaching of language arts and a review of the current literature on this topic, the committee pinpointed two basic questions that they felt were at the heart of the district's problem.

1. How can the structure of the English language be taught more efficiently and effectively?
2. How can the ability of students to express themselves in written language be improved?

The committee's recommendation to pursue answers to these two questions was adopted by a majority of the staff after several report meetings had been held at both the elementary and secondary levels.

The original committee was asked to continue with the project. The first step was to develop specific instructional objectives involved in teaching the structure of language and its use in composition writing. Next a program of studies to achieve these objectives had to be developed or identified. The committee decided that the development of such a program was an undertaking too extensive for a teaching staff at the local school level and began to examine newly published language programs. They eventually chose the Roberts Language Arts Series published by Harcourt Brace Jovanovich as presenting a curricular program that was compatible with the instructional objectives that had been identified. The committee then established a three-year pilot study of these materials to compare learning outcomes with the language arts program presently in force.

The pilot program was instituted at the third-grade and seventh-grade levels. Two schools were involved at each of these two grade levels; one set of matched experimental and control classes was established in each school. The Roberts Language Program was used in experimental classes and the school's current language program was retained for the control groups. A consultant was hired to assist with the development of the experimental design and the application of statistical techniques. An outline of the pilot project for the first year follows.

1. Fall—collect baseline data.
   a. Collect 250-word writing samples from third-grade students.
   b. Collect 500-word writing samples from seventh-grade students.
   c. Statistically analyze compositions according to method devised by Kellogg W. Hunt.[1]
2. Spring—collect data concerning program effects.
   a. Administer achievement tests compatible with programs presented in experimental and control classes. Analyze learning accomplishments against stated behavioral goals of instruction for each group.
   b. Collect 250-word writing samples from third-grade students.
   c. Collect 250-word writing samples from seventh-grade students.
   d. Statistically analyze compositions according to Hunt's method and run statistical analysis with baseline data to determine changes and their statistical significance. All data to be analyzed by instruction method, by grade level, by class, by school, and by sex.
   e. Administer opinionnaire to assess student reactions to program studied.

---

1. Kellogg W. Hunt, *Grammatical Structures Written at Three Grade Levels*, NCTE Research Report No. 3 (Champaign, Ill.: National Council of Teachers of English, 1965), p. 157.

f. Administer teacher opinionnaire to assess reactions to programs being taught.

In the second and third years the same procedures were followed except that it was not necessary to collect baseline data in the fall. Since this was a longitudinal study, the educational outcomes were assessed against those prevailing in the year immediately preceding.

The committee made program appraisals at the end of each year and reported these to the staff. Subsequent program decisions were based on these reports. Although the process required a good deal of time, this project represented the efforts of one staff to institute program changes on the basis of specific data regarding educational outcomes.

SELECTED
BIBLIOGRAPHY

Alexander, W. M., and V. A. Hines. *Independent Study in Secondary Schools*. New York: Holt, Rinehart and Winston, Inc., 1967.

Alexander, W. M., et al. *The Emergent Middle School*, 2nd ed. New York: Holt, Rinehart and Winston, Inc., 1969.

Allen, D., and K. Ryan. *Microteaching*. Reading, Mass.: Addison-Wesley, 1969.

American Association of School Administrators. *Administrative Technology & the School Executive*. Washington, D.C.: AASA, 1969.

American Association of School Administrators. *Profiles of the Administrative Team*. Washington, D.C.: AASA, 1971.

Association for Supervision and Curriculum Development. *Individualizing Instruction*, 1964 Yearbook. Washington, D.C.: ASCD, 1964.

Association for Supervision and Curriculum Development. *Learning and Mental Health in the School*, 1966 Yearbook. Washington, D.C.: ASCD, 1966.

Association for Supervision and Curriculum Development. *Learning and the Teacher*, 1959 Yearbook. Washington, D.C.: ASCD, 1959.

Association for Supervision and Curriculum Development. *Life Skills in School and Society*. Washington, D.C.: ASCD, 1969.

Association for Supervision and Curriculum Development. *Perceiving, Behaving, Becoming*, 1962 Yearbook. Washington, D.C.: ASCD, 1962.

Association for Supervision and Curriculum Development. *To Nurture Humaneness: Commitment for the 70's,* 1970 Yearbook. Washington, D.C.: ASCD, 1970.

Beggs, D. W., and E. G. Buffie. *Evaluation as Feedback Guide.* Washington, D.C.: Association for Supervision and Curriculum Development, 1967.

Beggs, D. W., and E. G. Buffie. *Nongraded Schools in Action.* Bloomington, Ind.: Indiana University Press, 1967.

Beggs, D. W., and E. G. Buffie. *Programmed Instruction,* National Society for the Study of Education, 66th Yearbook. Chicago: University of Chicago Press, 1967.

Blount, Nathan S., and H. J. Klausmeier. *Teaching in the Secondary School,* 3rd ed. New York: Harper & Row Publishers, Inc., 1968.

Bondi, Joseph. *Developing Middle Schools.* Belmont, Calif.: Fearon Press, 1971.

Borg, W. R., et al. *Improving Educational Assessment & an Inventory of Measures of Affective Behavior.* Washington, D.C.: ASCD, 1969.

Borg, W. R., et al. *The Minicourse.* Beverly Hills, Calif.: Macmillan Educational Services, Inc., 1970.

Boutwell, W. D. "Our Leisure-Time Education," *Education Digest,* Vol. 35, December, 1969.

Cuff, W. A. "Can Middle Schools Cure a National Disgrace?" *American School Board Journal,* Vol. 157, November, 1969.

"Curriculum for the 70's," *Phi Delta Kappan,* Vol. 41, No. 7, March, 1970.

De Vita, Joseph, et al. *The Effective Middle School.* Englewood Cliffs, N.J.: Parker Publishing Co., 1970.

DiVirgilio, James. "Our Middle Schools Give the Kids a Break," *Today's Education,* Vol. 60, January, 1971.

Educational Leadership, Vol. 31, December, 1973. (Contains a series of fourteen articles on middle schools.)

Eichhorn, Donald H. *The Middle School.* New York: The Center for Applied Research in Education, 1966.

Flavell, John H. *Development Psychology of Jean Piaget.* Princeton, N.J.: Van Nostrand Reinhold, 1973.

Gardner, John W. *Self-Renewal: The Individual & the Innovative Society.* New York: Harper & Row Publishers, Inc., 1964.

George, Paul S. "Unresolved Issues in Education for the Middle Years," *Clearing House,* Vol. 47, March, 1973.

Goodlad, John I., ed. *The Changing American School,* National Society for the Study of Education, 65th Yearbook, Pt. 2. Chicago: University of Chicago Press, 1966.

Grooms, M. Ann. *Perspectives on the Middle School.* Columbus, Ohio: Charles E. Merrill Books, Inc., 1967.

Gruhn, William T., and Harl R. Douglass. *Modern Junior High School,* 3rd ed. New York: Roland Press Co., 1971.

Hall, John S. *Selected Bibliography on Student Activism in the Public Schools.* Eugene, Oregon: ERIC Clearinghouse on Educational Administration, 1969.

Hansen, John, and Arthur Hearn. *The Middle School Program.* Chicago: Rand McNally & Company, 1971.

Havighurst, Robert J. *Human Development and Education.* New York: Longman, Inc., 1953.

Heller, M. P. "School Activities Need an Open Door Policy," *Clearing House,* Vol. 40, September, 1965.

Hilgard, Ernest R., ed. *Theories of Learning & Instruction.* National Society for the Study of Education, 63rd Yearbook, Pt. 1. Chicago: University of Chicago Press, 1964.

Howard, Alvin W. *Teaching in Middle Schools.* Scranton, Pa.: Intext Educational Publishers, 1968.

Howard, Alvin W., and George C. Stoumbis. *The Junior High School & Middle School: Issues and Practices.* Scranton, Pa.: Intext Educational Publishers, 1970.

Hunt, J. M. *Intelligence & Experience.* New York: The Ronald Press, 1961.

Individually Guided Education in the Multi-Unit Elementary School. Madison, Wis.: Center for Cognitive Learning, University of Wisconsin, 1968.

Kealy, R. P., and H. T. Fillmer. "Preparing Middle School Teachers," *Peabody Journal of Education,* Vol. 47, March, 1970.

Kindred, Leslie W., ed. *The Intermediate Schools.* Englewood Cliffs, N.J.: Prentice-Hall, Inc., 1968.

Kratzner, Roland, and Nancy Mannies. "Individualized Learning for Middle School Pupils," *Clearing House,* Vol. 47, March, 1973.

Maier, Henry W. *Three Theories of Child Development,* 2nd ed. New York: Harper & Row Publishers, Inc., 1969.

McCarthy, Robert J. *How to Organize & Operate an Ungraded Middle School.* Englewood Cliffs, N.J.: Prentice-Hall, Inc., 1967.

"Middle School Dilemma: Still Searching for Identity," *Nation's Schools,* Vol. 86, December, 1970.

Morphet, Edgar L., et al., eds. *Designing Education for the Future.* New York: Scholastic Book Service, 1969.

Moss, Theodore C. *Middle School.* Boston: Houghton Mifflin Co., 1969.

"Multi Media," *Saturday Review*, January 30, 1971.

National School Public Relations Association. *Differentiated Staffing in Schools.* Washington, D.C.: NPRA, 1970.

"One Room Schoolhouse 1972 Style," *School Management*, Vol. 15, April, 1971.

Overly, Donald E., Jon Rye Kinghorn, and Richard L. Preston. *Middle School: Humanizing Education for Youth.* Worthington, Ohio: Charles A. Jones Publishing Co., 1972.

Passow, A. Harry, and Robert R. Leeper, eds. *Intellectual Development: Another Look.* Washington, D.C.: Association for Supervision and Curriculum Development, 1964.

Pennsylvania Department of Education. *Student Unrest.* Harrisburg, Pa.: PDE, 1970.

Popham, W. James, Elliot W. Eisner, Howard J. Sullivan, and Louise Tyler. *Instructional Objectives*, American Educational Research Association Monograph No. 3. Chicago: Rand McNally & Co., 1969.

Popper, S. H. "Why Don't Elementary School Principals Raise Some Hell?" *The National Elementary Principal*, Vol. 49, April 1970.

Prescott, Stephan E. "A Strategy for Determining Unmet Needs of Youth: To Establish Co-Curricular Programs for Junior High Schools," Western Reserve University, unpublished dissertation, 1967.

Pulaski, Mary Ann. *Understanding Piaget: An Introduction to Children's Cognitive Development.* New York: Harper & Row Publishers, Inc., 1971.

"REACT" (Relevant Educational Applications of Computer Technology), *Northwest Report* (Northwest Regional Educational Laboratory, Portland, Ore.), December, 1970.

Regional Educational Laboratory for the Carolinas and Virginia. *Educational Development*, Vol. 2, No. 2, Durham, N.C.: RELCV, 1970.

"Report II, Random Access Information Center," Oak Park and River Forest High School, Illinois, September, 1968.

Romano, Louis G., et al., eds. *The Middle School.* Chicago, Ill.: Nelson-Hall Co., 1973.

Schoo, Philip H. "Optimum Setting for the Early Adolescent: Junior High or Middle School?" *North Central Association Quarterly*, Vol. 48, Spring, 1974.

"School of the Month: Beloit-Turner Middle School," *Nation's Schools*, Vol. 85, April, 1970.

Stoumbis, George C., and Alvin Howard, eds. *Schools for the Middle Years: Readings.* Scranton, Pa.: Intext Educational Publishers, 1969.

Stradley, William. *Practical Guide to the Middle School.* Englewood Cliffs, N.J.: Prentice-Hall, Inc., 1971.

Stroup, H. "Extra-Activities Curriculum: What Student Needs Must Be Met?" *Liberal Education*, Vol. 53, March, 1967.

Taba, Hilda. *Curriculum Development: Theory & Practice.* New York: Harcourt Brace Jovanovich, 1962.

"Twenty-Eight Ways to Build Mistakes Out of Your Middle School," *American School Board Journal*, Vol. 158, July, 1970.

Tyler, Ralph W. *Basic Principles of Curriculum & Instruction.* Chicago: University of Chicago Press, 1969.

Van Til, William, Gordon F. Vars, and John H. Lounsbury. *Modern Education for the Junior High School Years*, rev. ed. Indianapolis, Ind.: The Bobbs-Merrill Co., Inc., 1967.

Vars, Gordon F., ed. *Common Learnings: Core & Interdisciplinary Team Approaches.* Scranton, Pa.: Intext Educational Publishers, 1961.

Wattenberg, William W. "The Middle School as One Psychologist Sees It," *The High School Journal*, Vol. 53, December, 1969.

Wilson, M. T., and S. H. Popper. "What About the Middle School? Opinions Differ," *Today's Education*, Vol. 58, November, 1969.

❧ INDEX ❦

Moss, Theodore C., 220
Moyer, James, 139, 140
Murphy, Lois Barclay, 15
Musical activities, 144–145

n

National Association of Secondary School Principals, 107
National Commission on Teacher Education and Professional Standards, 99
National Council for the Social Studies, 8
National School Public Relations Association, 220
National Science Foundation, 8, 129
National Society for the Study of Education, 126
Nation's Schools, 219, 221
Ninth grade, placement of, 70–71
Noar, Gertrude, 29, 30
Nongraded instruction, 108–114
Norelco, 131
Northwest Regional Laboratory, 135
Northwest Report, 220

o

Oakleaf Elementary School, 121
Oak Park and River Forest High School, Oak Park, Illinois, 134–135, 220
Objectives:
  behavioral, 56–58
  chief function of, 53–54
  curricular, 56–58
  vs. goals, 52
  intermediate, 56
Observation, as evaluative device, 191–192
Open classroom, 8
Organization:
  criteria for, 178
  grade-level, 3, 70–71, 109
  in Laguna Beach Unified School District, 179, 181, 182

at Russell H. Conwell Middle Magnet School, 179
Outdoor education, 145–146
Overly, Donald E., 220

p

Passow, A. Harry, 60, 62, 220
Patrick, Robert, 139, 140
Patterns in Arithmetic, 119
Patterson, F. K., 66, 67
Pendleton, William C., 11
Pennsylvania Department of Education, 220
Personal and social needs, 32–33
Personality inventories, 197
Phi Delta Kappan, 120, 218
Philadelphia desegregation plan, 3
Physical development of pupils, 25–26, 33–34
Piaget, Jean, 26, 42, 43, 44, 45, 48, 59
Piaget's stages of intellectual development, 43–44
Pleasant Hills report card, 206
Plowman, Paul D., 57
Popham, W. James, 220
Popper, Samuel H., 220, 221
Pratte, Richard, 4
Prescott, Stephan E., 220
Preston, Richard L., 200
Principal's role, in team teaching, 165–166
Program, planning of, 92–93
Program for Learning in Accordance with Need, 120–121
Publications, 143–144
Pulaski, Mary Ann, 220
Pupils (*see* Middle school students)

q

Quantitative Approach in Elementary School Science, 130

r

Radio Corporation of America, 131
Raymer, Joe T., 2, 70

Readiness approach to learning, 7

Reed Union School District, Tiburon, California, 82, 83
report card for, 209, 210, 211

Regional Educational Laboratory for the Carolinas and Virginia, 119, 120, 135, 220

Regional laboratories, 135–136

Report cards, 205–211

Reporting student performance, 205–211

Required subjects, 72–73

Research for Better Schools, 121, 123, 135

Resource personnel, 171–172

Robert Language Arts Series, 215

Rogers, Carl R., 19

Romano, Louis G., 220

Rosenthal, Robert, 95, 96

Russell H. Conwell Middle Magnet School, 179, 180

Ryan, K., 217

S

Sarnoff, David, 23

Saturday Review, 220

Scheduling, 177–178
of activity program, 146–147
modular, 78–79

Schoo, Philip H., 220

School Management, 220

School size, 71

Science Curriculum Improvement Study, 129–130

Science laboratories, 129–130

Scope:
determination of, 47–48
meaning of, 58

Self-actualization, 13–14

Self-development, 55

Self-direction, 14–15

Self-government, 148–152

Self-reporting devices, 192

Seminar groups, 100–102

Sequence:
determination of, 59
meaning of, 59–60

Sesame Street, 24

Shikellamy Middle School, Shikellamy, Pennsylvania, 99

Simulations, meaning of, 65–66

Situational tasks, as evaluative device, 193–194

Skill development, 16–17, 37–38, 46–47

Social activities, 154–155

Social development, 28–29

Social Science Curriculum Project, 66

Society, changes in, 9–13

Sony, 131

Special resource personnel, 171–172

Spiraling, meaning of, 59–61

Staff (*see also* Aides; Teachers):
qualifications of, 174–178
responsibilities of in team teaching, 166–167

Stoumbis, George C., 219, 221

Stradley, William, 221

Strategy:
in curriculum design, 63–66
defined, 63, 91, 92
in individualizing instruction, 91–94

Stratemeyer, Florence B., 60, 62

Stroup, H., 221

Student council, 150–152

Student-needs approach to curriculum design, 62–63

Students (*see* Middle school students)

Study carrels, 133–134

Subject matter, structure of, 61–62

Subject matter–based curriculum, 61–62

Subjects:
elective, 72–77
mini-, 75–77
required, 72–73

Sullivan, Howard J., 220

Systems for learning (*see* Instructional systems)

t

Taba, Hilda, 67, 221